The Parents' Guide
to Raising Twins

The Parents' Guide to Raising

TWINS

By Elizabeth Friedrich
and Cherry Rowland

Americanization by
Anne Marie Mueser, Ed.D.

St. Martin's Griffin
New York

Design by Victoria Hartman

Library of Congress Cataloging in Publication Data

Friedrich, Elizabeth.
    The parents' guide to raising twins.

    Includes index.
    1. Twins.   2. Child rearing.   3. Infants—Care and
hygiene.   4. Pregnancy.   I. Rowland, Cherry.   II. Mueser,
Anne Marie.   III. Title.
HQ777.35.F74   1984   649'.144   83-26847
ISBN 0-312-03906-9 (Pbk.)

The Parents' Guide to Raising Twins is a revised version of *The Twins Handbook*, which was published in Great Britain in 1983 by Robson Books Ltd.

10

To our twins
Philip and Ben
Sam and Rebecca

Contents

Acknowledgments

This book is a composite of impressions and information gathered here and there, formally and informally—we wish to thank everyone who has ever talked with us about twins. Most of all we are indebted to the adult twins and the parents and children of the many families we interviewed. What they had to say is often retold in their own words. The book is theirs as much as ours.

We would like to express our gratitude to the doctors and health-care professionals we consulted: Bridget Baker, Elizabeth Bryan, Katherina Dalton, Anne Ford, Peter Huntingford, Michael Pawson, Barbara Pickard and Humphrey Ward. We would especially like to thank Elizabeth Bryan for her unfailing help and support and Averil Clegg for her shared interest and her help with sources.

Our thanks go, also, to Sue Cran and Pam Sterling for their support and encouragement in the early stages of this project and for putting us in touch with a number of families. Mona Arscott, Joan Hartje and Sophie Sanford have helped out with typing and photocopying, often at very short notice. We are most grateful to them.

Last but by no means least we want to thank our families— Stephen, Rebecca, Sam, Toby and Lotte Friedrich and Richard, Ben, Philip and Tessa Rowland for their patience and support during the long time it has taken us to do the book. Without them we would not and could not have done it.

Foreword

For most parents the news that they are to have twins comes as both a surprise and a shock. Few of us ever imagine having twins or more. Few of us, certainly, have seriously thought about what is involved in looking after more than one baby at the same time.

I know that many parents who are suddenly faced with this challenge find it hard to get the advice and information they need. They seldom know other parents of twins, and doctors and nurses are often at a loss when it comes to providing detailed practical guidance. Parents want information on twins and why they happen; on what to expect in their pregnancy and labor; on how twins grow and develop as compared with single children. They want advice on how to feed, how to carry and, most important of all, how to relate to two babies at the same time.

The Parents' Guide to Raising Twins by Cherry Rowland and Elizabeth Friedrich admirably fills all these needs. It is enriched not only by their personal experiences as mothers of twins themselves but also by a wealth of information gleaned from their many painstaking interviews with other parents.

I am sure that this book will be valued not only by parents of twins but also by the many people such as midwives and health visitors, family doctors and pediatricians, play-group leaders and primary school teachers, who are concerned with their care.

Elizabeth M. Bryan MD, MRCP, DCH
Consultant Pediatrician
President of the Twins Clubs Association,
Great Britain

To Parents

This is a book by parents for parents. We both found, when we were expecting twins, that there was virtually nothing practical to read on the subject. There were the psychological studies and the medical books but otherwise just a few pages in general books on pregnancy, birth and childcare. Once we had emerged from the first few years of total childcare we set out to write our own book, which would cover the period from conception to starting school.

We have tried to convey some of the joy and satisfaction that can come from having twins or more; but no one needs advice when things are going well, so we inevitably concentrate largely on the difficulties and dilemmas that can arise. Many of the problems we deal with might be encountered by parents of singletons, but they are compounded with twins.

Naturally we have drawn on the experiences we've had with our own sets of twins, but we gathered most of our material from detailed interviews with 35 families. They were from a variety of backgrounds and included not only families with twins but also those with triplets; there was a family with quads, and single-parent families. Most of the children were between two and five, though some were still babies and a few had started school. We also talked to many more parents about specific problems or experiences. We were not attempting any kind of sociological study. Our intention was to focus on the individual experiences and feelings of parents who had to deal with the impact of twins or more on their family and on the practical solutions they devised to problems.

Interviews with adult twins provided a critical perspective on the early years of twins' lives, showing just how crucial they are and how the issues that arise then can continue to be important into adulthood. Discussions with obstetric, pediatric and other specialists contributed useful material, especially to the early chapters. Much research into twin behavior is done to support a particular psychological theory. We have referred to studies only where they have looked at twins in their family setting and where they appear to illuminate or add to parents' own experience.

In all quotations from interviews, names have been changed to preserve anonymity. Though we sometimes make specific reference to triplets or more, our use of the word twin is usually intended to cover both twins and supertwins. When referring to "a child" we have sometimes used "he" and sometimes "she" as we feel that consistent use of only one pronoun inevitably suggests the exclusion of the other sex. The majority of interviews were with mothers, though where possible we talked to both parents. Some sections of the book are devoted especially to the needs of the mother because in all the families we met, the mother was the primary caretaker of the children.

Because we wanted this to be a practical book, we have quoted extensively from parents' experience. What works for one family will not always work for another, but all the strategies we suggest have worked for someone. Some of the things we suggest may seem very simple and obvious, but one of the difficulties faced by parents whose resources may be stretched to the limit, just coping from day to day, is that they lack the energy to devise even quite simple solutions to problems.

We have often found it difficult to be parents of twins, and we know that hearing of the wonderful ways other parents have dealt with problems can sometimes make you feel more inadequate. But we hope that other peoples' ways of coping will give you ideas and encouragement and that, at the very least, you will get some comfort from the fact that others have shared your difficulties—and survived!

Cherry Rowland and Elizabeth Friedrich

· 1 ·

Twins: How? Why? Who?

The news that twins are expected is likely to be greeted with surprise. Why should we be singled out for this privilege—or for this dilemma? Relatives on both sides begin unearthing twins in the remotest corners of the families in an effort to give some explanation or to claim some credit for this phenomenon. The possibilities of the outcome have multiplied. Will they be girls, boys, mixed sex, identical or fraternal?

Though this book is primarily about caring for twins, in this chapter we aim to answer briefly some of the questions parents ask about the biology of twins. A knowledge of the facts will not enable you to predict the outcome of your pregnancy with any certainty, but it will dispel some of the many myths and misunderstandings that surround multiple births.

Incidence of multiple births

Twins are not common. The number of sets born in both the United States and Great Britain stands at about one in a hundred births.

A German statistician by the name of Hellin produced a formula for calculating the odds of higher multiples. Assuming twins occur once in every 100 births, the probability for triplets, he claimed, is the number of twins squared; i.e., 100^2 (one in 10,000) and for quads 100^3 (one in 1,000,000). Hellin's law is valid only as a rough guide among mothers not using fertility drugs; quints are very rare indeed, occurring once in every twenty to forty million births.

The incidence of higher multiple births has increased in recent years with the use of fertility drugs. Unfortunately, parents are not always told the extent of the increased risks that use of such drugs entails. A mother taking Clomid, for example, has a 7 per 100 chance of having twins, 5 per 1,000 for triplets, 3 per 1,000 for quadruplets, and over 1 per 1,000 for quintuplets.

The mystery of the vanishing twin
With the advent of improved ultrasound scanning techniques, it has been found that at least twice as many pairs of twins are conceived as are born. Scans taken in the first three months of pregnancy have revealed two fetal sacs in women who are found at a 14–15 week scan to have only one baby; one twin embryo has vanished, leaving no trace. The earlier the scan is taken, the higher the likelihood of detecting an extra fetal sac that may subsequently disappear. It is only once the pregnancy has reached 14–15 weeks that a scan will reliably reveal the number of viable fetuses. What causes this phenomenon is not understood, but it is believed that the so-called vanishing twin is reabsorbed into the uterus.

Occasionally one twin is lost at eight or twelve weeks when the mother has bleeding and what appears to be a threatened or even complete miscarriage. She may be delighted to find, however, that she is still pregnant, unaware (unless she has had an early scan) that she has lost a twin.

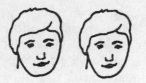

Boy and boy

Girl and girl

One egg + one sperm = same sex

Twin types

Identical

Identical twins account for about a third of all twin births in this country. Half of them will be girl pairs and half boy pairs. Identical or monozygotic (one egg) twins come from one egg that has been fertilized by a sperm and has then divided to form two separate cells or cell masses. It is not yet known why these cells sometimes divide to produce two children from the same set of genes.

Whether the cells divide immediately or later has an impact on the way the placentas will form and on the development of the twins in the uterus. If the cells divide to form two separate cells or cell masses soon after conception, then each fetus will have its own outer sac (chorion), its own inner sac (amnion) and its own placenta. They will move separately down the fallopian tube and may implant close together or far apart when they reach the uterus. If they are close together, then the placentas and the chorion may become fused.

Separate but fused placentas **Separate placentas**

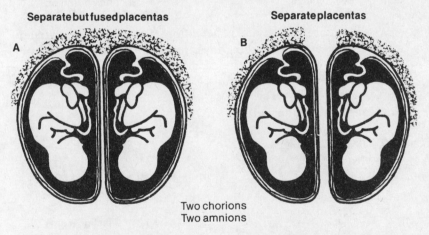

Two chorions
Two amnions

If the separation does not occur at this early stage, the egg will continue to divide and form new cells just as for a single child. The membrane that will form the outer sac, or chorion, is completely formed by the time the cell mass implants itself on the wall of the uterus at about six or seven days after conception. If the cells then separate at this stage the resulting embryos will share the outer sac and a placenta, but each will develop its own inner sac, or amnion. The amnion is the inner membrane that contains the fluid in which the fetus grows. The majority of identical twins are formed at this stage.

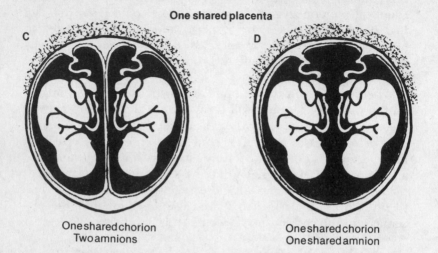

One shared placenta

C

D

One shared chorion
Two amnions

One shared chorion
One shared amnion

When separation takes place after the amnion has been formed, i.e., after about 14 days, the embryos will share one amnion, one chorion and the placenta. Only a very small proportion of identical twins divide as late as this.

Non-identical (Fraternal)

Dissimilar boys

Dissimilar girls

Boy and girl

Two eggs + two sperms = same sex *or* different sex

Non-identical twins, also described as fraternal or dizygotic (two-egg) twins, make up the other two-thirds of the twin population in this country. Half the pairs will be of mixed sex, a quarter will be both girls and a quarter both boys.

Usually only one egg is shed from a woman's ovaries in each menstrual cycle. If two eggs are released from one or both ovaries, and both are fertilized by sperms, then each will continue to develop into children who will be as alike or as different as any two brothers or sisters. The two fertilized eggs may implant themselves into the wall of the uterus close together or far apart. If they are far apart, the placentas will be completely separate. If they are close together, the placentas and chorions may fuse.

Separate placentas   Separate but fused placentas

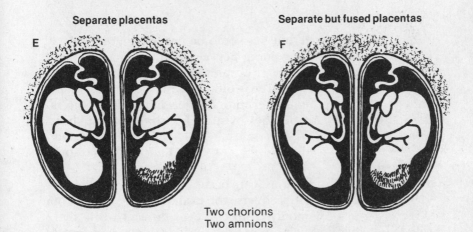

Two chorions
Two amnions

The two ova are probably fertilized at about the same time, but there have been cases recorded in which a woman has borne twins by different men. (An instance has been recorded of a mother producing one black and one white baby. In other cases, paternity has been established by blood-typing.) It is possible that a double conception may take place with a gap of as much as two or three days. In the past it was thought that non-identical twins could originate from eggs shed and fertilized in different menstrual cycles, but the possibility of this occurring is now believed to be extremely remote as the hormones of a pregnant woman inhibit ovulation.

Table 1. Chances of composition of twins

⅓ both girls $\begin{cases} \text{⅙ identical girls} \\ \text{⅙ fraternal girls} \end{cases}$

⅓ both boys $\begin{cases} \text{⅙ identical boys} \\ \text{⅙ fraternal boys} \end{cases}$

⅓ mixed sex

The chances of having mixed sex, both girls or both boys are approximately the same.

A third type?

It has been suggested, but has yet to be proved, that there may be a third type of twin coming between identical and fraternal types. This could, in theory, occur where one egg is fertilized by two sperms. The children would have an identical genetic endowment from the mother and a different one from the father. If such a twin type does exist, its occurrence must be extremely rare.

Supertwins

Triplets, quads and quints can occur in any combination of identical and fraternal. Triplets, for example, may come from three eggs; less commonly from two eggs, in which case there will be one identical pair among the three children; and in rare cases from one egg—after the initial division of cells, one will divide again.

Table 2. Possible combinations of triplets
(I = identical; F = Fraternal)

Conception   *Birth*

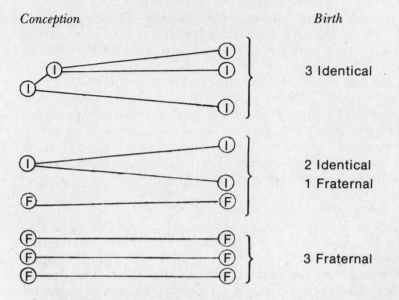

3 Identical

2 Identical
1 Fraternal

3 Fraternal

If both eggs divide again, the result will be identical quads. Identical quads can, in very rare cases, also be formed when, after the initial division, only one egg goes on to divide again twice, as for identical triplets. The most famous of all super-twins, the Dionne quints of Canada, were all believed to be identical.

Fertility drugs
Fertility drugs act by stimulating the ovaries to shed their eggs. Sometimes, when more than one is shed and they are fertilized, a multiple birth will occur. The babies will be non-identical, each with its own placenta, which may fuse with another or others as in the case of any non-identical fetuses.

Determining twin types
For a third of twins, boy/girl pairs, there is no problem in identifying the type—they are non-identical.

For the rest, a close examination of the placenta can give some answers. If there is only one outer sac (chorion), the twins are identical. This still leaves a very large number with separate placentas or with fused placentas, the majority of which will be non-identical and a smaller proportion identical. A fused placenta may pass as a large single placenta. The twin type has often been incorrectly determined; parents have been told that their twins are identical because there was one placenta, or non-identical because there were two.

The only method of determining zygosity when there are two placentas or fused placentas is by a series of blood tests. Blood can be taken after birth from the umbilical cord of each baby and from each placenta. Blood characteristics are genetically determined. If no differences are found in any of a series of tests, then there is a very high probability that the twins are identical. If there is even one difference, then the twins must be non-identical.

Who has twins?

An inherited tendency?
Fraternal twins run in the family. A woman with non-identical twins on her mother's side has a higher than average chance of having twins. Women who release more than one egg in a cycle are thought to produce higher levels of the hormone that stimulates the release of eggs from the ovaries. Why some women should produce more of this hormone is not known, but it is believed that it is this tendency that is passed on through the mother. There is no evidence to suggest that fathers have an influence on twinning.

The popular belief that twins skip a generation has no foundation. This may or may not occur. A mother we interviewed was a twin herself and believed she was "immune"—until her own twins were diagnosed.

Identical twins are on the whole believed to be a chance event with no hereditary factor, but it is now thought that in a very few families a tendency to have identical twins may be passed on.

Racial differences
Twinning rates vary according to a mother's racial origins. The lowest rates occur in the Far East and the highest in Africa,

with Europeans and Indians coming somewhere between. The Yoruba tribe in Nigeria has the highest twinning rate in the world.

Table 3 shows that identical twinning is remarkably constant throughout the world, which supports the theory that such twinning is a random occurrence and not determined by heredity.

Table 3. Number of twins per thousand births

	Total	Non-identical	Identical
Nigeria	46.2	42.3	3.9
England & Wales	11.2	7.5	3.7
Japan	6.4	3.1	3.3

In the United States, the number of identical twins per thousand births is usually between three and four, while the number of fraternal twins stands at somewhere between six and eight per thousand. This averages out to be approximately one in a hundred chance of twins in a given pregnancy.

Mother's age
The likelihood of a mother having non-identical (fraternal) twins increases as she gets older, reaches a peak when she is in her mid thirties, and then gradually falls away. A forty-year-old mother is more likely to have twins than a twenty-year-old mother.

Number of previous births
A woman is least likely to have fraternal twins in her first pregnancy. The likelihood increases with each successive birth. This occurs in mothers of all ages and therefore is not necessarily a factor of maternal age. Both factors are thought to be caused by hormonal changes.

Height and weight
Studies have shown that women who have fraternal twins tend to be taller and heavier than average.

Fertility

There are a number of studies that suggest that twinning is related to fertility. Studies in the United States and in Italy have shown that where there has been a sudden increase in the birth rate following the return of troops from war, the twinning rate rose early, suggesting that twins are likely to be born to women who conceive promptly. Certainly among the mothers we saw, most conceived their children, both twins and singletons, within the first month or two of trying.

Are my twins identical?

Parents often find it difficult to tell at birth whether their twins are identical or fraternal. It usually becomes clearer as the babies develop and grow more, or less, alike. In a few cases, doubt persists well into childhood as some identical pairs can be fairly easily differentiated, while some fraternal pairs can be very similar.

Placentas

It is often assumed that if there is only one placenta the twins are identical and if there are two they are not. While this is true more often than not, it is a totally unreliable way of establishing twin types (see pages 7–8).

Sex

Twins of different sex are always fraternal. Twins of the same sex may be either fraternal or identical.

Size

Weight and size at birth can be misleading as it is more likely there will be a large weight discrepancy in identical rather than in fraternal pairs. This may be due to the effects of the twin blood transfusion syndrome (see page 35). The difference can be considerable. A mother we interviewed had identical girls weighing 7 lb. and 3½ lb. Later, identicals are likely to be closer to each other in weight, and fraternals to diverge more.

Hair

One woman gave birth to an identical pair, one with a dark mop and the other bald! Hair texture and color are initially less reliable indicators than the way the hair grows. If both twins have cowlicks, double crowns or other similar growth patterns, there is a good chance they are identical.

Facial features
Any marked variation, even in only one feature, will mean they are not identical. Ears, with their intricate shapes, are a good guide—but, in the early days, make allowances for ears pushed forward or down because of an awkward position in the uterus.

Hands and feet
Again, any marked variation in shape will mean they are not identical. Palm and foot prints are never identical, but in identical pairs they are likely to follow a similar pattern.

Mirror image
Some identical twins may resemble each other as in a mirror image and have special traits such as a birth mark or hair pattern on opposite sides.

These are just guidelines. Apart from the sex difference, none of these criteria is foolproof. If your twins are alike on all or most of these features, it is very likely they are identical. There are only two reliable ways of establishing that a pair of older twins are identical—a successful cross-twin skin graft, and matching their blood. Apart from the difficulties of taking blood samples from small children, the blood tests are costly and not usually undertaken except for research or medical reasons. In cases where one twin has a hereditary illness or disorder, it can be very useful to know if the other is also at risk, but blood tests or skin grafts are not done simply to satisfy parental curiosity.

Insurance

Very few parents insure against twins, although it is possible to do so. Lloyds of London, the first to offer such insurance, is still the major supplier of insurance policies that pay off in the event of a multiple birth. If you decide to purchase such insurance, you must act quickly because the policy must be secured before multiples are diagnosed, which means within the first trimester (three months) of pregnancy. Chances are, by the time you read this book, it would be too late to obtain twins insurance.

The availability of insurance and the premium depends on a number of factors, including the family history of multiple births on both sides, the mother's age and the mother's previous pregnancies, especially if she has already borne one or more sets of twins.

No firm is likely to accept parents who have undergone treatment for fertility, though a broker stated there was a small chance of being accepted if it was only the father who had received treatment.

Unmarried mothers may meet with some difficulty, and may only be accepted if the father gives the history of twins in his family and signs the declaration too.

Parents most likely to want to insure are those who have already had twins, if they can find a firm that offers a reasonable premium. One such mother commented, "It is one of the rare situations in life where you win either way. If you have twins, you've got the money to pay for the help you know you'll need. And if you have only one, you're only too delighted to forgo what you've paid out."

If you wish to insure against twins, and it is not too late in your pregnancy to do so, we suggest that you contact the agent who handles your family's other insurance business. Although this agent may not handle twins insurance, he or she can probably put you in touch with someone who does. Any broker who deals with Lloyds of London should be able to assist you.

· 2 ·

Pregnancy

"You're expecting twins, how marvelous—two for the price of one!" cry your friends. Perhaps you are not so sure. Something tells you that maybe it is not that simple.

For some women a twin pregnancy proves straightforward and enjoyable, though most experience some of the discomforts or problems that can arise when producing two or more babies in a system that is basically geared to one at a time. While you will not want to spend your whole pregnancy worrying about possible complications, it is helpful to be aware of the problems that can occur, particularly in the latter part of the pregnancy, and be prepared to take things easy.

Diagnosis

Early suspicions
The only certain positive diagnosis of twins is by ultrasound scan or X ray, but there are a number of factors that could make you or your doctor suspect that you are carrying twins before it is confirmed by one of these methods. Regular prenatal visits to your doctor or clinic and the use of ultrasound early in any pregnancy in which multiples are suspected will reduce the chances of twins being undiagnosed. Nevertheless, some twin mothers are not diagnosed until the last two months of pregnancy, and it is still possible to give birth to undiagnosed twins. It is not easy to diagnose twins without ultrasound or X ray. Twin pregnancies are rare enough for some doctors to have had only limited experience in dealing with them—so the first step in diagnosis may well be your own suspicions.

Size

The most significant factor in diagnosing twins is the size of your uterus, especially early in pregnancy. Almost every mother we talked to confirmed that it was her size in the early months that made her (and often friends and relations, too) suspicious. "I was only three months and I looked six," "Suddenly I had this great basketball" were typical comments. Some mothers had not thought of themselves as especially large but found that it was others who commented on their size. One went to try on a maternity dress at six months (her twins as yet undiagnosed) and was disconcerted when the salesperson eyed her professionally and said, "You're due soon, I suppose."

Shape can also be an indication. To accommodate the extra baby, the abdomen tends to expand sideways, making the bulge look round rather than oval.

It is not how large you look but the size of your uterus in relation to the date of the beginning of your pregnancy that is important. The height of the fundus (the top of the uterus) can be felt quite clearly by a doctor or midwife (and you can learn to feel it for yourself). It is a pretty accurate indication of the stage of your pregnancy. As the following diagram shows, there is little difference in the height of the fundus in a singleton and a twin pregnancy initially, but by 16 weeks in a twin pregnancy the fundus has already reached the height of a singleton pregnancy at 20 weeks.

Early weight gain

In a singleton pregnancy there is usually a weight gain of only a few pounds in the first three months, and sometimes no increase at all. In a twin pregnancy there is often a significant weight gain at this stage so that you may be told that you are putting on too much weight and must limit your caloric intake. This is not a good idea if you suspect you are carrying twins.

Lots of limbs

As your pregnancy advances, you may feel that there are a lot of odd lumps and bumps. Your doctor may be able to feel more than one baby, but to be sure she must be able to feel at least three "poles," that is, heads or bottoms, and the heads will

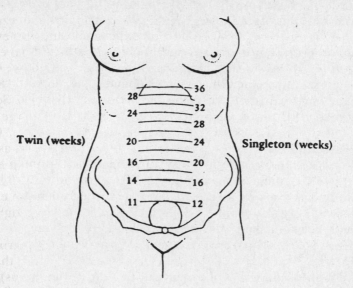

The height of the fundus at different stages of pregnancy, shown in weeks

probably feel relatively small. But babies can adopt all sorts of strange positions and if one is lying behind the other, nothing unusual can be felt, so the fact that two babies cannot be felt or "palpated" does not rule out twins.

Only you can feel the movements of your babies. Individual babies vary greatly in their activity, so it is not so much quantity of movement as movement in three different areas at once that indicates twins. However, movement cannot be felt through the placenta which, though usually sited at the back of the uterus, may be toward the front, especially if there are two. For this reason, the absence of lots of movement does not rule out twins.

Self-diagnosis

A number of mothers we talked to had suspected that they might be carrying twins but were told that "It is just one big baby," "You have probably got your dates wrong," "You should cut down on carbohydrates." If you meet this kind of response, do not be put off. In a large clinic, where you may not see the same doctor twice, it can be difficult to persuade anyone to take you seriously, but if you are certain of your dates and have one or more of the signs of twin pregnancy described above, then do persist in asking for a second opinion and an ultrasound scan. Obviously, the earlier you and your doctor know that you are expecting twins, the better.

Ultrasound

An ultrasound scan uses very high-frequency sound waves, beyond the range of the human ear. These sound waves can be directed as a beam into the abdomen and when the beam meets different organs—your bladder, the wall of your uterus, a placenta, a baby's skull—"echoes" are bounced back into the machine, which then converts them into a picture on a small screen.

The procedure is quite painless, though it may be uncomfortable if you have been asked to drink a pint of water—this makes it easier to get a good picture in early pregnancy. You lie on a couch, your abdomen is oiled and the device that emits and picks up the sound waves is moved backward and forward.

During a scan it is usually impossible for a mother to make sense of the lines on the screen, though sometimes the doctor will interpret the picture for you. The clearest diagnosis of twins is a picture of the two heads together—a sure sign. Occasionally, a Polaroid photo is taken from the screen for reference, and if you are lucky you may be given one—your first snapshot of your twins!

Although twins can be detected as early as eight weeks, because of the "vanishing twin" syndrome (see page 2), at this stage you cannot reliably predict that both fetuses will develop. Some doctors advise against a scan this early as it has not yet been positively proved to be safe in the early, most vulnerable, stages of a baby's development. Some doctors offer a routine scan at about 16 weeks, and that is when most twins are now diagnosed.

Although a scan after 14 or 15 weeks can give a positive diagnosis of twins or more, they can be missed if one baby is lying in front of the other. If you have had a scan that showed just one baby and still feel that you have the signs of a twin pregnancy, then you are justified in pressing for an additional scan. A mother of quints had a series of scans and each time another baby was identified, the fifth appearing only on an X ray. She had been taking a fertility drug, and anyone doing so should be very carefully checked for a multiple pregnancy.

X ray

If your twins are diagnosed late in your pregnancy you may be sent for an X ray. This is usually carried out only after seven months, when it is considered less dangerous. If you are x-rayed you may be asked to lie on your stomach—an apparently impossible feat, but it can be done, albeit with a certain amount of discomfort. An X ray is particularly useful in establishing the position of the twins and in confirming the number of babies you are carrying if it is more than two. When you go for an ultrasound scan or X ray, you will probably be told then and there how many babies can be seen. Strictly speaking, the results of an ultrasound scan or X ray, like any other test, are supposed to go to your doctor and through him or her to you, so you may find that the person operating the machine is not prepared to discuss them with you in any detail.

Good news—or bad?

Reactions from the mothers we interviewed to the news that they were expecting twins varied from delight to horror. Most of those for whom it was their first pregnancy were pleased, especially older mothers who had postponed having children for a long time. Annie was thirty-three when her twins were diagnosed at seven months:

> "I felt very elated. I was so excited I went straight to the nearest phone to tell David. In spite of my large lump, I felt as if I was walking on air. A friend later said it was like winning the lottery, and that's how it felt—a totally unexpected bonus!"

Not all first-time mothers were pleased, however. Some shared Eleanor's feelings:

"We'd waited several years before having children, and it was all carefully planned. I was looking forward to this cozy relationship with a 'baby.' I felt twins were the end of the world and thought what have I done to deserve this—why me? I just want to be ordinary and normal."

Most mothers who already had young children, and therefore had some idea of what would be involved in looking after two tiny babies, were not enthusiastic. Anita's reaction was fairly typical:

"I nearly fell through the floor. A woman came out of the next cubicle and said 'Congratulations!' and I just thought, oh God! As I drove home my knees were knocking so much I kept stalling the car and all the traffic was piling up behind me and I felt like getting out and saying—'You should worry behind me, you don't know what I've got to worry about.'"

If the prospect of two babies at once is daunting, then three might seem impossible. Helen had thought she was having twins, but shortly before they were delivered, it was discovered that they were to be triplets:

"I remember saying, 'But how can I love three babies? I won't even be able to hold them. I only have two arms!' What worried me more than anything . . . was that I would not be able to fall in love three times over. I had fallen in love with Louisa [her four-year-old] after a few weeks. . . . I had found it possible to believe that I would fall in love with the two babies at once, but to fall in love threefold seemed a bit like promiscuity!"

But some mothers with older children were pleased. Gillian already had three children, loves babies and is a foster parent in addition to rearing her (now) five children. She was thrilled when she was told she was having twins:

"I was over the moon. . . . I don't know how I got home. I had the photo [from the ultrasound] on the seat beside me and I thought—'If a policeman stops me for speeding—I'll show him the photo and he'll be sure to let me off.'"

Even if they were upset that they were expecting twins, most mothers had adjusted to the idea by the time the babies were born. Many agreed that they began to feel they were rather clever, and so did many fathers—despite the fact that all the evidence seems to indicate that the father plays no part in twinning!

When a mother gives birth to undiagnosed twins, parents can find the experience traumatic. Sarah had already had to come to terms with an unplanned pregnancy and was concerned as to how her 21-month-old son would cope with a new baby. She decided to have the baby at home, where labor progressed easily:

> "I saw Emma being born. It was a positive and wonderful experience . . . the midwife gave her to me, I put her to the breast straightaway, then the midwife said, 'I think there's another one there,' and I thought, 'Oh God! No'—I'd just had the perfect birth. James felt the same. The first birth was so right, I felt overwhelming resentment that it was being spoiled. I knew I had to get the second one out. I started pushing; it was a great effort. The baby was bigger, and I was tired. I was thinking, 'I hope it's dead.' Martha came out pink and blonde and cherubic and as soon as she was born, it was all right. She was accepted—it was only that moment . . ."

Ideally, twins should not go undiagnosed. Early diagnosis means that the pregnancy can be closely supervised and gives parents time to adjust to the idea of two babies, as well as to make the practical preparations that are necessary.

Taking care of yourself

However fit and healthy you are at the beginning of pregnancy, carrying twins or other multiples is bound to put a strain on your physical resources. If you recognize this, you can set out to compensate for it through adequate rest, good diet and keeping fit. Taking good care of yourself cannot guarantee a problem-free pregnancy, but it will certainly give your babies the best possible chance and leave you in better shape at the end of the pregnancy.

Weight and diet

After a fairly rapid weight gain in the first weeks of pregnancy, you will continue to put on more weight than a singleton mother. The extra weight is not only that of the second baby and its placenta and amniotic fluid but also extra maternal body fluid. There is no ideal weight gain in pregnancy—it will vary greatly from one mother to another. Until recently, women were being advised to keep their weight down. In the past, some authorities suggested 21 lb. as the optimum weight gain in a singleton pregnancy and 28 lb.—only 7 lb. more—in a twin pregnancy. Although a few doctors still follow these guidelines, most now realize the importance of good nutrition during pregnancy even though this may involve a greater weight gain than was previously suggested. In the past, it was also believed that the baby was a parasite that took what it needed from the mother's body and was thus not affected by any inadequacy in her diet. Studies around the world have produced evidence to challenge these views. Women who are poorly nourished tend to give birth to underweight and often premature babies.

Tom Brewer, M.D., and Gail S. Brewer, M.A., conducted a long-term study of nutrition and its effects on pregnancy. The results of their work are published in their book, *What Every Pregnant Woman Should Know—The Truth About Diet and Drugs in Pregnancy* (New York: Random House, 1977). The Brewers maintain that twin mothers who eat correctly can have babies of normal birth weight at term. They found that some mothers, particularly if they were underweight at the beginning of pregnancy, put on as much as 50 or 60 lb., while others who were overweight put on very little.

Eating well for three

A pregnant woman's greatest nutritional need is for protein. Some nutritionists recommend up to 2½ or 3 oz. per day, and Dr. Brewer suggests that a mother expecting twins needs another ounce on top of this (an extra two pints of milk a day, for instance). Details of the Brewers' diet for pregnant women can be found in their book mentioned above.

Any diet can only provide guidelines to quantities of food, as every mother will have her own individual needs. Nutritionists increasingly stress balance and variety in diet. If you aim to have a diet of mainly fresh, unprocessed whole foods varying what you eat, especially proteins and vegetables, from day to day and week to week, then you need not worry that your body will be lacking in any important nutrient. Such a diet should provide all the vitamins and minerals necessary for your health and that of the babies. The following gives guidelines for a healthy diet: Select foods from each group every day.

Diet in Pregnancy

Milk and milk products 3–4 helpings or more a day — 1 quart of milk at least—some can be taken as yogurt or used in cooking; cheese; butter and cream only in small quantities

Meat, fish, eggs, legumes 2 helpings a day — beef, pork, lamb, poultry; heart, kidney, liver (at least once a week for its iron); fish or shellfish; eggs; nuts, seeds, peas, beans, lentils (check for balance to provide complete protein if you are vegetarian)

Bread and cereals 4–5 helpings a day — whole-grain bread, crackers or biscuits; whole-grain cereals, porridge; whole-wheat or enriched pasta, brown rice

Vegetables and fruit 4–5 helpings a day— some fresh, some raw — onions, leeks, peppers, tomatoes; *root vegetables*: potatoes, carrots, parsnips, turnips; *green leafy vegetables* (one helping each day): lettuce, spinach, broccoli, watercress, cabbage, brussells sprouts, green beans; *fresh fruit* (one helping each day): apples, pears, bananas, grapes, melon, soft fruit, dried fruit (some fruit can be taken as unsweetened juice)

| Fats | — unrefined cold pressed olive, |
| moderate quantities | corn, sunflower oil, margarine |

Stimulants such as tea and, more especially, coffee should be drunk only in moderation and can be replaced by herb teas, fruit juice or milk. Alcohol should be drunk only in small amounts, if at all. It is best to avoid spirits altogether. The U.S. Surgeon General recommends that pregnant women eliminate alcoholic beverages from their diet entirely. If you have a problem with this, ask your doctor for help.

There is no place in your diet for sweets, cakes, cookies and fizzy drinks. Not only do they provide empty calories and perhaps extra weight, but also they take away your appetite for more nutritious foods.

If your diet follows these suggested guidelines, you probably won't need multivitamin or mineral supplements, although many physicians recommend them as an added safeguard. Even with careful attention to diet, however, many mothers of multiples do need iron supplements that will be prescribed as necessary.

Toward the end of pregnancy, it may be a problem to eat enough. The increasing pressure of your uterus may make you feel perpetually full, and you may experience heartburn or indigestion. Yet this is a time when your babies are growing rapidly, and you should be building yourself up for labor and after. You may find it easier to do what Dr. Brewer calls "graze" rather than attempt the conventional three meals a day, eating small nutritious snacks throughout the day and even at night.

By adding skim milk, soy flour, wheat germ, and brewers' yeast to recipes where appropriate, you can add extra nutrients without having to eat more bulk. Or you can add them to milk drinks. Sheila Kitzinger, author of many books on childbirth, suggests this "nine-month protein cocktail," which provides 50 grams of protein:

    1 cup whole milk
    ⅓ cup instant non-fat dried milk powder
    4 tablespoons soy powder (available from health-food shops)

1 banana
1 tablespoon honey

Blend all ingredients until smooth.

You can try various concoctions along the same lines using, for instance, concentrated orange juice instead of bananas, an egg instead of soy powder.

More babies means that you need even better nutrition. Obviously, there is a limit to how much you can or should eat, but if you find you are becoming increasingly thinner as your tummy gets larger, a Kitzinger cocktail or two or extra protein in another form will help you keep up your strength and energy.

Nausea

Some obstetricians believe that twin mothers are more likely to suffer from nausea. Not all the mothers we interviewed suffered from it, and some who had had a previous pregnancy found it no worse with twins. There were quite a number, however, who experienced severe nausea and several who said that it was this that made them suspect they were having twins:

> "I was so sick morning, noon and night. I said to my mother, 'I feel so awful, I wonder if I'm having a double dose.' Despite being sick, I put on a lot of weight and was told off by my doctor. . . . The sickness stopped at about 13 or 14 weeks."

Tiredness will make nausea worse, as will hunger. Small frequent meals of bland food will often help, and many mothers find they prefer starchy foods during this period:

> "I never went anywhere without half a dozen cream crackers in my bag. Whenever I started to feel hungry—and sick—I would fish one out. It may not have been the healthiest diet, but it helped me get through the day."

Nausea usually disappears by three or four months, so if you can face only a very restricted diet at this time, you can make up for it later. Any food is better than no food. In very severe cases there are drugs available, but most tend to have the side effect of making you drowsy as well as being a potential hazard to your unborn babies. Vitamin B6 and vitamin C have been found helpful. Both are better taken through food than as tablets. The best dietary sources of B6 include soybeans, brewers' yeast, wheat germ, blackstrap molasses, liver and other organ meats, brown rice, peanuts, salmon, mackerel, herring, sardines, and whole-grain breads or cereals. Vitamin B6 is also found in potatoes, bananas, meat, eggs and beans. Sources of vitamin C include citrus fruits and leafy green vegetables.

Smoking
There is universal agreement about the adverse effects of smoking on the developing fetus and the way in which it can inhibit growth in a singleton. The effect on twins will be even less desirable. Mothers who smoke tend to have more frequent miscarriages, stillbirths, and babies with low birth weight than mothers who do not smoke. If you find it impossible to give up smoking completely, you need to pay extra attention to eating well as smoking is an appetite suppressor. And you might consider taking extra vitamin C, as one of the effects of smoking is to destroy vitamin C in the body.

Rest
Most mothers experience the compulsive tiredness of early pregnancy and find no difficulty in having early nights and a nap whenever there is an opportunity. For some, this feeling of tiredness may continue into the second trimester (three months) of pregnancy, especially if they have a demanding toddler to care for, but most mothers feel better and fairly energetic during this time. Even though you may be feeling well, extra rest is sensible at this stage. At 5½ months you will be the size of a singleton mother at 7 months. Whether you are out at work or at home with other children, half an hour's rest or more after lunch and in the early evening will be valuable, as will regular early nights.

It is during the last trimester that rest becomes especially important. As you become bigger, you will probably find that your size naturally limits your activities. Bearing in mind that by 30 weeks you will be the size of a singleton mother at term, ideally you should not work beyond 28 weeks. If financial necessity or arrangements for maternity leave mean working beyond this date, then you can discuss with your doctor the possibility of having a disability certificate when work becomes a strain.

Some doctors still prescribe extensive periods of bed rest for the last weeks of a multiple pregnancy, although current research suggests that prolonged periods of inactivity do not prevent premature delivery and may actually increase the mother's blood pressure and chances of harmful blood clots. In Britain, with its National Health Service, mothers expecting twins are often admitted to the hospital for rest during the last trimester. This practice is not followed in the United States, however, because of the costs involved and because it has not been found to be beneficial. Particularly if the mother has other young children at home, the disruption caused by hospitalization or rigorously enforced bed rest at home may actually be more stressful than moderate activity with short rest periods during the day.

If your pregnancy presents special medical reasons for extraordinary intervention, your doctor should be willing to discuss the matter with you fully. Feel free to ask any questions you may have. The fact that twins are on the way does not, by itself, mean that unusual measures are indicated or that problems are inevitable.

Once you are at home, work out ways to cut down on housework and take at least two or three hours' rest each day. If you already have a small child or family, now is the time to organize help that can continue after the twins are born (see page 72).

A couple of mothers felt strongly that rest (or the lack of it) had played an important part in the onset of labor:

"I'd had contractions at 32 weeks, but they stopped with the rest, and from then on I felt I was sitting on the babies, willing them to stay in. I held on until 34 weeks."

"I had had a lot of prodding from medical students the day before, some of them none too gentle. That day I was the only one on the ward not on bed rest, so I kept hopping in and out of bed on various errands. I realized that whenever I moved around I had a flurry of increasingly strong Braxton Hicks contractions [the 'practice' contractions many women experience in pregnancy]—I knew I should have stayed in bed. . . . That evening the contractions got stronger and stronger, and they were born the next day."

Another mother attributed the fact that she had carried her twins—weighing 6 lb. 14 oz. and 6 lb. 11 oz.—beyond 38 weeks to the care she had taken of herself during pregnancy:

"I was very careful and quite strict about my diet. . . . I ate fish and liver regularly and lots of fruit.I drank at least a pint of milk a day—I usually had it at the office instead of tea or coffee. And I made a point of putting my feet up every lunch hour while I was still working. . . . I stopped working at 28 weeks . . . until they were born I really took things easy and rested for several hours each afternoon."

Getting comfortable
Deciding to lie down and rest is one thing, getting comfortable is quite another. The basic problem, lying or sitting, is to find a way of giving your uterus as much space as possible. As you get bigger you may find you can rest your bulge on your lap. Find yourself a really comfortable chair at home—a hard upright one may be better than a more obviously comfortable one with cushions. One mother found a garden lounger, where she could adjust the back and foot to any angle, the most comfortable, although she needed help getting on and off in the last few weeks.

Finding a comfortable position in bed at night can also be difficult. You may find, when lying on your side, that a pillow between your knees or supporting your upper leg is helpful. Some mothers also like a pillow or cushion under the bulge. Alternatively, you may find it more comfortable to be in a sitting position propped up on pillows, perhaps with an extra one under the knees. By the time you have arranged yourself, your bulge and the extra pillows, there is not much space in the bed for anyone else, and you can get the feeling that these twins are beginning to come between you and your partner!

Bigger and bigger

For most of the mothers we interviewed, the most difficult thing to cope with in pregnancy was their ever-increasing size and its associated problems. Most reported themselves to be huge by the end of their pregnancy. Breathlessness, indigestion and backache may be caused by the expansion of the uterus. A baby squashed up high under your rib cage can cause a lot of discomfort. Maria summed up the feelings of many mothers in the last months:

> "Oh, it was awful! I couldn't reach my feet . . . I was always so hot, I suppose because I was so big. I had lots of backache—I think it was the size, it seemed to pull on everything else."

But for some mothers, once the bulge had reached a certain size, it became more comfortable again:

> "I was much more comfortable at eight months than at six. By then the bulge was big enough to rest on my lap when I sat down—though when I sat upright it practically reached my knees!"

Bathing can be a hazard toward the end:

> "I was like a stranded whale . . . I always left the bathroom door unlocked in case I finally couldn't make it out of the bath."

As they got bigger, several mothers said they used to walk around with their hands clasped under the bulge to support it. A few found a maternity girdle useful at some stage, though most such garments will not expand enough to be worn in comfort at the end of pregnancy. Some mothers who delivered 12 or 14 lb. of babies had not found any extra support necessary. If you feel really desperate you could try a sling tied round your neck and under the abdomen. These are used in the West Indies and African countries by women carrying twins.

If you find your ever-increasing girth alarming, others may find it even more so. At eight months Clare, who had been shopping, went to get on her bus at the terminal:

"The driver was sitting talking to the conductor. He took one
look at me as I got on, put out his cigarette and said, 'I think
we should get you home' and drove off at top speed. The
conductor refused my fare and watched me anxiously all the
way to my stop."

What to wear

Finding suitable clothes to accommodate your girth may be a
problem. A dress or trousers that fit comfortably at six months
will probably be useless by eight. Buy or make only the loosest
of dresses or pinafores and adjustable trousers several sizes
larger than you think you will need. You may find that as your
skin becomes very stretched it may become very sensitive and
you will not want to wear anything tight around your middle,
so loose-fitting overalls may be a better investment than trousers.

Stretch marks

Stretch marks can appear in any pregnancy, and most women
carrying twins find that these will appear as purplish marks on
the abdomen in the later months. These gradually fade after
the babies are born and remain as fine white lines. There are
creams and oils on the market that claim to prevent stretch
marks: these will help to keep your skin supple and prevent it
from drying out (it tends to become dry and flaky in pregnancy), but they will not prevent stretch marks.

Keeping fit

Although your increasing size will impose severe limitations on
most forms of exercise late in pregnancy, there is no need to
anticipate becoming a semi-invalid. It is important to make
sure you keep fit and supple. You can continue most sports for
as long as you find it comfortable, but toward the end of pregnancy you will probably find that walking is the most energetic
activity you can undertake. Swimming, if you can brave the as-
tonished sidelong looks at your fertility-goddess proportions, is
both good exercise and a wonderful way to forget the extra
weight you are carrying.

Yoga classes for pregnant women are becoming increasingly

popular, and many of the exercises taught there can be carried on until the end of the pregnancy.

With an extra baby to support, your pelvic floor (the area of tissue and muscle that encloses your urethra, vagina and anus and supports your abdominal contents) is subjected to extra strain. It is especially important to do pelvic floor exercises, tightening and relaxing these muscles, regularly throughout pregnancy to tone up this area and help it get back to normal after the babies are born. Muscles that have become very slack can lead to a prolapsed uterus later in life.

As your uterus expands, you may find it quite difficult to pull in these muscles when sitting or standing. It is easier to do the exercises lying down with a cushion under your buttocks, or your feet up on a chair, to raise your hips and tip the weight of your uterus and babies off the pelvic floor.

Your back can also become very vulnerable, so it is important to avoid bending down and lifting weights—such as toddlers—using your back as a lever. If you find it difficult to follow the advice often given to crouch down and get up using your thigh muscles, try stepping forward bending both knees and lifting with a continuous scooping movement.

Good posture, standing with your weight evenly distributed over both feet and your buttocks tucked in can help to avoid backache. Your abdominal muscles will be extra stretched, so avoid putting extra strain on them. Always roll onto your side before getting up from a lying position; draw up your knees and push up with your arms and hands. Never do any leg-raising exercises. Far from strengthening the abdominal muscles, such exercises may pull them apart and strain the lower back.

Childbirth preparation classes
Other useful exercises as well as breathing techniques, general discussions of pregnancy, labor and caring for the babies are provided in childbirth preparation classes. These classes are usually available at the hospital or local clinic. Your doctor or midwife will direct you to classes in your area. Regardless of where you plan to attend classes, arrange them to start sooner than you would in a singleton pregnancy. Most mothers we

talked to missed some or all of their classes either because their babies were born early or because they spent a period in the hospital before the birth. Classes are usually designed to occupy the last couple of months of pregnancy, but anyone expecting twins should aim to start classes between 20 and 24 weeks in order to get a full course well before labor is likely to begin.

Travel

Because of the increased risk of premature labor or other complications, most doctors would advise against traveling too far from home after about 30 weeks. An airline would probably not take you after this date. Obviously you should not spend what might be two months of your pregnancy anticipating premature labor at any moment, but it can happen very fast and must be dealt with in the hospital so that the babies receive immediate care. It is inadvisable, therefore, to go off and camp in the wilds.

Susie's experience is certainly not typical, but it does give an example of the possible consequences of traveling during the last trimester of a twin pregnancy:

> "I was thirty weeks pregnant, staying with my parents in the country, when my waters broke in the middle of the night. The family doctor wasn't very interested and didn't examine me. He said I could get to the hospital in the city where I was booked. The ambulance driver had never been to the city and couldn't find the hospital. I directed them using a street map. I had an occasional pain on the journey. We arrived at five A.M. on Sunday morning and I was put on a drip to slow down labor and given an injection to mature the babies' lungs."

The babies were delivered 48 hours later and weighed 2 lb. and 3 lb. respectively. After eight weeks in the neonatal unit they went home, each weighing around 5 lb.

Sex

A great deal has been written about sex in pregnancy. Most doctors agree that in a straightforward pregnancy there is no reason why the couple should not continue making love as long as they wish.

Some women find that pregnancy increases their interest in sex, others have the opposite reaction. And some men find the pregnant shape very attractive, others less so. The only reason for avoiding sex is a history of miscarriages, any bleeding or signs of premature labor. In these instances you should consult your doctor. The only special problem in a twin pregnancy is how to get near each other toward the end of pregnancy. Obviously you will want to avoid putting any pressure on your abdomen, so now is the time to experiment with ingenious positions.

Fears and anxieties

If you are anxious about any particular aspects of coping with two or more babies at a time, it may help to talk to mothers who are already experienced. The best way to make contact is through a Mothers of Twins Club. These are organized locally on a self-help basis, and if you are lucky enough to have one near you, you are almost certain to find yourself welcomed as a pregnant mother. (See Appendix 1 for the address of the national office of this organization, which can refer you to your nearest local chapter.)

Irrational fears about your baby dying or being born with a deformity are common to all pregnant women. Mothers carrying twins are perhaps more likely to be anxious with two babies to worry about and knowing that a twin pregnancy can be more hazardous than a singleton.

A number of mothers we talked to were certain, right up until the babies' birth, that something would be wrong with one or both twins. One mother had seen an X ray showing one twin to be smaller than the other and was convinced it would die. Another felt little movement on one side and was convinced there was something wrong with one baby. Both mothers had healthy babies. Probably nothing would have stopped these mothers from worrying. If you suffer from irrational fears, then no amount of reassurance will help. It has been suggested that mothers who admit their fears to themselves, or who dream about deformed babies, are more relaxed and cope better with labor itself. It seems that everyone has these anxieties, and it is better to let them out than bottle them up.

Hospital care

If, prior to your twins being diagnosed, you contemplated a home delivery, you need to face the fact that you will be better off in a hospital and plan accordingly. If you were booked into a small local maternity unit without a special-care unit close at hand, your doctor may advise transferring to a larger hospital if this is possible. Many twin deliveries are straightforward and the twins a good weight, but there is a possibility that complications might affect either mother or babies and so twins are almost always delivered in the hospital. We did not find any mother, even among those enthusiastic about home delivery for singletons, who said that she would choose to have her twins at home. As one put it, "Knowing the risks, I wouldn't take the chance. How would you ever forgive yourself if something went wrong?"

Prenatal care

You are likely to be checked more frequently in a twin pregnancy: probably every three weeks from 20 to 26 weeks, once every two weeks until 30 weeks and then weekly until the babies are born. The more babies you are expecting the more intensive the care you will receive and the more likely you are to be admitted to the hospital before the end of pregnancy.

In the course of your prenatal care, in addition to the routine checks of a singleton pregnancy, extra tests may be made to guard against anemia, and you will be watched carefully for any signs of pre-eclampsia (see pages 35–36). Both are more common in twin pregnancy.

Do make sure that at some stage you visit the labor ward where the babies will be delivered. Being familiar with it will help to make you feel more relaxed when you go into the hospital in labor. You can either arrange a visit following a prenatal check—most hospitals are very willing to show you around—or it may be part of the childbirth preparation classes at the hospital. Ask to see the special-care nursery as well. This is where premature and small babies are cared for as well as those who have special problems or who have had a difficult birth. They may spend just a few hours there or it may be many weeks. Twins are more likely than singletons to be in the special-care nursery, and it is well to be prepared for the idea that you could be separated from one or both babies—even only for a short time. This is less upsetting if you have seen where they will be cared for and have perhaps met some of the staff.

Amniocentesis

Amniocentesis is a procedure that is increasingly being offered to women of 35 and over and those who have a family history of certain abnormalities. It is carried out at about 16 weeks and involves using a fine needle to draw out a small quantity of the fluid surrounding the baby. An analysis of this sample can confirm a number of abnormalities, the two most common being spina bifida and Down's syndrome (mongolism).

Mothers of twins who are offered amniocentesis face a number of problems. It is technically more difficult to carry out, so there is a higher (though still small) risk of inducing abortion. Sometimes it will provide information about only one twin because it is not always possible to reach the second sac of fluid. If an abnormality is detected, except in the case of an identical pair with Down's syndrome, only one baby is likely to be affected. Parents may feel that they are faced with an impossible decision: either to have the pregnancy terminated, thus aborting a normal fetus as well as an abnormal one, or to go ahead with the pregnancy knowing that one baby will have an abnormality. You need to be very certain that you can cope with making this decision before you have amniocentesis. Both parents should be offered counseling on the moral and emotional implications of the procedure before it is carried out.

Techniques are being developed that will allow the termination of just one fetus, though it will have to be carried to term, but this may not make the decision any easier for parents.

Complications in pregnancy

Certain problems that can arise in any pregnancy are more likely to occur the more babies you are carrying. Apart from prematurity they include anemia, bleeding, hydramnios and, most commonly, raised blood pressure and pre-eclampsia. They are all conditions that can become serious for mother and babies and may require medical attention and perhaps even early admission to the hospital.

Anemia

Many women become mildly anemic during pregnancy. Anemia is a reduction in the blood of the red blood cells or the amount of hemoglobin in them. Anemia can be caused simply by the increase in fluid in the blood during early pregnancy without a corresponding increase in red blood cells. Later the demands of the babies can deplete the mother's reserves of iron. In severe cases, a mother can become very tired and weak and prone to dizzy spells. The babies may also be affected as they receive less oxygen through the placenta, and premature labor can result.

While a diet rich in iron—liver, egg yolk, whole-grain cereals, raisins, prunes, apricots and nuts—is sometimes sufficient to prevent anemia, you may need extra supplements of iron and folic acid prescribed by your doctor when meeting the needs of two or more babies. If your hemoglobin level is very low after 30 weeks, you might be given iron injections.

Bleeding

Slight bleeding in the early months of pregnancy at times when you would have a period is not uncommon. Any bleeding with fresh, bright red blood should always be taken seriously and you should call your doctor and go to bed. Bleeding sometimes occurs at about 28 weeks or shortly after, when the lower part of the uterus begins to thin out and part of the placenta can become detached and cause bleeding. This antepartum hemorrhage usually stops spontaneously and the placenta reattaches itself. In rare cases a placenta may be very low down (placenta previa), completely obstructing the neck of the womb, in which case delivery by cesarean section will be necessary. Bleeding is always frightening and often looks more serious than it is. A number of mothers we spoke to had problems at some stage of their pregnancy but went on to have a normal labor and healthy babies. It is important to remember that any blood you lose during pregnancy is from your circulation and never from the babies'.

Hydramnios
This is a condition in which an excessive amount of the fluid surrounding the babies is produced. Usually it develops gradually, but it can happen quite suddenly. It is much more likely to happen in a twin pregnancy than in a singleton. Most cases, however, are fairly mild, so if you develop it you may not need any treatment at all. In a more serious case you may have to rest, since the condition can lead to premature labor if it becomes severe.

The babies usually show no ill effects from mild hydramnios, though you may find it very uncomfortable to have your already greatly enlarged uterus extended still further. In certain fairly rare cases, hydramnios is associated with the "twin transfusion syndrome." This is a condition that can affect identical twins sharing a placenta. The circulation of one twin pumps blood into the other, thus reducing its own blood supply and producing too much for its co-twin. This results in one small and one large baby, both of whom may need special care.

Raised blood pressure
If your blood pressure goes up and stays up toward the end of your pregnancy, you are likely to be taken into the hospital for complete bed rest. If the problem is less serious, you may be allowed to rest at home. High blood pressure is bad for the babies because it reduces the efficiency of the placenta. It is also the first symptom of pre-eclampsia.

Pre-eclampsia
The symptoms of pre-eclampsia (sometimes called toxemia) are raised blood pressure, protein in the urine and edema (swelling of the legs, hands and face). Untreated pre-eclampsia can lead to eclampsia, a condition in which the mother develops severe headaches and, finally, convulsions. Such convulsions in pregnancy or labor are very rare because pre-eclampsia is treated swiftly by bed rest and, if necessary, sedation. Where severe

pre-eclampsia is diagnosed, the babies will be induced or in serious cases delivered by cesarean section.

About 10 percent of all mothers develop pre-eclampsia, but the likelihood is greater in mothers expecting twins or other multiples, and in a first pregnancy. It is because mild pre-eclampsia can quickly become severe that if you develop raised blood pressure you will be closely monitored and perhaps even admitted to the hospital if more conservative measures do not bring improvement.

Preparing for change

A note to fathers

As a father you will have to make the same emotional adjustment as a mother to the news of an unexpected increase in the size of your family:

> "It came as quite a bit of a shock. I felt something had conspired against us as we hadn't even planned to have another child, let alone two. It would have been easier to accept if the pregnancy had been planned. But we just got on with it—there is no point in being bitter, and I got used to the idea during the pregnancy. By the time they were born I was quite happy about it."

Some fathers may feel anxious at the prospect of having to support their partner through what could be a difficult and tiring pregnancy. There may also be financial worries, especially if your partner is giving up work. If it's a first pregnancy, a family may jump from two people on two incomes to four on one income.

It is useful to attend childbirth preparation classes together if at all possible. This provides an opportunity not only to learn about the practical details of caring for the twins but also to share some of the natural anxieties you may both have about coping with and relating to two babies at once. Nearly all the fathers we talked to found themselves very involved with the babies right from the start. One of them wanted to pass on a warning for other prospective fathers of twins:

"You're going to lose quite a lot of sleep when you help with night feedings, and it's going to have an effect on the way you work. I'd suggest that fathers don't undertake any new projects in the months immediately following the birth and that they also let colleagues or a boss know in advance that they will not be as available as they were before and may need some support."

During pregnancy you can help by taking on extra household tasks to give your partner more rest, especially toward the end of the pregnancy. If you already have a child, it is a good time for you both to plan ways in which to give him or her more attention to compensate for the time that will be taken up by the twins. The birth of a second baby is often a time when a father builds up a close relationship with the first child. You will be especially important when two arrive at once.

Other children
All children need some help in adjusting to a new arrival in the family, but to be displaced by two at once is very hard, especially for the child under three years of age. Apart from preparing the child for the arrival of two babies, it is important to make arrangements for his care. Whoever is to look after him while you are in the hospital should get to know him (if it is not a close friend or familiar relative) well in advance of your expected delivery date, and if possible be available to come if you have to go into the hospital before the twins are born. If you are lucky you may be away from home for only a few days after the babies are born, but you could be away for weeks beforehand, and continuity of care for older children can help to make your absence easier for them to cope with.

If a young child is due to start at a playgroup or nursery school around the time of the twins' birth, it is a good idea to get him settled in before you are likely to have to go into the hospital. If this is not possible, it may be wise to wait until the babies are well into their first year so that the older child does not have to make more than one major adjustment at a time.

Practical preparations

A check list

• *Help.* How are you going to arrange for the maximum help after the babies are born (see Chapter 4, pages 72–75)?

• *Finances.* Make certain that you are getting all the allowances to which you are entitled. If your income is low enough to qualify you for supplemental assistance, check with social services to make sure that your benefits are correct. You may be entitled to nutritional assistance from WIC (see page 91). Find out what your health insurance will pay for twin prenatal care and delivery.

• *Decorating the house.* If you are planning to decorate or alter your house or apartment, remember that twins tend to arrive early and there will be very little time after the birth.

• *Buying equipment.* You may feel superstitious about buying two sets of clothes or ordering a twin carriage, but there will be little time for shopping after the babies are born. By the end of the pregnancy, you may have to rest and will probably not feel like undertaking tiring shopping expeditions, so prepare the basics in advance.

Suggested minimum clothing and equipment for twins

Where possible try to borrow as much as you can. You are unlikely to need two of everything again.

Clothes

These are minimum quantities. Some babies may need more, and you will want more jackets and hats in winter.

6–7 baby undershirts
6–7 stretch suits (first size) or nightgowns for tiny babies
2–4 hats
4 or more jackets or cardigans
2–4 shawls or blankets suitable for wrapping babies, or
2–4 sleeping bags—knitted or fabric (with hoods for winter). These are useful in replacing shawls as the babies get older.

Diapers and changing

Disposables: a good supply of first size with elasticized legs
plastic bags for disposal

Cloth Diapers: 3–4 dozen (seconds of quality brands are good value)
diaper liners
8–10 pairs waterproof pants—elasticized or tie-on
pail to soak diapers
sterilizing fluid or powder

Toiletries: baby lotion, cotton wool, diaper cream/ petroleum jelly

Changing mat on firm surface

Bathing
Baby bath or large dish pan
Toiletries: soap, cream, baby lotion
2 towels

Sleeping
2 bassinets/portable cribs/carrying baskets
and/or 1 crib—later 2 cribs
6–8 sheets (preferably fitted)
quilts
and/or 2–4 blankets (buy crib size and fold to fit bassinets/ carriages)

Transport
portable cribs/baskets
large twin carriage/convertible stroller
babysling(s)
federally approved car restraints

Feeding (bottle)
6–14 bottles (depending on method of preparation)
bottle brush and salt for cleaning
large pot for sterilizing

    You will also need 2 bouncing cradles or baby relax chairs. If your finances permit, an automatic washing machine and a tumble dryer will make life a lot easier. A discussion of the pros and cons of various types of clothing and equipment can be found in Chapter 4.

Thinking of names

There is a tendency for parents to give twins, particularly girl pairs, related names: either names that sound alike (Lucy/Elisa) or those that begin with the same initial (Jennifer/John) or names with a close association (Christopher/Robin), (Charles/ Diana), (Heather/Daisy). Having similar names can be a nuisance for twins later when there is a risk of letters, exam papers or official forms being confused. Even worse, though, is the confusion they will constantly have to sort out in their social lives. People regard names as labels or symbols of identity and will be helped to know your twins as individuals if the names themselves have their own identity. A Heather and a Daisy will not thank you when they become collectively known as "the little flowers."

For the twins themselves, their name is an important part of their identity, their uniqueness. Address any two- or three-year-olds by the wrong name and they will be indignant at the affront to their newly found selves. Twins have to share so much that they—perhaps more than anyone—need to have a name they can consider wholly their own.

The choice of names does matter and deserves thought and care. The more close-sounding they are, the more likely it is that they will be used inadvertently when a child is called or referred to in speech—even by the parents. Names that look very different on paper may sound surprisingly alike.. A Christopher and a Charles are less likely to be accidentally called by the wrong name, for example, than a Christopher and a Nicholas—names with a very similar rhythm.

The more different the names are in all respects—sound, rhythm, length, spelling, initial—the easier it will be for everyone to get them right most of the time.

·3·

Birth and After

Much of the process of a twin delivery is like that of a singleton. We assume that the reader has basic knowledge of labor and delivery, and concentrate on aspects that are particularly relevant to the birth of twins or more. We recommend general books on pregnancy and labor in Appendix 4, pages 293–294.

Provided your twins were diagnosed reasonably early in your pregnancy, you will have had time to adjust to the fact that obstetrically you are in a special category. The delivery of twins is becoming safer all the time through better prenatal care, improved obstetric techniques and increasingly sophisticated care of premature babies.

Nevertheless, there are still a number of factors that can make a twin delivery more difficult: twins tend to be small (averaging 5½ lb.), more are breech, and more are delivered by forceps or cesarean section. Even when there are no obvious difficulties, there is always particular concern about the second twin, who has to experience the strong expulsive contractions of the second stage twice over.

Although these facts are true of twins' deliveries in general, they cannot tell you anything about your delivery in particular. They do, however, account for the very cautious approach of hospitals to twin labor and birth.

The babies' positions
During pregnancy, twins can and do adopt a variety of positions in the uterus. They may continue moving around until labor begins. Several mothers we talked to had the second twin diagnosed as a breech (bottom first) late in the pregnancy only

to find that it had turned to vertex (head first) by the start of labor—though the reverse can happen:

> "While I was resting in the hospital there was an almighty upheaval on my left side, usually the quieter side. It was Paul somersaulting into a breech position, and there he stayed until he emerged—foot first."

The "presentation" of a baby in labor is important. Because head first is the easiest and safest way for a baby to be born, sometimes a doctor will try to turn a singleton breech before delivery. This is not possible with twins. There is insufficient room in the uterus, and attempting to turn a baby might damage the placenta(s).

By the beginning of labor, most twins will have sorted out which will be born first, and the first baby will sometimes have his or her head or bottom tucked down in the pelvis so low that "it felt as though the first baby would just fall out." In over 40 percent of deliveries both twins are vertex. In over 30 percent the first is vertex and the second breech. The remainder are in a variety of positions: breech then vertex, both breech or, rarely, the first baby may be transverse (lying horizontally across the pelvis). See the diagram that follows for illustrations of these positions.

Although the first twin will usually be lined up more or less vertically by the beginning of labor, the second may not do so until after the first is born.

As long as the first twin is vertex and there are no other complications, you can expect to have a vaginal delivery. If the first baby is transverse, delivery has to be by cesarean section. This may also be recommended if the first baby is breech.

Labor—the first stage

A spontaneous start
Labor may begin with a show, mild contractions, backache or with the waters breaking. The latter is much more common in a twin labor than in that of a singleton. Labor started in this way for about half of the mothers we talked to.

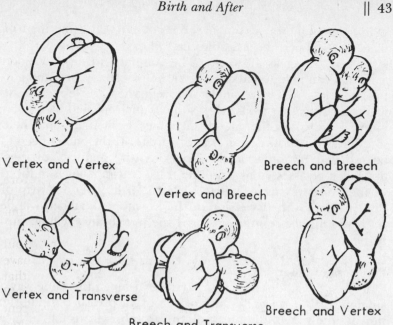

Vertex and Vertex

Vertex and Breech

Breech and Breech

Vertex and Transverse

Breech and Transverse

Breech and Vertex

You will probably be told to go to the hospital when the waters break or when the contractions have become regular. Different obstetricians suggest different criteria for established labor, but contractions coming every five minutes and lasting about 45 seconds is a general guideline in a singleton labor. With twins you may be told to go to the hospital as soon as you feel that labor has started so that the babies' positions and well-being can be checked.

A number of mothers in our survey started their labor in the hospital because they were already in the prenatal ward. Many mothers had spent time there at some point in their pregnancy. Several mentioned this as a bonus when they returned to the hospital or went to the labor ward. "It made a lot of difference seeing some friendly faces and knowing my way around; I felt much more confident."

Induction
The point at which your twins are considered overdue will depend on the views of your obstetrician. Some feel that 38 weeks

is long enough for a twin pregnancy and that after this the placentas will become less efficient. Others may be prepared to let it go as long as 40 weeks. The standard urine and blood tests that can help to indicate when the placenta is beginning to function less well in a singleton pregnancy are less accurate when investigating twins. Ultrasonic scans repeated at regular intervals will show the rate of the babies' growth and may help to indicate when induction is appropriate. If the babies need to be induced for other medical reasons, the maturity of their lungs can be assessed by amniocentesis. A twin labor is induced in the same way as a singleton labor. An intravenous drip of Pitocin (the synthetic version of the hormone oxytocin) will be set up to induce contractions, and the membranes will be ruptured.

Progress of labor
Once labor is under way, it progresses in much the same way a singleton labor does. Because of the extra pressure inside the uterus, the cervix (the neck of the womb) will usually efface (thin out) more quickly, but it may then open more slowly. Contractions are stimulated by the pressure of the first baby's head on the cervix. With two of them crowded together the first baby may not be in the best position to stimulate really effective contractions. If you keep as upright as possible, you will make the best use of gravity to help improve contractions.

Although the different parts of the first stage of labor may proceed at a different rate from a singleton delivery, the overall length of time is much the same: an *average* of 12 hours (within a range of 3 or 4 hours to 18 or even 24 hours) for a first baby and an average of 6 hours with a second or subsequent baby.

The progress of labor will be dictated by the position of the first baby, as in a singleton labor. If the baby's head is in an awkward position or its back is toward your back rather than toward the front, labor will tend to be a little longer.

Monitoring the babies
There is always concern in a twin labor to monitor both babies to see how they are coping with contractions. Their hearts will

therefore be checked frequently. It is often more difficult to pick up the second twin's heartbeat since he or she may be tucked behind the first. Although both hearts can be picked up with the fetal stethoscope, it is usually easier on an electronic fetal monitor, which also provides the benefit of a continuous printout. To monitor both twins, two machines must be used.

One machine will monitor the mother's contractions externally with a pressure gauge strapped to her abdomen. The same machine can also monitor the first baby's heart either externally, with a transducer strapped to the mother's abdomen, or internally with an electrode that is passed through the vagina and clipped to the baby's head. The second baby can only be monitored externally on another machine. (If only one baby is monitored electronically, the other will be checked frequently by the labor nurse or midwife.

One of the benefits of electronic monitoring for the mother is that as well as reassuring her about the condition of the babies, it avoids having two nurses trying to find each baby's heart simultaneously:

> "I had the midwife and the medical student clambering all over me with their little ear trumpets, often during a contraction, trying to keep tabs on the babies' heartbeats. It was pretty uncomfortable and disturbing. Eventually they started marking the position of the babies with little blue crosses—it took a week to get the ink marks off!"

A drawback of electronic monitoring is that it immobilizes the mother. Mobility and keeping in an upright position using gravity to help stimulate contractions have been shown to shorten labor and to produce babies in better condition. Conversely, lying supine can prolong labor and lead to a more difficult delivery. Lying on your back can also constrict major blood vessels, a particular hazard for a twin mother with her extra-heavy uterus. If you have an electronic monitor there is no need to lie down. You can sit propped up on the bed with lots of pillows or on a chair. You can even be on hands and knees. You need to get into the most comfortable position before the monitors are attached.

Pain relief

During the first stage of labor, the breathing and relaxation techniques you have learned in childbirth preparation classes will help you to cope with the contractions. If possible, a mother expecting twins or more should avoid medication or anesthesia. There is a greater chance of multiples being premature or of low birth weight, and thus more vulnerable to the effects of anything the mother might take during labor. Some hospitals may offer (or even encourage) use of a muscle relaxant or inhalation gas during the first stage of labor, but these should be used only if absolutely necessary, not simply because they are available.

Epidural

If anesthesia is required during delivery, the use of an epidural is more advisable than a general anesthesia. With an epidural, the pelvic area is numbed by a local anesthetic that is introduced through a fine catheter into the epidural space of the spine. It allows an obstetrician to carry out forceps deliveries, manipulation of the babies and even a cesarean without distress to the mother and is done while she is conscious. It is often recommended for twin mothers because of the increased likelihood of some complication in the delivery. However, the use of an epidural has been found to increase the possibility of need for instruments to assist delivery because the epidural may slow down the contractions and impede the mother's ability to push. So although an epidural makes the mother ready should complications occur, it also adds to the possibility of certain of these complications.

Once an epidural is set up, the mother remains on the bed. She will have monitors for each baby's heart and her own contractions and probably a drip set up so that her contractions can be augmented with a synthetic hormone should they slow down. It is sometimes possible to taper off or reduce the quantity of anesthetic so that a mother is able to respond to the pressure of the baby's head on her perineum and to push him out. This cannot always be done, however, and in most hospitals there is a considerably higher incidence of forceps delivery with an epidural.

Because of the higher risk of a complicated delivery with twins, some mothers feel that a labor dependent on technical aids is a small price to pay for the certainty of being conscious and alert for their babies' delivery and the knowledge that the twins could be delivered speedily:

> "I was quite happy to have an epidural. As an older mother and having lost one baby, I felt I couldn't take any chances. The twins were so very special. I felt I might not get another chance, and I was prepared to take all the help I could get. The monitors were very reassuring, we had fun identifying which was the one that always kicked most. . . . The epidural worked well. I wasn't worried by being confined to bed—I was so huge that I don't think I could have stood or moved to save my life. The first baby was stuck at the end, and they used a ventouse [a vacuum cup attached to the baby's head] on him. Minutes later, the second baby popped out without any trouble. I was wide awake for the delivery and they were both given to me and both sucked at the breast."

If you plan to have an epidural you should be aware that occasionally they do not work, either because it is not possible to insert the needle in the right place or because the anesthetic does not work correctly and only partially removes sensation. If this happens, it can be disconcerting and you should be prepared to use breathing and relaxation techniques and other methods of pain relief if necessary.

Delivery—the second stage

Spontaneous
If both babies are head down they can usually be born without any intervention. Ideally, you will be able to touch and hold the first until contractions start again, probably after ten minutes or so, sometimes sooner:

> "Sian was born quite easily—after a minute she was put into my arms still slimy, wrapped in a towel and I held her with the help of a nurse while contractions started again. There was a moment of anxiety when Paedar's heartbeat was lost, but it was because he was going through the pelvis. I felt his head and shoulders delivered and then 12 minutes after Sian

was born, Paedar was handed to me and I had them both in my arms. It was a tremendous experience."

After the birth of the first baby the midwife or doctor will feel your tummy to check on the position of the second baby and if necessary encourage it to adopt a vertex or breech position. If contractions do not start spontaneously after about ten minutes, the membranes of the second twin will be artificially ruptured to speed things up. Sometimes this is routine after the first birth.

Few doctors like an interval of more than 20 minutes between the birth of the first and second twin. Once the first baby is born the uterus begins to contract down, making the area where the placenta attached smaller. As an obstetrician described it: "It is like having a postage stamp stuck inside a balloon and beginning to let it down." With its blood supply partially reduced, the second twin may begin to use up its reserves of oxygen.

Although most second twins spontaneously line themselves up to be delivered, sometimes one will take considerable persuasion:

> "It seemed as if they had to squeeze her out. There were several sets of hands on my stomach . . . she was lying sideways quite high up and they pushed her down hand over hand, preventing her from turning back. They tried to turn her head down, but she came out a breech after about ten minutes."

Forceps

Forceps are much more likely to be used in a multiple birth than in the delivery of a singleton, especially for the second twin, who may not be in such a good position to go through the pelvis. They may also be used to protect the heads of breech or premature babies.

If you have already had an epidural, then a forceps delivery can be done quickly, although your physician may first want to slightly increase the level of anesthetic. Otherwise you will probably be given an injection of local anesthetic in the perineum for a low forceps delivery and higher into the vagina for a more complicated delivery. If it becomes really difficult, it is likely that you will be given a general anesthetic.

Forceps delivery is often glossed over in childbirth preparation class so that a mother may have no idea what to expect:

> "I was utterly confused about what was going on and felt I took no part in the delivery of the babies."

It need not be like that, however:

> "Although it was a forceps delivery, the doctor explained what he was doing at every stage and told me when to push so that I still felt that I had delivered the baby."

By the time it becomes apparent that a mother needs a forceps delivery, it will probably be difficult for her to articulate what she feels and wants; indeed she may not care too much about anything. It is up to her partner, then, to remind the doctor to explain why forceps are being used, to tell her what is happening and how she can best cooperate.

Even a difficult delivery can be a rewarding experience:

> "Right at the end I was asked to push. Nothing happened. (I learned later that Tom was oblique and there was an added complication because Robin's foot was in the way.) They tried to move Tom's head manually and that was extremely painful and so I welcomed the general anesthetic when it was suggested. Both were delivered with fairly high forceps. . . . When I began to come round in the delivery room I heard a nurse say, "Wake up, Mrs. Harris, you've got two lovely boys." I was also vaguely aware of Peter talking to the babies in the background. I drifted off again and then woke up. The first thing I asked was not "Are they OK?" but "Are they identical?" There was no need for a reply. Peter was holding Robin, who was awake, and Tom was asleep in a cot beside me—they were very different. Peter and I were left on our own with them for about twenty minutes before we were all taken up to the ward. The hospital photographer was there, and we have a photo of all of us when they were only two or three hours old."

Who will be present?

In a large hospital you may find that there could be quite a number of people in the room for the delivery of your babies. If the delivery is complicated, then the most senior doctor available will be there, possibly with an anesthetist standing by. There may be one or, if available, two pediatricians, especially if the babies are premature or expected to be small. In higher multiples there may be a pediatric team for each baby. Because the birth of twins and more is regarded as an exciting event, there may be a small crowd of medical students, student nurses as well as any nurses who are free. One father dispatched outside the delivery room for a possible forceps delivery heard a shout, "Quickly—there are twins being born!" and his wife counted 14 people in the delivery room.

Some mothers did not mind the numbers:

> "There were quite a lot of people at the delivery but most of those who had come to watch were pupil midwives and students that I had got to know on the prenatal ward so it was a very friendly affair."

Others found it upsetting:

> "There were at least ten people at the delivery. At the time, I was too involved in what was going on to object, but afterward I was angry about it. I felt I was just a public spectacle."

If you feel that you want your birth to be an intimate affair, then you should say so, preferably at the start of labor—it is much more difficult to ask people to leave once they have arrived. In a straightforward delivery there is no reason for extra people to be in the room. And the argument that twin births are few and far between and everyone needs to learn about them is not a valid one. Videotapes of twin births can be used for teaching purposes.

Cesarean

Elective
If the first twin is in a breech or transverse position toward the end of the pregnancy, it may be suggested that your babies should be delivered by cesarean section. An increasing number of obstetricians like to deliver singleton breeches by cesarean, and many more feel that it is desirable with twin breeches. Factors such as the size of your pelvis, whether this is your first

delivery and the size of the babies will also be taken into account.

A planned cesarean will also be carried out if there are clear signs that the placentas are not functioning well and the babies are not growing, or if your blood pressure is dangerously raised or you have symptoms of pre-eclampsia or other medical problems that would make labor dangerous for you or the babies.

If you agree to an elective cesarean, then you may be offered the option of a cesarean with an epidural. This method of doing a cesarean is becoming increasingly popular. The mother recovers more quickly when she does not have the aftereffects of a general anesthetic to contend with. From a mother's point of view, it can be a very satisfying delivery: "It was quite a hassle setting the whole thing up, but I'm glad I persevered. It was marvelous to see and touch them both as they were delivered."

Some obstetricians are happy to have a father present during the delivery. He does not watch the operation—his place is at the other end of the table. From this position, like the mother, he cannot see past the screen placed in front of her tummy.

You may not want an epidural—one may not be available—or it may not be suitable for you for medical reasons, or occasionally it may simply not take. In these instances you will have a general anesthetic.

Emergency

An emergency cesarean will be done in the first stage of labor if the babies become distressed or if there is no progress. In the second stage, it will be done when a forceps delivery is not possible. In recent years there has been a tendency to deliver the second twin by cesarean rather than attempt a difficult forceps delivery.

If you already have an epidural, it is often possible to have an emergency cesarean using this form of anesthetic, but it may be done under a general anesthetic. You are given the smallest possible dose of anesthetic so that very little goes through to the babies, who are usually well and alert after delivery. The delivery is very quick, often less than five minutes from the start of surgery to the delivery of the first baby.

Even though you may be unconscious when the babies are

born, their father can still hold them if they are well enough, or at least see them. Not only will he have had the pleasure of greeting them on their arrival into the world but he will be able to talk to you about them, helping you to begin to relate to them.

Although you will become conscious again within an hour or so of the operation done under general anesthesia, most mothers drift in and out of a doze for several hours, and you may feel weak and confused and perhaps sick for most of the day. It may therefore be some time before you can really take notice of your babies.

The third stage

The delivery of the placenta is not usually of particular significance following the birth of just one baby. Parents of twins may hope that it will tell them whether their twins are identical. We explained in Chapter 1 (pages 7–10) the difficulty in telling just by examining the placenta, though you may be interested to see it for yourself. Some parents will be happy to wait and see if it becomes clear as the babies develop whether or not they are identical. If you want to know for certain, then you could ask if tests described on pages 7–8 can be done on blood taken from the babies' umbilical cords after delivery.

Premature labor

In a singleton pregnancy, 40 weeks is regarded as term and before 37 weeks would usually be considered premature, but as there is no precise agreement on what is term for a twin pregnancy there is no exact definition of prematurity. Concern about babies being born early has less to do with the length of pregnancy than the size and maturity of the babies. Twins born at 36 weeks weighing 5½ lb. will give less cause for concern than a singleton of the same weight born at 37 weeks.

If you begin to have contractions before 34–35 weeks and the waters have not broken, then you are likely to be put on bed rest in the hospital. This is often enough to stop the contractions. You might also be given an injection or put on a drip containing a muscle relaxant, which may slow down or stop labor. You may be given an injection of a steroid to help ma-

ture the babies' lungs. This reduces the risk of respiratory difficulties or infection when they are born. Lung maturity may be
tested by amniocentesis.

Sometimes complete rest can be enough to delay labor for
days or even weeks, but once the waters have broken or your
cervix is opening, labor will proceed as for term babies. Because the babies tend to be small, premature labor is usually
quicker. In some hospitals it is routine to deliver all premature
babies with forceps in order to protect the still-soft bones of
their heads. When the babies are delivered, there will probably
be a pediatrician, resuscitation equipment and incubators ready
to receive them.

It is alarming to realize that the contractions are not going to
stop and the babies will be born before they are "ready." You
may not feel ready for labor, either. Most mothers feel that
they are not psychologically prepared to give birth; and what is
more, the house is not decorated, the baby carriage has not
been ordered and childbirth preparation classes have only just
begun. When told, "start your breathing now, dear," a mother
of triplets born, one of them undiagnosed, at 32 weeks, said
ruefully, "Well, we were going to learn that at next week's
class."

Active birth

Some mothers feel that the best birth for them and their babies
will be achieved by their remaining as active as possible in labor
with the least possible intervention.

Given the "just-in-case" attitude of most hospitals to a twin
delivery, you have to be very determined to get agreement to
this kind of approach. Two mothers who had both already had
babies felt very strongly about what they wanted in their second labor. They were confident of their ability to give birth to
their babies and very determined to do it their way. Both had
supportive partners with them during the delivery.

Jane's delivery:

> "I'd been having contractions on and off from thirty-two
> weeks. At thirty-four weeks my waters began to leak but there
> were no contractions and I went to bed. At six-thirty next
> morning I phoned the hospital and they said come in. I had a

headache and thought I'd just lie down to try and get rid of it and fell asleep. When I awoke it was nine-forty-five! By the time I got into the hospital contractions had started and I was four-to-five cm. dilated. . . . The nurse tried to persuade me to have an epidural. She even took Eddie aside to try and get him to persuade me to have one. They said I'd be very tired by the time it came to pushing out the second twin, but I felt that if I wanted to push I could. They also said that although the second was head down, he might turn into a different position and they would have to use forceps, which would be very uncomfortable for me. I thought that if I had an epidural they would probably have to use forceps anyhow.

"I felt that with monitors *and* an epidural, the whole labor would be taken away, it would be nothing to do with me at all. I felt in a real quandary—they made me feel I was going to have an awful birth and I felt that if I was left alone I would be just fine. I wasn't sure whether to listen to them or to myself. But I felt that if anything went seriously wrong with the second twin they would just knock me out anyhow and at least I would have been there for one and that would have been something.

"I went straight to the delivery room, and they fitted monitors with a scalp clip and two belts. I was sitting upright and having strong contractions. They asked me to lie on my side because one of the machines wasn't working very well and I said, 'No, I'm sorry. I don't work very well on my side!' The nurse was quite annoyed, and they had to use a manual machine!

"After that the midwives were very encouraging. They said I was having good contractions and doing well. They didn't press medication when I said I didn't want it. When I wanted to push they said, 'Are you sure?' and went to get the doctor. They apparently decided I looked too calm and collected and said, 'Oh no, not yet' and went out. Next minute everyone was getting into a whirl because they could see the head and I was trying not to push, waiting for a helping hand.

"Next thing I knew there were sixteen people in the room, but I didn't mind because I was doing it myself. I couldn't have stood having them there if I had had an epidural. The midwife was about to do an episiotomy but the head was too low. The first baby was born and I touched his feet, then they broke the waters for the second and he was born ten minutes later.

"Everyone was very excited. It was the first spontaneous delivery of twins at the hospital for six years!

"I felt really good about the birth. Having no episiotomy and soreness and having breast-fed before they went to the neonatal unit all helped me to cope."

Paula's delivery:

"I didn't want an epidural—I'd had one before and I didn't like it. I had a couple of arguments in the prenatal clinic and I asked to see the consultant. I went with my husband and we talked to him about what we wanted and he was very bland and just said 'Yes' to everything and next time I went the senior registrar came to see me and said, 'Now, what are all the questions you have about your labor?' I was quite unprepared and rather angry and I was on my own so I said, very politely, 'If we are going to discuss it again I'd like my husband to be there so can we talk next time?' So we both went again. He put a lot of pressure on us and said if I decided not to have an epidural it was my decision and I must accept the fact that if anything went wrong it was my responsibility, which was a bit scary.

"He did say grudgingly, 'Well, you've proved us right so far' (I'd persuaded them not to take me in for rest prenatally but to let me rest at home so I needn't be separated from Simon [her four-year-old]).

"When I was in labor and my blood pressure went up they were very nice. They didn't push the epidural and gave me an injection instead. It was good because they had taken notice of what I'd wanted.

"I talked about monitoring during the prenatal visits—they had said how they worried about the second baby and I had said, 'But what if I want to sit right up or even squat?' When I was actually in labor we talked about it again and the midwife was really helpful and said, 'If you want to move around, we will take it off. We just need to monitor the babies every so often.' We were really amazed how flexible they were. They used the fetal stethoscopes to check the hearts until I was well into labor and ready to sit on the bed anyhow. Then they attached belt monitors. They took them off when I needed to pee—it was good to be encouraged to walk to the bathroom rather than struggling onto a bedpan.

"They discussed everything with me in terms of 'What shall we do?' including breaking the waters to speed things up when I was beginning to get tired. I had said I didn't want hundreds of people at the delivery and they asked if I'd mind two medical students, so there was them and three staff and I felt very positive about them.

"The midwife asked if I was ready to push and when I said I wasn't she said fine, she'd wait and I thought, oh, that's lovely, no one is going to bully me. About 30 seconds later I felt the baby move down and yelled, 'This baby's coming.' I had an episiotomy because she was facing the wrong way, then Claire was out in half a dozen pushes. . . . They cut her cord, quickly weighed her and gave her to me. She was all pink and looked lovely. . . . I had her for about ten minutes, then gave her to Bob. The midwife felt to see how the second one was lying. It was all very relaxed. People were laughing and smiling, then Jack was out in a couple of pushes. He came out crying. When the pediatrician checked him, he peed all over her! Then he was given to me.

"When we were ready to go down to the ward they had the two little cribs by the bed and the nurse looked at the midwife and said, 'Oh, we can't separate them, can we?' Then she turned to me and said, 'What do you think?' So they put them side by side in one crib. The nurse said, 'They'll give us hell on the ward for doing this.' I was really touched by that. The two of them lay there, and Jack's hand was immediately in Claire's mouth and she was sucking it."

Getting the birth you want

Safety first
While mothers giving birth to twins have every reason to be grateful for the technology that can come to their aid during labor should it be needed, a number of those we interviewed felt that the concern of the hospital for the safety of their babies had excluded concern for their emotional welfare as mothers:

"I felt that the joy of delivery was taken away. They put me into lithotomy poles to do a forceps delivery, though I hadn't wanted this because I had felt the head coming down. I couldn't push properly in that position, but even so the first one was born as the doctor came into the room to do the forceps. They tried to turn the second, but he went back and

was born normally as a breech with the next contraction. . . .
It was an easy birth but everyone flapped around in panic
because the second stage was so quick. I felt that my wishes
were of no importance, only the babies mattered."

Concern for the safety of the babies and the need for medical intervention in labor should not exclude concern with the
emotional aspects of giving birth. Feeling good about labor and
the delivery of your babies is not just an optional extra for parents, it is the beginning of a good relationship with them.

Making your wishes known

If you have questions that are not answered satisfactorily in
your regular prenatal visits or if you are concerned about a
particular aspect of the birth, you can ask for a special appoint-
ment to see your obstetrician. Taking your partner or a close
friend will give you moral support. It helps to prepare in advance a list of questions you want answered about the routine
conduct of a twin labor and what sort of choices you might be
offered. You can also find out in what circumstances you might
be separated from the babies. Make sure any special requests
or concerns are entered in your notes.

You will need to make the same points again when you go
into the hospital in labor. Mothers have found, as Paula did,
that even when they did not get a very positive response to
some of their requests in the prenatal visits, staff on the labor
ward were more sympathetic.

You are likely to feel much more positive about the birth of
your babies—even if the delivery is a complicated one—if you
have been involved in decisions about what should happen. If
you make it clear to all the staff from the obstetrician down
that you are not only concerned about the safety of your babies
but about the quality of your delivery, there is a good chance
that your wishes will be respected whenever possible.

Triplets, quads and quints

The more babies you are carrying the earlier they are likely to be
delivered. Triplets are usually born at about 35 weeks, though
some will be earlier and a few may be born as late as 36 or 37

weeks. Quads are born at about 33 weeks, again with considerable variation. Although triplets will be delivered vaginally whenever possible, most triplets, two-thirds of the deliveries or more, will be by cesarean section. Occasionally, undiagnosed quads or quints are born vaginally—otherwise they are usually born by cesarean.

It is the condition of the smallest baby that dictates when the cesarean will be carried out:

> "There was concern that the one lodged up in my rib cage might be in such cramped conditions that first of all it might not be able to develop properly, and secondly it might not be able to survive a natural birth when it would be subject to a lot of stress and be the last one out."

After carrying out amniocentesis to check the state of the babies, Helen's triplets were delivered by cesarean at about 34 weeks.

The birth weight of triplets averages around 4 lb., though they may reach more at 35 weeks or beyond. Those delivered earlier are likely to be smaller and spend longer in the neonatal unit. Quads and quints will be correspondingly smaller still.

Parents of triplets and more will undoubtedly be made only too aware of the potential hazards of a multiple birth and will probably focus on delivering the babies safely. It is wise to be prepared for a cesarean delivery as a strong possibility. A straightforward vaginal delivery will be a bonus.

Your first contact with your babies is also likely to be delayed, since nearly all triplets will be in special care immediately after delivery and will probably remain there for a number of weeks. Getting to know three or more babies as individuals is bound to be a very gradual process.

First contact with the baby

Ideally, your babies are delivered gently one at a time onto your tummy and then into your waiting arms before being given to their father to hold. One of the bonuses of having two is that you each have a baby to cuddle! The reality may not always be like that.

It is not only babies who are ill or were distressed during delivery who may need attention in the special-care unit. Babies of low birth weight are also routinely taken to the unit, and this will include many twins. Such a baby is one that weighs less than 5½ lb., and most twins born before 37 weeks will go into this category. A number of twins born after this time also weigh less than 5½ lb., although it may only be one of a pair. It is not uncommon to find a difference of one or two pounds between twins. In a few cases one may weigh twice as much as the other. Virtually all triplets and more will be of low birth weight.

Babies who weigh close to or over 5½ lb. and who are healthy and feeding well may spend only a few days in the unit. Smaller babies lack enough fat to give them good insulation and can suffer from heat loss. They need the extra warmth of the special-care unit (a temperature of above 80° F—just right for the babies but not so good for visiting parents!) while they put on extra ounces or pounds before they are discharged.

Tiny babies of 2 or 3 lb. may need help with breathing and are kept under close observation. With the sophisticated skills and equipment available in special-care units, even very tiny twins have a good chance of surviving to become healthy children.

Contact may be delayed for many reasons: If you have had a general anesthetic, you are not even "there" for the birth. Luckily as a species we do not, like some animals, have a critical period after which we will not accept an infant as our own, but there is no doubt that the sooner the process of bonding begins the easier it is to get to know and love our babies.

A mother who is tired and perhaps dopey with drugs may not feel able to make the effort to greet her babies, and staff busy with the welfare of the babies may not think of her. Several mothers whose babies went into the special-care unit regretted this lack of early contact:

> "When the first baby was born they whisked her away. They gave me the second all wrapped up. I was stranded with my feet in lithotomy poles and couldn't hold him properly. I asked about her, and they eventually said she was bruised from the forceps and I could see her later. I naturally

thought there must be something awfully wrong if she looked so bad that they couldn't show her to me. When I finally saw her, she looked OK—all the anxiety was for nothing."

"The delivery was quite easy but all a bit hazy. I was more aware of my stomach collapsing and becoming all horrible and crumpled than with the birth of the second baby. They were both cleaned up, given some oxygen, then taken to the premie unit. I felt too weak to visit them that day so I didn't hold them until the next day. I really wished I had insisted on holding them when they were born."

In situations such as these a father who is there during labor and delivery can do much to remind staff tactfully about the mother's need to hold or at least see *both* babies. Sometimes it is assumed that as long as parents have seen or held *one* baby, that is all right.

Sometimes there are urgent medical reasons why a baby must be taken straight to the neonatal unit and not handled, but such occasions are rare and it is usually only very tiny two- or three-pounders who need instant and continuing help with breathing. Larger premies may be surprisingly responsive:

"I had touched them both as they were born, then they took them away to check them and were about to take them down to the premie unit when I asked if I could have them to breast-feed. 'Oh,' they said, looking surprised, 'you can if you like. But don't be surprised if they don't suck; they're so small.' [They were 4 lb. 12 oz. and 5 lb. 3 oz.]. But perhaps because I hadn't had any drugs they both sucked strongly. It was really important having that contact with them. That and having a good delivery I'm sure helped me to cope with their being in the neonatal unit for five days."

If you are separated from your babies at birth because they are small, they or you are ill or you have had a general anesthetic, then do not be surprised if it takes time to feel that they are yours:

"After 48 hours I was wheeled down to see them. I still felt very weak. They held up these babies and said how nice they were. I didn't know what to say. I couldn't feel anything at all—not until the next day when I went to feed Belinda.

When I got her in my arms I felt better. I felt as if she was mine. It was another day before I held Tara, and I didn't feel as if I could get attached to her. . . . It took some time to get used to her. I didn't say anything to anyone, but I did wonder when it would come right. After a few weeks it did."

When you are not able to visit your babies for several days, a Polaroid snapshot of them can be very valuable. Some special-care units have a camera. It also helps if their father is able to visit the babies frequently and report on them to you.

Premature babies

Parents are often surprised at the appearance of their newborn. He or she is seldom a picture-book baby and probably bears no relation to the fantasy baby imagined in pregnancy. The appearance of premature babies can be even more startling. Very tiny babies often have an "unfinished" look. Because they have so little body fat, their facial features may be very prominent and their arms and legs may look fragile and scrawny.

A mother of triplets wrote about her first meeting with her 4½ lb. babies:

"They were tiny and funny with their little bony faces topped with stockinette hats [to help maintain body temperature]. . . . Even the miniature nighties swamped them . . . I held each in turn . . . I laid them in the crook of my lap with their head cradled in my hand. They only reached the length of my forearm . . . I drew up their nighties to inspect their legs and chest. The muscle and skin was so soft and fragile that it hung loosely on their skeleton, and their bottoms were so small that they could easily even at this stage kick themselves free of their diapers with their constantly working legs."

Many premature babies initially spend a great deal of their time sleeping as they develop and catch up on the time they would have spent in the uterus. It may take a while before parents feel that they and their babies are beginning to respond to one another.

On the ward

A mother who delivers a singleton can reasonably expect to have him with her in the maternity ward. Only one-third of the mothers we interviewed actually went to the maternity ward with both babies, though three-quarters of this number had one or both with them after two or three days.

The size of the maternity ward will depend on the design of the particular hospital you are in and may be anything between four and ten or more beds. Many maternity facilities have semi-private and private rooms available as well. Some hospitals make a point of offering single rooms if they are available to twin mothers. Several mothers were lucky enough to have this facility. One mother was even given a suite that included a separate nursery:

> "It was absolutely wonderful. They wanted me to get used to my babies in peace and quiet, although they knew it wouldn't be like that at home. They felt I should have a good start in the hospital. They couldn't have been more helpful. They ran me in gently, helped with bathing and washing them and at first a nurse helped with feedings. By the time I left, I was able to do everything."

One of the difficulties mothers found on a ward was that there was not enough space for themselves and two cribs. If you find yourself hopelessly cramped, you can ask to be moved to a better position or to a side ward or single room.

Getting back on your feet

You are in the hospital not just for the babies' sake but also for your own. Your needs are as important as theirs even though sometimes it may not seem like that:

> "It was rather a shock after the labor ward where all the emphasis was on our welfare. On the ward afterward everyone seemed concerned about the babies and not nearly so interested in us mothers."

After delivering twins or triplets, it may take longer to recover than after the birth of a singleton. Many mothers are very tired by the end of their pregnancy and their resources may be low. Your body needs time to recover before you are launched into caring for your babies at home. Eat well and rest.

Getting some rest

With two babies to care for, you need all the rest you can get. You should not feel apologetic about asking for help. Sometimes staff simply do not realize what is involved in looking after two babies at once, especially when it is all new and you have not had a chance to work out the strategies and skills that you will develop later.

A few mothers encountered responses such as "It's no use us doing it for you, you're going to have to look after them yourself at home." But it is to be hoped you will not have to do it all yourself. You will have arranged for help for the first few weeks or months at home, and you will also be fitter and stronger by then, so accept and—if necessary—ask for, all the help you can get. If problems do arise and you are too exhausted or upset to deal with them, get your partner to ask the head nurse to help you sort things out.

Although you will probably want to feed the babies yourself, it saves a great deal of time if a nurse will change them for you, and when you are pressed for time, she could give an occasional bottle feed. Should you become very tired, ask for a night without the babies. They can be fed in the nursery with either a bottle of milk or, if you are breast-feeding, a bottle of dextrose. When you are breast-feeding you cannot do this often without impairing your milk supply, but just once in a while may be worth it for the extra rest. If the babies are restless, you can ask for them to be in the nursery for the night and you can be wakened to feed them.

Most hospitals have a rest period in the afternoon. Feeding two babies can often spill over into this time, but do try to make it a priority. Five minutes of complete, conscious relaxation can set you up for the rest of the day.

Visiting time

You have managed to feed the babies, get into the bathroom, have a few mouthfuls of lunch, and are just thinking of having a nap for ten minutes when the troop of visitors eager to admire you and your babies begins to stream into the ward—a familiar scene for many mothers. When you have so much to cope with, too many visitors can be the last straw. If you establish beforehand that all arrangements to visit you should be made through your partner, you can see only those you wish to see while you are in the hospital. It is much easier to cope with visitors and well-wishers once you are at home—as long as there is someone else to do the entertaining.

Back in shape

Do not expect too much too soon from your overstretched tummy. More than one newly delivered mother of twins has been asked when she was expecting her baby. Many mothers commented to us on their dismay when they first viewed their tummy:

> "A couple of days after the birth I had a look at myself sideways in the cruel mirror in the hospital bathroom. This great lump of flabby wrinkled flesh that was my tummy hung down in folds. I pulled my muscles in to give it some kind of shape . . . nothing happened. . . . It was never quite the same again, but not so bad that I couldn't wear a bikini—though not a brief one—three months later."

Patient, gentle exercising will eventually restore your shape. The simplest and most effective is just to pull your tummy muscles in slowly and firmly, concentrating on each part of your abdomen, and then let them out again. More violent exercises, especially those involving raising your legs, can damage your already overstretched muscles.

The effects of a multiple pregnancy and delivery on your pelvic floor are less immediately visible. It may only be when you find you have no control over your bladder as you sneeze that you realize things are not quite right. Continuing with the pelvic floor exercises you did in pregnancy will eventually restore muscle tone to this area, but they must be done regularly.

Tummy and pelvic floor exercises should be started as soon as possible even though you feel nothing is happening when you first try to use the muscles. Although there are many pressures both in the hospital and when you take the babies home, making a ten-minute space for yourself should be a high priority.

For information about exercises during pregnancy and after delivery (with special suggestions for mothers of multiples and those who have had a cesarean section), try reading *Essential Exercises for the Childbearing Year,* by Elizabeth Noble (see Appendix 4, page 293).

An episiotomy, bruising from forceps or a cesarean scar can be sources of considerable discomfort. Frequent salt baths are healing and soothing.

Starting breast-feeding

You should receive every help and encouragement from staff in establishing breast-feeding. If their support seems less than wholehearted or their advice conflicting, it may well be because they have never seen a mother breast-feed twins and are uncertain how it can be done. In these circumstances you need to be very confident and determined and clear in your own mind how to set about it. We discuss the principles and methods of feeding in Chapter 4. An excellent publication on breast-feeding twins is available from the Center for the Study of Multiple Gestation. (See Appendix 4, page 295.)

However determined you are and clear about the theoretical principles of feeding, there is no doubt that the right help and advice is important when it comes to dealing with real live babies who perhaps fall asleep at each feed or suck too fast and get upset. Rachel, whose twins were her first babies and were delivered by cesarean under general anesthetic, felt that the help she had received was crucial in her success:

> "Everyone meant very well, but I got hopelessly conflicting advice: the doctor in charge of breast-feeding would come along and advise one thing, then the nurse another, and a student nurse would suggest something else. It was terrible, and I saw other women become discouraged and give up. Then this wonderful woman came on night duty. She was a middle-aged West Indian nurse who had five children, all delivered by cesarean and all breast-fed. She exuded confidence and she would sit with me at night through a whole feeding.

She calmed me and the babies down. I could see them relaxing when she touched them. She gave me all kinds of useful advice and reassurance. She was on duty for a week, and by the end of that time I was feeding them confidently. I'm sure I couldn't have succeeded without her."

Several mothers felt very self-conscious while they were learning to feed two together. Inevitably staff and other mothers were intrigued to see how it was done:

"One day there were several people round my bed at feeding time and they were saying, 'How are you going to do it—we've never seen twins being fed before. Can we watch how it's done?' But I didn't know how it was done, I was still trying to work it out."

"I felt really uncomfortable for the first few feedings—I got all tense and sweaty trying to arrange them—then I thought, this is ridiculous, and pulled the curtain round the bed—and it was much better."

Your babies are likely to be small and may need feeding every two or three hours. Small, frequent feedings will stimulate your supply and are less likely to lead to sore nipples. You may want to feed each baby separately on some occasions, especially if this is the first time you have breast-fed, but feeding them simultaneously is an added stimulus to your milk supply and should be attempted while you are in the hospital. You will need help arranging the babies and latching them on, especially when one comes off in the middle of the feeding. It is also useful to have someone to burp the first baby until you learn to manage this yourself. This means having someone with you throughout a feeding, and you may have to ask for this to be arranged.

A hospital bed is normally too narrow to allow you to have a baby on either side of you, so it is better to sit sideways on the bed with your feet on a chair or in a chair with low arms on which you can rest the pillows and the babies. You cannot feed properly if you are uncomfortable, so make sure you are given a rubber ring to sit on if you have a sore perineum after an episiotomy.

The best treatment for soreness is exposing your nipples to the air as much as possible (not always easy in the hospital). If they get very sore, you can try feeding the babies through a rubber teat held over the nipple, though this may mean feeding them separately. Most mothers found that soreness lasted only a few days or perhaps a week. If you have serious problems with feeding, contact the La Leche League breast-feeding counselor (see Appendix 2, page 290), who will give you advice on the phone or may be able to come and visit you.

You may have to give complementary bottles (*after* a breast-feeding) in the hospital either because your babies are very small or because your milk supply is slow to build up. Once the babies reach a reasonable weight and your supply is established, you will be able to phase these out. If either parent suffers from allergies, the babies could be allergic to cows' milk. If there is no bank of expressed breast milk in the hospital, your local La Leche League may be able to supply it or you can arrange for a soy-based milk to be brought in.

Should you encounter problems that you cannot resolve— difficulties trying to fit feeding your babies into a hospital schedule or a lack of support and help with feeding—ask to see your pediatrician. She should be able to advise you and establish with the nursing staff how they can best help you.

Babies in special care

Most mothers we saw whose babies went to the special-care unit had them with them on the ward if not in a few hours, then in a few days. If your babies are not with you in an hour or so, you will be encouraged to go and see them. Staff in the neonatal unit make a point of encouraging parents to hold their babies, or, if they are not well enough to be picked up, to touch them. Babies thrive not only on warmth and food but also on loving handling.

While the babies are in the unit, you will be encouraged to feed them and handle them as much as you like. If the babies are too small to suck, they will be fed through a fine tube that is inserted through the nose down into the stomach.

Babies who are under 5 lb. or very weak may not have the

stamina to suck for a whole feeding and will need to be introduced to the breast or bottle gradually. If you plan to breast-feed, you can stimulate your supply by using an electric pump, and the expressed milk can be fed to the babies. Most mothers who did this felt it was worthwhile: "I felt it was something I could do for them, and it provided a link."

The few mothers who did not have their babies at all in the maternity ward found it a strange experience:

"It was a very peculiar feeling to have your children taken away soon after they were born. After a day or two I really wasn't very interested. There was no point of contact and I was taken up with my own discomfort after the cesarean."

"It didn't upset me not having the babies with me, though I did find it odd being surrounded by flowers and congratulations and having nothing to show for it. I felt pretty ill, and although the neonatal unit encouraged me to visit, it was an awful effort to get down and back up the three floors. The nursery was so hot that I always felt faint. I only went down when my husband came in the evenings. I suppose I could have gone more often, but I felt a bit detached from them. I was relieved that they were being cared for so well. They were often asleep when we were there or were tube-fed. I felt there wasn't really anything I could do for them."

Sometimes only one baby needs to go to the unit or one baby becomes unwell after both have been with you on the ward. Some hospitals have a policy of keeping twins together and will admit both babies. It is much easier for the mother both physically and emotionally when both babies are in one place. If this is not the policy in your hospital or there is not space for both, see if it is possible to have a room for you and the well baby as near as possible to the unit.

Mothers who had one baby on the ward and one in special care found it exhausting, especially if they were trying to breast-feed. Marilyn's experience was typical:

"It was all so hectic. I wanted to breast-feed, so I decided to give each the breast at alternate feeds while they were in different places. . . . I would dash down and feed Tessa, and by the time I'd finished it was time to come up and feed Patrick.

I could hardly find time to sit down and eat, do exercises and get a rest. . . . I asked if I need not feed Patrick on the ward at night because of going down to feed Tessa, and they were quite reluctant about agreeing. I had to negotiate it with each new shift. I didn't worry so much about Tessa as there was such a high ratio of staff to babies in the unit, but I was concerned about Patrick when I wasn't there. One night when I came up from feeding her, expecting that he would have been given the bottle, there it was, still stuck in the end of the crib."

Many neonatal units encourage fathers as well as mothers to visit whenever they can. This can be a great help for a tired mother and a bonus for the father:

"I found it very tiring having to go up and down to the unit to visit them and several evenings after visiting time, Ian took my expressed breast milk up and fed and changed them both. He had a wonderful time with them."

Going home

Leaving babies in the hospital

A hospital will often encourage a mother to stay a few days longer than she needs if it means she and her babies can leave together, but few have facilities for a long stay. Most units like parents to visit as often and for as long as they wish and will encourage breast-feeding mothers to express milk, arranging for them to have an electric pump at home. Such pumps can be rented if necessary. Your local La Leche League will have the required information.

Sometimes one baby is ready to go home before the other. In many units it is the policy to keep both until they can leave together. A few still suggest that bringing them home one at a time will help the mother, gently introducing her to caring for two. Few mothers agreed with this:

"The doctor wanted us to leave Emily behind because she was still quite small and fragile, but I felt very strongly that once I was home with just Helen I might get used to having one and be unable to cope with two. Also, I just didn't want to be parted from her, so we took them both."

There are times, however, when one baby will have to come home without the other either because there is a shortage of beds in the unit or because the second twin needs a fairly long stay in the hospital. Visiting can be difficult, especially if you are some distance away, but it is very important to keep in touch with the baby in the hospital.

Being separated from one baby while you develop a relationship with the other can cause problems. Most mothers dealt with it successfully. One mother who visited daily and gave one (sometimes two) breast-feedings to the baby who was still in the hospital felt that this helped her to keep in touch with him. She was able to get both babies onto total breast-feeding within a few weeks of getting the second baby home.

Going home without either baby may seem odd, especially if you have had only a limited contact with them in the special-care unit and have not yet begun to care for them:

> "It was a strange, suspended state. There I was, a new mother and no babies. I didn't know what to do with myself, I hadn't any role. My brother came to visit me, and we went out for a drink. It felt all wrong. I didn't know how to behave. We visited them every day. It was so artificial going in and saying, "Hello, babies." They just lay there. I don't think either of us felt they were really ours. They were hospital property. The staff were super, very kind and always answered questions, but I was told off one day for looking at the notes on the end of the crib. I think the first time I felt they were mine was when we came in one evening and Luke was crying for a feeding and there wasn't a bottle ready. I felt a real stirring of maternal instinct. It was my baby that was hungry and I wanted to feed him."

If you have to go home without your babies, then you can take time to concentrate on getting yourself fit and well to care for them when they do arrive. Several mothers were ill or just exhausted after their babies were born. One mother of triplets described herself as "haggard and drawn," another "like a scarecrow." Helen felt it was only because she had worked hard to regain her strength that she was able to cope when her triplets came home from the hospital:

> "I was worried by this physical weakness; I had been very anemic, so I really looked after myself in those two weeks at

home. I did almost nothing but rest and drink lots of Guinness, and I did all the things I thought would make me strong. By the time they came out I was really feeling quite prepared."

When the babies are finally discharged it is not uncommon for parents to feel that they are not quite ready for the responsibility of taking them home:

"The nurses had been talking about them going home 'quite soon' for some time and then we went in one evening and they said, 'You can take them home tomorrow if you like.' We just looked at each other and gulped. Then, 'Well—no, we couldn't do that—their room isn't ready and we haven't got any bottles.' I don't think we would ever have felt ready, though. It seems such a big thing, suddenly assuming responsibility for these tiny things."

Home at last
Several mothers who had spent some time in the prenatal ward or had a long stay after the babies were born confessed to feeling institutionalized and being quite reluctant to return home:

"I got very depressed in the hospital. I felt very tired and weak, and I'm usually very healthy. I felt I'd never get out and if I did I wouldn't be able to cope with me, let alone the babies. The nurse was wonderful. She was very reassuring and sent us out together for an afternoon while I was still in the maternity ward. We went to the park and I was dazzled by the green of the trees—it was early spring when I went into the hospital. Then we went home for a few hours. I just lay on the bed and had a good cry, and it was then that I realized I *did* want to come home."

Eventually all babies and mothers are discharged, leaving the safe confines of the hospital to embark on their new life. It can be a very exciting moment:

"I'll never forget the drive home with them as long as I live. It was dark, and to me High Street looked as though it had been decorated for Christmas with garlands and fairy lights. I was absolutely high."

· 4 ·

Practical Management— the Early Months

Getting organized

A new mother with just one baby usually finds that caring for the infant occupies her whole day. How then can anyone cope with two, or even three or four? In order to not merely cope but actually have some time to enjoy their babies, mothers generally agreed that two things were necessary: to have as much help as possible and to organize themselves and the babies into a routine.

Help
Mothers of multiples require additional help, especially at the start, and it's best to organize plans for this in advance if at all possible. Unlike Britain, where home help for mothers of newborn twins or other multiples can routinely be arranged for most families through social services, the United States has no program of public assistance for which families qualify simply because a multiple birth has occurred. As a result, the parents of multiples must make their own arrangements for assistance, and this help can prove to be quite costly. Because few families can afford the luxury of full-time paid household help, parents of multiples must often rely on an informal network of friends, neighbors and relatives.

More than half of the mothers we talked to had no regular help while their babies were small beyond the first few weeks, yet the overwhelming response to a question about what would have made caring for the babies easier was: "more help," "another pair of hands," "someone else around the house." Others shared the feelings expressed by one mother:

> "I really wished I could have the first few months over again. I let myself get so bogged down in the difficulties that I really didn't have time to enjoy the babies."

Mothers whose twins were their second or subsequent children were generally far better organized than mothers whose twins were their first, presumably because they had a much clearer idea of what would be involved in caring for two babies.

It may be that few mothers organized help because they did not realize in advance that they would need it, and once they were involved in caring for the babies they had neither the time nor the energy to arrange things differently. Another explanation may be that the right kind of help was not available at the right time. A survey carried out in Canada by the Parents of Multiple Births Association looked at the stresses on parents caused by the arrival of twins or more and found that having help at home could reduce stress but *only* as long as:

—the mother is assured this does not reflect on her adequacy as a mother;

—*she* determines the areas where the help is needed;

—having an extra person in the house does not increase the physical work.

Our discussions with mothers bore out the findings of this survey. Several mentioned their difficulty in accepting help when it was offered because they felt a need to prove that they could cope. The feeling of needing to prove oneself as a mother is understandable, but if you can distinguish those things that are part of mothering your babies—feeding, changing, bathing, cuddling—from those that are not—cooking, washing, cleaning, shopping—then you can accept help with the non-mothering tasks without feeling threatened.

Mothers of higher multiples do need help with mothering as well—and so will mothers of twins at times. Everyone handles children in different ways. Once you have made it clear what you want on issues that are important to you, such as the way you deal with crying, it is then wise to have a relaxed and tolerant approach to details. Babies are usually not bothered about such things as a different style of diaper pinning or wearing the wrong jacket.

Some mothers may experience very mixed feelings about the help they cannot manage without:

> "When the 'helper' came at breakfast time she would be down there with some of our children [quads], playing with them, giving them the bottle, giving them toast, talking to them, and you could hear them laughing and all I wanted to do was say, 'Get out of the house! They're our children!' I used to hate it, but there was no other way."

Determining the areas where you need help is obviously essential. Everyone will have different priorities, but if you are someone who usually has a sparkling house, ironed sheets, and produces elaborate meals at the drop of a hat, you may have to resign yourself to lowering your standards just for a while. If you find it difficult or even embarrassing to ask someone else to do your household chores, it may help to write out a list of tasks in order of urgency.

Utilizing your help sensibly can often mean that you need to be quite firm. As one mother put it ruefully: "Everyone wants to help with the babies and no one wants to wash the floor."

The third criterion for help—that the person should not actually create extra work—excludes the mother or mother-in-law who comes to stay intent on giving helpful advice on baby care and expecting a three-course meal every evening. Any offer of help that would not really serve your best interests must be politely but firmly refused.

While it is clear to everyone that a mother with twins and more needs help during the first weeks or months, there is an assumption—often shared by the mother herself—that at some point she will take over and manage on her own. Many mothers do. It *is* possible to care for the babies, run the house and do the cooking unaided, but invariably at considerable personal cost. Although the physical demands of the babies decrease, the emotional demands do not, and most mothers agree that caring for two or more at a time remains a very demanding task until well beyond the toddler years. Help for a mother of multiples should, then, extend long beyond these early months. The need for help with practical tasks becomes a need for respite from the demands of several children.

Evolving a routine
To some mothers, it is self-evident that looking after a baby means having a routine. To others, the idea of a "routine" is too reminiscent of an older generation's approach to mothering— the "if-you-keep-picking-them-up-you'll-spoil-them" school. Certainly, contemporary baby books endorse a relaxed and spontaneous attitude to mothering. This is fine for one baby, but it can be a recipe for chaos with two. As Jane, whose approach to her first baby had been very relaxed, put it:

> "It's quite different with two. You need a routine, not necessarily a strict one, but you need to know what is happening next."

Most mothers agreed that they had to have some kind of predictable shape to their day so that they could at least get through the basics and occasionally have an occasional spare hour as a bonus, though in the early weeks this was rare.

If you have heard horror stories from friends or have had a baby of your own who was "difficult" you may wonder if it is possible to organize babies at all, but most mothers we saw had no problem in working out some kind of routine:

> "I came to realize that babies tend to expand to fill out the time available. It would not have been any use if one of them had been endlessly difficult and demanding; there just wasn't time."

Of course, you cannot make babies feed or sleep, but a regular pattern of feeding, handling and talking to them, then putting them down for a nap helps to coax them into a routine.

The following is an example of Louise's day when her twins were about seven weeks old:

6:00 A.M. Alarm rings. Reluctantly creep from bed to get bottles from fridge, put to warm. Make cup of tea. Back into bed and wait for sounds of waking baby.

6:15 Noise from babies' room. Fetch Luke and feed.

6:30 Rachel wakes, prod Simon awake to feed her. Change Luke, take downstairs to sit in baby relax chair while make another cup of tea, let in cats, etc.

7:30 Take Luke upstairs to watch while changing Rachel. Simon shaves, dresses, has breakfast, puts diapers in machine to rinse, makes up new solution. Leaves for work.

8:00 Put babies in baskets to sleep. Have quick breakfast. Rinse bottles ready to put in sterilizing fluid. Get out sterilized bottles. Measure out and mix formula for 24 hours. Make up new sterilizing solution.

9:30 Quick wash, get dressed, pull up bedclothes.

10:00 Put bottles to warm. Look at babies. Luke stirring so pick up and feed.

10:10 Rachel wakes, give pacifier.

10:20 Luke into bouncing cradle. Feed Rachel.

10:45 Grab cup of coffee, talk to and play with babies.

11:00 Take babies up to bathroom, one at a time. Put Rachel on floor to kick, with large plant nearby to look at, while change and wash Luke.

11:20 Swap round and change and wash Rachel.

11:45 Bring both back to cribs to sleep.

12:00 P.M. Hang diapers on line, sort through washing, put load in machine. Fold and put away previous day's washing and diapers.

1:00 Make self quick lunch.

1:30 Sounds from a baby. Pick Luke up and cuddle, carry round while practicing well-known maternal skill of doing everything with one hand; get out formula and warm.

1:45 Wake Rachel. Put both in bouncing cradles. Feed together as want to get out this afternoon, otherwise would do it separately. Lay Luke across knee to burp while Rachel finishes bottle.

2:20 Take both up to bathroom and change, put into

knitted sleeping bags (wonderful garments), ready to go out.

2:40   Curl up on bed, with Luke lying beside me, Rachel on tummy; she dozes, he gazes around. Doze myself.

3:05   Put babies into carriage. Walk to small local park, collecting some shopping on the way. Meet another mother who often wheels baby in park. Chat briefly.

5:00   Home. Babies asleep in carriage. Grab cup of tea. Phone mother for a chat. Look hopefully in freezer for supper, get out spaghetti bolognese to thaw. Put away shopping. Debate whether to wake a baby in case husband not home in time for feed and end up with two yelling. Decide to wait and enjoy peace for five more minutes.

6:10   Luke wakes. Put baby in bouncing cradle with pacifier while warm bottles.

6:15   Rachel wakes, seems urgently hungry, so feed while rocking Luke, who begins to show signs of impatience.

6:20   Relief at hand, husband arrives home, feeds Luke.

6:45   Luke changed and situated to watch husband bathing Rachel (they have turns so each has a bath every 4–5 days–they don't enjoy it much). I putter in kitchen and organize supper.

8:00   Both babies in bed and quiet. Eat supper, collapse in front of TV.

9:45   Prepare for bed, washing into dryer.

10:10   Both babies stir. Feed, change, straight back to bed, prepare night bottles.

11:15   Asleep as soon as head touches the pillow.

2:15 A.M. Luke wakes, both stagger out of bed. Rachel looks sound asleep but not confident she will last until nearly morning and don't want them on completely different schedules, so wake her and we feed both. Rachel very sleepy and only takes half her bottle. Change Luke because jumpsuit wet, but not Rachel.

2:50   Fall back into bed.

6:00   Alarm, etc. . . . .

For many mothers life was not quite as straightforward or organized. Janet's experience was not unusual:

"In the beginning I had decided they should be demand-fed like any single baby. That was fine while my mother was there to help. Once she had gone, feedings were sometimes hectic. Their feeding pattern wasn't synchronized—one needed seven a day and the other six—and I'd sometimes get caught out when they coincided unexpectedly. One would wake and I'd just settle into feeding him when the other would start grizzling. Sometimes he'd be calmed by a pacifier or by my pushing his cradle back and forth with my foot, but sometimes he'd yell so desperately that I'd interrupt the first one's feeding (or put him and his bottle in a baby relax chair) while I got the second one's bottle. It was all very unsatisfactory and I hated it. It was only when they had settled into a similar pattern when they were about three months that it was much better!"

Louise admitted that she found it quite easy to be so organized because her twins were born six weeks prematurely and therefore spent three weeks in the neonatal unit:

"They came out of the hospital programmed like little computers to wake up every four hours for a feeding, though Luke always woke first. The best thing about their going for so long between feedings was that I only had to do two feedings on my own."

It is clear that there is not much space in such a routine for anything but the babies, but the mother is able to find time to have a brief rest during the day, get out of the house, and deal with the basic chores. If the babies were breast-fed, feedings would probably be more frequent, but if the babies were mostly fed together, it would not take as long. Since the mother has to do all the feeding with breast-fed babies, fathers can usefully take over the burping and changing whenever possible.

If the schedule at seven weeks looks pretty daunting, then it may be encouraging to see the routine Barbara, a single parent, found suited her when her twins, Polly and Owen, were nearly a year old:

6:45 A.M.   Try not to get up before this, though twins often wake earlier—can hear them muttering and laughing. Give them their breakfast.

7:30   Twins back in bed. Sometimes they go to sleep, sometimes not, but they are quite happy to entertain themselves for an hour. If they fall asleep will probably not wake until 10:00. Meanwhile, I get dressed and have breakfast in peace.

10:00   Get twins dressed. Mother's helper takes them out for a walk, usually for 1½ hours but only ½ hour if it is very cold.

12:00 P.M.   Lunch for Owen and Polly, followed by nap. If they have not slept after breakfast, will sleep for two hours; if they have slept, don't put them down until a bit later and they will sleep for perhaps 1½ hours.

2:30   Get twins up, maybe go out to park or to visit some-one. Maybe stay in and play, or friends visit. Possibly give them bread and jam if hungry mid-afternoon.

5:00   Suppertime, followed by bath. A favorite activity—they love it.

6:00   Bedtime. Each gets own sleeping bag and snuggles in. Feed and cuddle Polly and then Owen.

Barbara commented on her routine:

> "This suits me and them very well. Just recently, I got in a muddle and they were very fractious. . . . Now we are in a routine again; they are getting enough sleep and are much easier. Much as I love them I do find it more restful not to eat with them, and I do like to have a reasonable evening time to myself, so I am prepared to start the day quite early to achieve that."

The more babies you have the more important a routine becomes, and mothers with three, four and five babies found that they needed a well-planned day far beyond the toddler years.

Feeding

General principles

In the early months, feeding is the main activity of the day and—for a while—the night, and provides your main source of contact with the babies. The most important aspect of feeding, whether it is breast or bottle, is that you should evolve a routine that allows you to have as much contact as possible with each baby and at least some time in the day when feeding can be totally relaxed and unhurried.

If you arrive home from the hospital with some kind of pattern to feeding, then you are doing well; if not, you are like most mothers of twins. Once you are home you can decide how you want to feed them: always separately; sometimes together; always together. Most mothers of singletons, especially if they are breast-feeding, expect to feed on demand; with twins or more, this may be possible and desirable for the first few days in the hospital and if you are building up a supply of breast milk, but later, demand feeding could lead to feeding all day and you would become utterly exhausted. Most mothers adopt a modified demand approach, feeding the first baby to wake and then waking the second (if necessary) so that both have roughly the same feeding times, though a number did give an extra feeding to a baby who needed it. Most babies can be coaxed into a routine of feeding every three or four hours, depending on their size and appetite. If your babies are very different weights, it may take some time to evolve a timetable that suits both. It is quite easy to forget which baby you fed last. A number of mothers kept a note of when each baby was fed and who gave the feeding.

Although you may want to give your babies as much sucking time as they would like—and some would like a great deal—this may not be possible at every feeding. Whether feeding from breast or bottle, most babies have taken as much as they need in fifteen minutes and later on may take it in as little as five or six minutes. If you have another hungry baby waiting for a meal, then a pacifier is very useful to give the first some extra sucking. Similarly, it can help calm the baby who is waiting for a feeding. Many mothers who admitted that they disliked the idea of pacifiers recognized their use when it came to feeding twins.

Feeding takes up so much time in the early months that there are bound to be interruptions: visitors arriving, the delivery person wanting to be paid, the telephone ringing. If you are feeding the babies together, then you cannot get up to deal with any interruptions. You can leave a notice on your door, "Feeding in progress until 3:00," and many mothers leave the phone off the hook.

Breast-feeding

We recommend a number of books on the general principles of breast-feeding in *Appendix 4* (page 294). Most of the advice on feeding singletons applies to feeding twins, so we deal here only with the aspects of breast-feeding that specifically relate to feeding two.

For twins the particular advantage in being breast-fed is that once breast-feeding is established, the babies can be fed together without either losing close physical contact with the mother. Breast milk is particularly valuable for small and premature babies, and many twins come into this category.

It is quite possible for a mother to produce enough milk for two babies—breast-feeding is a system of demand and supply. To provide enough milk for two babies, you need to have the kind of well-balanced varied diet we recommend in Chapter 2 (pages 21–22). You can help to improve your milk supply by increasing your intake of food containing B vitamins, including whole-grain cereals and bread, yeast products, milk, liver, eggs. This is when a pint of Guinness really is good for you. The brewer's yeast in this beverage provides some nutrition, while the fluid helps replenish your body fluids along with providing some relaxation. Enjoy! You need plenty of fluid. Drink whenever you are thirsty. Rest is important, too.

One mother made the point that:

> "People do still tend to think one's ability to produce milk must somehow be related to the size of one's breasts. I'm normally a 34A and I've been feeding my two for nine months without any problems, so maybe that could be an encouragement to some mothers."

Many mothers breast-feeding their first baby do encounter problems of one kind or another and find feeding their second much easier. This is also true of feeding twins, so although it is entirely possible to breast-feed first-born twins, you should recognize that it requires a good deal of commitment and support. Some women produce prodigious quantities of milk, and if you are lucky enough to be one of these, you may encounter no problems at all, but most women produce just enough, and the supply will go up and down depending on their physical and emotional state. If you seriously want to breast-feed your twins, especially if they are your first babies, then it is probably realistic to think in terms of organizing some kind of help every day for the first six weeks and being prepared to devote your time largely to yourself and the babies (hopefully giving the poor father some attention as well!)

Support for your desire to feed the babies yourself is another very important factor. Your partner is one crucial source of support: if he doubts your ability to feed or fails to recognize how important it is to you, then your confidence will almost certainly be undermined. Another source of support could be a twin mother who has successfully breast-fed her own babies. She can give you confidence and practical advice. It is worth making considerable efforts to find someone who lives near you either through a Mothers of Twins Club, your family doctor or the hospital. Visiting another mother, talking to her and seeing her feed her babies will help you to feel it can be done. In one study, where great efforts were made to provide this sort of contact for mothers expecting twins, the success rate, especially for first-time mothers feeding their twins, went up significantly.

Feeding two together

It has been claimed that the let-down reflex, so important in ensuring that the milk flows freely, is especially strongly stimulated when there is a baby sucking at each breast, and that when both breasts are emptied together there is a greater stimulus to the milk supply. This suggests that it may be particularly important to feed the babies together at least some of the time in the hospital when you are establishing the supply, or whenever you need to build up your supply. Although most babies fed together quite happily, we did come across a few who seemed to object to each other's presence after a few weeks and preferred to be fed alone.

Positioning the babies

You will need to experiment to find the most comfortable position for you and the babies. The most popular ones are illustrated above. Positioning the babies one on each side with their heads to the front and their legs under your arms may be the easiest way to breast-feed newborns. Feeding them together will inevitably feel very awkward at the beginning, but it becomes easier as their neck muscles become stronger and you become more adept at arranging them. You will certainly need help at first in latching them on and refixing them if they come off. It is a great help if there is also someone to burp the first baby to finish, though later you will find you can do it yourself, turning her over to lie across your knee to bring up the bubble or scooping her over your shoulder without dislodging the second baby.

It is very important to get yourself comfortable before the

feeding because once the babies are fixed, you cannot move much. Some mothers found it best to sit in bed propped up with lots of pillows. You will need a pillow under each baby, at least one behind your back and possibly one under your knees. Others liked to sit on the edge of the bed with their feet on a chair or stool. Some preferred a sofa, and others found it easiest on the floor with lots of cushions. A V-shaped pillow usually sold as an "orthopillow" or by a similar name may be very useful either to prop yourself up or to support the babies. One resourceful father sculpted foam rubber supports for the babies.

If you are still sore from an episiotomy when you get home from the hospital, try to borrow a rubber ring similar to that used in the hospital; your doctor or midwife might be able to help you. The smallest size of child's inflatable swimming ring is an alternative. When feeding two, it is very difficult to do anything other than sit directly on your sore area.

Do you swap breasts, or does each baby have its own? Some mothers liked to swap around at each feeding (provided they could remember!), but most preferred to let each have its own breast. Babies are bound to have different appetites and different requirements, and as each breast makes its own supply to some extent independently of the other, the baby can build up its own supply to meet its demands. This may result in your sometimes being a little lopsided!

Complementary bottles

If you feel basically confident about feeding your babies but need more time to build up your milk supply when you get home, then complementary bottles may solve the problem. These are given only after a baby has had time at the breast and if one or both still seem hungry. Several mothers who did this recommended using Playtex bottles, which have nipples designed so that the baby uses a sucking action similar to that used at the breast. A conventional bottle requires a completely different sucking action that is far less energetic and sometimes leads to babies showing an eventual preference for the bottle over the breast. A number of mothers used a complementary bottle for a week or two and then went on to breast-feed successfully for many months.

Breast and bottle

Should you find that your milk supply does not build up enough to feed two, then you might decide to try alternating the breast and the bottle. Health professionals tend to advise against this, feeling that the mother has the limitations of both methods of feeding to contend with. Some mothers shared this view and made a complete switch to bottles. Others, keen to continue breast-feeding in some form, found that the combination of breast and bottle worked well. When alternating breast and bottle, it is best to switch at each feeding to avoid either baby developing a preference for one or the other, and Playtex bottles may also help to prevent this. Although it is usually for the bottle that a baby develops a preference, Barbara suddenly found herself with a baby who would only take the breast. She had been giving each baby 24 hours on the breast and then 24 on the bottle when at 2½ months one baby suddenly refused the bottle:

> "I tried every trick in the book but he wouldn't take it, so after much agonizing I decided to keep him on the breast and her on the bottle, but I do feel it isn't fair on her."

Such a situation is obviously a dilemma for the mother. It can arise through other circumstances, such as having one baby in hospital who has been bottle-fed for a period and has no interest in the breast. It poses the question that comes up again and again for parents of multiples: Do you, in the interests of "fairness," treat both the same, or do you try to meet the individual needs of each—whether it seems "fair" or not? There is no easy answer.

Triplets and more

Very few mothers are able to feed three babies solely on breast milk, but we talked to several women who had breast-fed their triplets by feeding two at the breast each feeding and giving one a bottle. One mother who did this for 4½ months admitted that she felt it would not have been possible for her if she had not had full-time help. She also found it difficult to constantly rotate the babies:

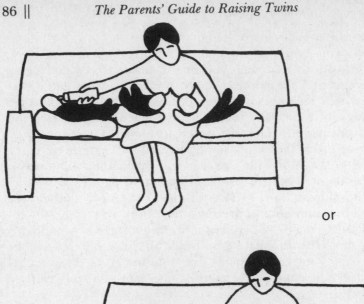

or

"I felt that my breasts never quite settled. I couldn't produce a supply that suited all of them. Sometimes one had too much and sometimes one too little. But I am glad I did it. It was really worthwhile. I remember looking down at these two little heads and them grinning up at me and thinking, this is marvelous."

Another mother decided to breast-feed her two smallest babies:

"The biggest one was putting on weight at a great rate, so I decided to feed the smaller ones. It was a difficult decision. I did feel guilty about it, but it seemed the best thing to do."

She breast-fed them for three months.

If you plan to feed triplets, then the problems are the same as for feeding twins, with the additional physical load of caring for a third baby. You may also find your reserves of energy very low after you have had the babies. Several triplet mothers commented on how thin they were after the delivery. Rest and nutrition are therefore of extra importance.

Since you can only feed two babies at a time it is understandable that most mothers of quads and quints do not even consider breast-feeding. A mother of quads breast-fed one baby at every feeding because she found it a valuable way of having individual contact and time with each baby. She had a great deal of help with bottle-feeding the others.

How long can you breast-feed?
Many of the mothers who breast-fed their twins continued to do so for as long as they would have breast-fed a singleton, weaning anywhere between six months and a year. A number of others who found feeding rather tiring breast-fed until three or four months, when they began to introduce solids.

If you feel uncertain of your ability to produce enough milk for two, rather than embarking uncertainly on an indefinite period of breast-feeding it may be better to make a series of short-term commitments. You might decide to devote all of your energies to building up your supply while you are in the hospital and then, if you feel that it is going well, feed for another month at home. If breast-feeding is going well, then you may feel happy to continue until the babies are, say, three months old and then review the situation again. If you feel when you come out of the hospital that breast-feeding is not for you or if you decide to stop after a month at home or to switch to breast and bottle, then you can feel that you have given your babies the benefits of breast-feeding in their first weeks, achieved what you have set out to do, and feel pleased with yourself.

Although you may recognize rationally that babies thrive and are perfectly happy on the bottle, once you have started to breast-feed, it is hard to stop without feelings of guilt and failure. These feelings are often tied up with fears about being an inadequate mother and a need to prove oneself capable. They should not, however, be allowed to get in the way of your making a clear decision about how to feed the babies. They and you will become miserable if you struggle with breast and bottle, not quite confident about either, as happened to a few mothers we talked to. Babies thrive best on love, physical contact and an atmosphere of confidence and calm. How they get this nourishment is less important to them.

Whenever you decide to wean your babies—or they decide to wean themselves—from the breast, you may share the mixture of relief and regret experienced by many mothers: "I was relieved because I had found it tiring, but at the same time I felt very sad." Patricia, who breast-fed her babies until they were 9½ months, summed up the pleasures of breast-feeding:

> "It took no longer than feeding just one. In fact it was easier because it avoided all that dribbling and leaking you get with one when you put it to the first side. And it was a marvelous feeling, feeding from both breasts."

Bottle-feeding

If you have decided that you do not want to breast-feed or for one reason or another it is not possible to do so, then you can enjoy the advantages of bottle-feeding.

Who feeds?

Perhaps the biggest advantage of bottle-feeding is that someone other than the mother can feed the babies. When this means that the night feedings can be shared and each baby has an opportunity to be fed regularly by his father or perhaps a competent older brother or sister, this is obviously a boon. In the early days, however, feeding a baby is an important source of contact—and part of the whole process of getting to know and love him. Constantly allowing any obliging visitor to feed one of the babies may interfere with this process and possibly unsettle the baby:

> "I know everyone meant well, but grandmothers especially would swoop in at feeding time and grab a baby and a bottle,

obviously convinced they were helping me—which in a way they were. I was close to tears sometimes. For one thing, I felt I wanted to show them I could cope with my babies myself, and for another, they didn't always get it right. One baby was a very fussy feeder and I would see someone holding him the wrong way or trying to burp him too soon—just getting it wrong and upsetting him. I found it very difficult, though, to say, 'Just leave us alone and we'll muddle through' when people obviously wanted to be helpful."

Another mother was more firm with well-intentioned visitors:

"Tom took ages to feed and used to get in a state so, despite lots of offers of help, we made a rule that only Peter, my mother or myself would feed him."

Of course, there will be times, especially with three or more babies, when you will want to use all the extra help that is available at feeding time. One triplet family continued to entertain friends, but they had to feed a baby before they got their own dinner.

A mother of quads or quints needs help at every feeding until the babies are old enough to feed themselves. A quad mother had a team of helpers from the local social services department who came around-the-clock to help with feedings, but this arrangement had its problems:

"I had this thing when the babies were tiny that they wouldn't know who their mother was. They had the helpers around just as much as I was. I thought, How on earth are they going to pick out their mother from all these people? So I used to try and work it that the babies saw me as often as they could and I avoided giving the same one to be fed breakfast, dinner and supper by the same helper."

There are many ways in which bottle-feeding can provide intimate contact, even when babies are fed together. Feedings in bed at night and in the early morning are opportunities for skin-to-skin contact with your babies; when the babies are fed separately they can be held close in a position where you can look at each other. When they are fed together, as will probably be necessary at times, they can be arranged either as for breast-feeding, on pillows facing you with their legs toward you, or sitting in bouncing cradles, in baby relax chairs (infant seats), or propped against cushions on a sofa so that you can look at and talk to both of them as they feed. Or you could try one of the arrangements illustrated on page 92. By experimenting, you will find the best positions for you and the babies.

If ever you need to arrange one baby with his bottle propped on a cushion, you must not leave him alone as he may choke.

Preparing bottles

Preparing bottles for feeding infants in today's world is not the monumental task it once was, although parents of twins do, to be sure, have twice as many bottles to prepare as parents of singletons do. The availability of commercially prepared, ready-to-feed formula has greatly reduced the effort involved in preparing bottles for feeding. Gone are the days when all the separate ingredients had to be assembled and mixed each day and the required procedures for sterilizing the equipment would nearly have suited standards for a hospital operating room.

Follow the advice of your pediatrician or clinic about the type of formula to use. If the brand used in the hospital worked well for your babies, there is no need to change. Infant formula can be purchased in most supermarkets, grocery stores and drugstores. Shop for price, which may well vary from one outlet to another. Inquire about quantity discounts, which may be available if you purchase several cases at one time.

The major brands of infant formula are available in 32 oz. or 8 oz. ready-to-feed cans, as well as concentrates that require the addition of an equal amount of water before feeding. Although the ready-to-feed version is somewhat more expensive than the concentrate, many parents feel that the effort saved in preparation is well worth the cost. If price is no object, ready-to-feed disposable bottles are the easiest of all, but the number needed each day for twins or higher multiples would be extremely costly. If the cost of feeding your babies is a problem for you, consult your local social services for information on any assistance for which you might be eligible. A federally funded program known as WIC (Women, Infants and Children) provides nutritional assistance, including information, counseling, food and formula for mothers and babies at risk. The Department of Health or some other social service agency in your area will be able to tell you whether you are eligible for WIC, for food stamps, or for any other supplemental assistance that could help you pay for feeding your babies.

There is considerable disagreement among health-care providers about the extent to which sterilization of bottles and equipment is necessary. Follow your own doctor's advice about this for your babies. While some physicians still recommend careful attention to sterilization for the first several months, others feel that such procedures are needed only during the first few weeks, if at all. Some doctors suggest that use of commercially prepared formula (which is sterile) in "dishwasher clean" bottles is sufficient care. Others advise boiling the bottles and nipples for five minutes or more as an added precaution before pouring in the formula. If you use the formula in concentrated form, boil the water you use to dilute the formula. This is especially important if there is any question about the purity of your water supply. Opened cans of formula and filled but unused bottles should be stored in the refrigerator and used within a day or two. Because twins will consume twice as much as one baby, there will be little need to store opened cans for very long.

If your doctor advises you to sterilize the bottles, the standard size sterilizing equipment will not be large enough to meet your needs conveniently. An enormous pot with a lid would probably be handier than a sterilizing unit that holds only six to eight bottles. Simply fill the pot with water, add the bottles, nipples and caps, and boil.

Giving up bottles
Twins may give up bottles later than many singletons do. One baby may be ready at nine or ten months, but if the other is not, then they will probably both continue for as long as either of them wants it, and give them up together.

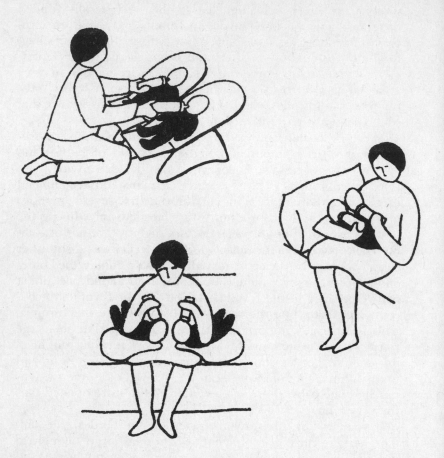

Introducing solids

In the families we interviewed, twins were given solids somewhere between three and six months. Current theories of baby
nutrition agree that babies should not be given solids before
three months, and most advocate four to six months as the
ideal starting time.

One mother introduced solids at three months because her
premature twins were gaining weight and growing at a great
rate and were already consuming the maximum quantities of
milk. "They obviously needed more and wolfed down every-

thing I gave them." Another mother who was breast-feeding felt she could not keep pace with the babies' demands at 12 weeks: "My doctor nagged me to put them on to bottles, saying they must not have solids until 16 weeks, but I started solids and was able to keep the breast-feeding going."

Fiddling with tiny baby-size portions of food for one baby can be irksome. Several mothers said they felt that preparing food for two or more seemed far more worthwhile and that they cooked things they might not have bothered with for one. A blender and a food mill were mentioned as being particularly useful.

Most mothers fed the babies solids together, sitting them side by side or facing each other. Some started with two bowls of food and two spoons but soon abandoned this as they realized that twins are constantly exposed to each other's germs. Sharing a bowl or even a spoon poses no serious health hazard!

> "I gave up worrying about which spoon was which. It was all I could do to keep up with them at feeding times—trying to spoon the right quantity into the right baby—I felt like a mother bird confronted by these two gaping little mouths."

As the babies became big enough to get food into their mouths themselves, most mothers felt that they should be encouraged to feed themselves and introduced finger foods as soon as the babies seemed ready. One pair of twins became adept at spooning food into each other's mouths some time before they were coordinated enough to get it into their own.

Two babies can make twice as much mess as one, and several mothers recommended a plastic tablecloth spread under the high chairs to catch the worst of it. This is especially useful in other people's houses, where the onslaught of two or three butter-fingered and inaccurate feeders may not be appreciated.

Sleeping

Child-care manuals may suggest that it is a good thing for a baby to be alert and lively, but nevertheless most parents are relieved if their baby is prepared to sleep the greater part of the day and night while it is tiny. Parents of twins or more have particular reason to be grateful for quiet spells between the often hectic times of feeding and changing.

Most of the parents we interviewed had established some sort of routine by six to eight weeks out of sheer necessity, and very few reported problems with non-sleeping babies.

Restless babies

If either or both of your babies find difficulty in relaxing and dropping off to sleep, then there are various techniques you might try. The use of a baby sling to carry one or both babies around with you, and a pacifier or comforter to provide the baby with an opportunity for some soothing sucking are both discussed under the section on "Crying." You could try a conventional rocking cradle if you can get hold of one, or try a fairly new piece of equipment of which we have had some enthusiastic reports: a Lullababy, which is basically a giant spring, suspended from the ceiling that holds a net into which a portable crib or basket can be fixed. The baby is then bounced up and down at just the right speed. There are also special tapes of a mother's heartbeat and one of white noise—a monotonous background noise—that work magically for some babies, though just running the vacuum cleaner is cheaper. Many respond to a musical box. Everything is worth investigating.

Daytime naps

Mothers usually found it best to have their babies near where they carried out most of their daytime activities. A number of mothers had a portable crib for each baby downstairs, or, if they could have a carriage conveniently indoors, they used that and one crib.

A similar arrangement may be useful for sleeping out in the garden. Babies may share a crib or carriage comfortably at first if they both sleep soundly, but most soon outgrow this.

Until they are old enough to roll over or crawl, babies can sleep in something that takes less space than a conventional crib. A number of mothers used either straw carrying baskets or something that is usually described as a cocoon. A cocoon is a small baby sleeping bag but has in addition a hard base and handles, unlike a baby nest, which has a soft base and can cause suffocation. Cocoons and carrying baskets can be put on a firm surface such as a table, sofa or bed and can then be put into a carriage or conveyed to a car (although the babies should be in approved car restraints until the destination is reached). Jane found her carrying basket particularly useful to quiet the baby who was waiting for his feed: she hooked her foot through the handles and rocked the basket while she fed the first baby. She did find one drawback to this method of transporting the babies, however:

> "One day I took them both into the greengrocer's and, obviously not thinking there could possibly be a baby in both baskets, he assumed the one on the floor was for shopping and dropped a pound of apples in on top of the sleeping baby."

Together or apart?

A number of parents felt that far from disturbing each other, on the whole the twins slept better in the same room. "They seemed reassured by each other's presence"; "They seem to like to hear each other's little snuffles" were typical comments. Surprisingly few mothers reported that their twins seemed to disturb each other. Separating them for daytime naps may not be difficult but having them in separate rooms at night may not be an option available to everyone. If it seems advisable to separate them temporarily, then one could sleep on a landing or in a bathroom or living room for a spell. If they will have to share a room at some point, then it may be better to have them together from the start. This may, however, entail the occasional confusion, such as the one encountered by this mother:

> "I woke up one night and heard one of them crying and groped my way to their room. Bleary-eyed, I bent over the cot and felt around for the pacifier and tried to put it into the baby's mouth. I couldn't understand why he wouldn't take it and why the crying went on. It was several minutes before I realized it was the wrong baby."

Sleeping at night

Some twins shared a crib in the early months with one at each end, others had a bassinet, portable crib, or crib each. Most mothers agreed that if possible it was better to duplicate sleeping arrangements for day and night rather than struggle up and down stairs with a succession of beds and babies.

With two or more babies to deal with during the day, sleep is very important for parents of multiples. It will be up to you whether you decide that only one of you gets up to feed the babies or whether you share the job. A mother who is breast-feeding has to feed the babies, but burping and, if necessary, changing them can be done by their father. The most important thing about feeding your babies at night is to disturb them and yourselves as little as possible. The babies may be encouraged to move toward the idea that nighttime is for sleeping if you keep everything very low-key, using only a dim light and putting the baby straight back to bed after a feeding. It may further encourage the babies to get back to sleep quickly if you do not change their diapers in the middle of the night unless they are dirty or their clothing soaked.

Later, the price many parents of singletons find they pay for a baby who sleeps soundly for 12 hours or so is that they are summoned loudly to provide breakfast anytime from 6:00 A.M. onward. A number of mothers felt that one of the bonuses of having twins sharing a room was that they would entertain each other for quite some time gurgling and laughing in their cribs, giving their parents a few more peaceful moments in bed.

Crying

Crying patterns

Crying was not a serious problem for most of the mothers we interviewed, despite the fact that twins may well have more cause to cry than a singleton, as one twin often has to wait while the other is attended to.

Every mother inevitably had hellish moments:

> "It didn't get me down very often, but I do remember times when they were all [twins and toddler] crying together and I was sitting in the middle of the floor crying as well, not knowing which to deal with first."

In general though, these twins, like many other pairs, stuck to their own crying patterns and did not seem to influence each other. The occasional crisis came when both happened to be crying together. The mother's feelings of hopelessness and helplessness, though acute at the time, were only temporary.

Several mothers reported that when one twin was particularly fractious with a cold or teething or just generally miserable, the other often demanded less attention. This pattern was surprisingly common among the twins we saw and persisted throughout the first year and beyond. Some mothers felt that each baby had an understanding of the other's needs. Whatever the reason, it is tremendously helpful to the mother when it happens.

Far less common, fortunately, were the twins who seemed to interact to ensure that their mother was perpetually tuned in to one or the other of the pair:

> "Because of my exhaustion, because I didn't respond as rapidly as I might have done to their needs, if one got tired the other would take over and in that way they carried on indefinitely because they would just take turns. Yes, they definitely colluded."

Occasionally one twin will set the other off. In the early days one may be startled and upset by the other's sudden loud shriek. If they share a carriage or crib, one may be disturbed as much by the body movements that accompany crying as by the yells themselves. In either case, separating them is the obvious solution. Conversely, some parents have found that putting a crying baby in the same crib as his twin has worked wonders.

Anticipating your babies' needs—such as having their bottles ready before they are likely to demand them and not preparing your own evening meal when they are likely to be fretful— goes a long way toward reducing the amount of crying and tension you and they will have to endure. Whereas a singleton mother can afford to take the day as it comes, a mother of twins cannot. Your babies will be much more contented with a well-planned routine.

When both are fretful

Many mothers were able to soothe two crying babies by holding them together, one on each shoulder, or by laying both across their lap. Others cradled one in each arm and rocked them in a rocking chair. Getting them into position when you are on your own takes practice. Any awkwardness may well induce louder yells until they are settled.

Each twin will tend to have less body contact with his mother than a singleton, but extra contact can be provided by a baby sling. Many a restless baby will settle down and drop off to sleep almost instantly when snuggled, against his mother in a sling. If both babies are fractious, you can have one in a sling and your arms free to hold and comfort the second baby. One mother managed to carry both babies in slings herself by arranging them diagonally from shoulder to hip.

If you have two slings, each parent can have a baby held close and you may have an evening's peace. The parents of a pair of twins who cried a lot in the early months used to put them in the car and go for a 40-minute drive to pick up a fast-food meal and then drive home. As long as the car was moving both babies were quiet, and the parents were able to relax and talk together.

If both babies are crying when you want to have a rest, take them to bed with you and place one on your chest and one across your tummy. A third, if you have triplets, could lie along your thighs. You are hardly likely to go to sleep with this string of babies along you, but if it stops them from screaming, you will at least be able to relax.

Several mothers found, if they had the presence of mind to

think of it, that taking the babies out for a walk gave them a break when both babies were crying. Complicated outdoor clothes will put off attempting this in a crisis. Just wrap each in a shawl or a blanket and ensure their ears are covered, and get moving. Better still, if there is someone else around, ask them to take the babies out so that you get a complete break from the stress.

Many mothers are reluctant to leave a fretful baby, let alone babies, with someone else. If your twins cry a lot in the early days, do take advantage of any offer of help. Remember the crying affects you much more than it will another person. While fretful spells are tiring but usually manageable for a singleton mother, a twin mother may find she has to have a break in order to preserve her sanity.

If there is no one around to take them off your hands—and this is more than likely in a crisis—then take yourself out. Shut the door on them, turn up the radio to drown them out, make yourself a cup of tea or coffee, take a few deep breaths, and let go of the tension. It need not be for long. With a bit of luck, one or both might have dropped off to sleep in your absence. If not, you can make a fresh start.

Comforters
One of the simplest ways of dealing with any baby's crying is to give a comforter to calm him or her. We feel quite strongly that some kind of comforter, whether it be pacifier, thumb or cloth,

can only be an asset for twins and their mother, and indeed the whole family. This feeling was shared by many of the mothers we interviewed: "It is good to have something to give them when you can't give them attention," "You can shove a comforter at one while you mop up the main difficulties"; "If one is upset and likely to upset the other, they can prevent escalation," "They keep them and me relaxed."

A few small babies are born with the ability to find their thumb or finger because they have already been sucking in the womb. Most, however, do not have the manipulative skill to get their thumbs to their mouths, or to reach for and fondle a cloth, till they are about three or four months old.

Unless you have a lot of help through the first few months you are very unlikely to have the time some mothers, particularly those of firstborn single babies, have to comfort their babies by giving them the breast:

> "One afternoon when they were about three and a half weeks old, Paul was niggly and crying. I let him suck at me and he was fine. He wasn't trying to feed. He just seemed to want something in his mouth to suck. Every time I removed my nipple he started crying again. I had to get on with something else eventually and put him down, and he was miserable yet again. That was when I made the final decision. It would have to be pacifiers. I just didn't have the time to sit around and pacify him. I had things to do in the house and David to see to as well. I had a pacifier on the shelf in the kitchen. I gave it to him there and then, and he settled. The next day I went out and bought some more."

Pacifiers or Thumbs?

Some of the parents we interviewed put their babies' thumbs in their mouths till they could do it themselves. Not many used pacifiers, and among those who did, some were apologetic. This was not surprising in view of the myths and taboos that surround the use of such devices. Most child-care books are fairly dismissive about them, often leaving parents with the feeling that they must only be used as a last resort.

Poor hygiene is the basis of some of the taboos. Pacifiers can be dirty—and so can fingers and thumbs. It is in fact easier to keep a pacifier clean. A pacifier can be boiled clean. Or it can be attached to the child with a short ribbon on a safety pin. (Never hang a pacifier on a ribbon around a child's neck.)

A new mother, still anxious to prove her worth, may find it particularly difficult to resort to what seems to be a totally artificial source of comfort. Anxiety about the artificiality, together with social taboos, has often caused many a caring mother to endure months of crying rather than "succumb" and try them out. That choice is fine if the amount of crying is not getting you and the babies down. If it is, take no notice of what your mother, the in-laws or Aunt Matilda will think or say. You and the babies matter far more than their opinions.

You may find that some small new babies reject pacifiers outright or lose them almost immediately. Some will never take to them. Some need a little time to get used to them, so if you feel your babies need them, do not give up after only one or two tries. Some will use them for only a few weeks or months and then reject them or transfer their affections to a thumb or cloth. Some will become so attached to them that you may begin to wonder if they will ever be able to do without. It is worth remembering that you will not be watching your twins at their eighteenth birthday party still with their pacifiers in their mouths, nor even going off to school with them secreted in a pocket at the age of five. A great many five-year-olds still suck their thumbs, however, and one or two 18-year-olds!

How often do you let them suck at a comforter? In the early days, quite simply as often as they need to. You will soon be able to gauge their needs by the amount of sucking movements they make or by their fretfulness. A pacifier will help to distract one while you deal with the other's needs. As we said earlier in this section, twins have to do a lot of waiting around. A pacifier will make it easier for them to tolerate the waiting and easier for you to get on with the one if the other is not screaming.

Later on, once they can amuse themselves more easily, you can restrict the use of pacifiers to certain times in the day. Excessive use of these devices can get in the way of a child exploring her world, which in the first year or two will be largely through her mouth. Excessive sucking of pacifiers or thumbs at a later age may push teeth forward, though this is more likely with thumbs.

Cloth comforters

Some babies begin to form an attachment to a blanket or sheet when they are a few weeks old. An alert mother will notice a small baby's hand or fingers working rhythmically over the chosen fabric at an early stage. Once formed, the attachment may last for many years. Having a toddler on each hip, each child holding a large gruĿby blanket, may be a grim thought. We suggest that you offer an alternative cloth as soon as you notice a small hand beginning to fondle an item of bedclothing. A men's handkerchief or washed muslin diaper is soft and is usually a very acceptable alternative for a baby. You can have stocks of them and thus keep them clean, and also avoid frantic searches at stressful times later on.

Needing help

Crying becomes a serious problem when the quantity overwhelms the mother or the parents to the extent that they are exhausted, unable to find any joy in their babies, and unable to think of a way out.

Veronica's firstborn identical girls were difficult from the very beginning:

> "As my mother said, both my girls just seemed to enjoy screaming and spitting out the bottle and not sleeping at nights. . . . It was just one problem after another. I just couldn't cope. I couldn't believe it because all I'd ever wanted was a baby and here they were and I couldn't do a thing with them. They wouldn't sleep. They wouldn't do anything, they just screamed all day long."

Veronica's husband was very understanding, and she felt she would not have got through the experience without his support:

> "He used to say, 'Go out and leave them with me,' and then when I came back he would snap at me and say, 'I don't know how you cope. I don't know how you can stand it.'"

Such stress can bring parents close to battering, however much they basically love and care for their children. Veronica told us:

"I always felt for them. I could never have hurt them. Sometimes I used to go, 'Please . . . stop it.' My husband once threw one into the crib, I mean, not to hurt her. We could neither of us ever hurt her. I can remember banging my hand against the wall and bruising it all down one side. My husband's done the same—just to stop ourselves. We've shut the door on them and gone out into the garden and said, 'To hell with you two.' They were just ruining our lives. But I could never have hit them."

When crying is anything like as bad as this, the family needs help. Very often this kind of situation is self-perpetuating. The babies' crying wears the mother down. She is exhausted and tense. Her tension is transmitted to the babies, who will continue their crying beyond the initial discomfort that caused it in the first place.

If you find yourself in this trap you are bound to feel totally inadequate, a failure as a parent. Do remind yourself that the best of mothers, including those with only one baby, have been ground down by relentless crying. If the next-week-when-it-will-all-begin-to-get-better never seems to come, the only positive thing to do is to seek help. This can be very hard, particularly if you are usually a competent person. Family doctors are familiar with this predicament and are usually understanding and helpful. It may be that getting it off your chest, some advice on establishing a routine, and help with giving you a break will be all that is necessary. Or it may be that some kind of medication is prescribed if your twins are old enough (see page 174).

If you feel that you can't cope, and that you might hurt your children, call Parents Anonymous, an organization founded by parents to help other parents under stress. The PA toll-free number is (800) 421-0353 except in California, where it is (800) 352-0386.

Play

Babies enjoy and thrive on all kinds of sensory stimuli from the moment they are born. Much of this will be provided, especially in the early weeks, in day-to-day caring such as feeding, bathing, and diaper changing. During these activities they see their mother's face, hear her voice, smell her breasts or the bottle she offers, taste the milk from them, feel the way she handles them. Twins are not likely to lose out on stimuli provided by basic caring if you are able at least some of the time not to rush through these activities. Because of the demands on your time, though, they are far less likely than a singleton to receive anything like the same amount of stimuli through play and physical contact unless you make a conscious effort to go some way toward redressing the balance.

While you cannot expect to be able to give each twin as much time and attention as you would a single baby, there is much you can do to ensure that your twins, separately and together, have opportunities for play with you. In this context, by play we mean not only looking at and exploring objects such as mobiles and rattles but also talking, stroking, cuddling, and rocking. In other words, intimate communication.

So when is there time to play?

In the early weeks when feeding and changing are the main activities in your day, an unhurried diaper change may be the chief or only opportunity for face-to-face contact, stroking or talking to each baby. Most mothers spontaneously play with their babies as they change them; when you are wilting with fatigue these niceties may be forgotten and the whole operation performed in weary silence. It is worth making the effort at these times to make this necessary contact with each baby into a rewarding few minutes for you both.

Finding the time for play continues to be the biggest hurdle. It is all too easy to use any spare moments, when neither baby is demanding your attention, to get the living room straight, start the next laundry load, peel the potatoes. . . . All of these and many other household chores have to be done and will be instead of play unless you are careful to make it a priority at some point during the day. If playtime occasionally has to be put aside because of other pressures, it is of no consequence as long as you and your twins are not missing out altogether. We do not want to make play sound compulsory or, even worse, yet another chore, but fatigue and other pressures can easily prevent you from finding space in which to relax and play with the babies.

A couple of mothers, each with two or three older children, found they had very little time for play with their twin babies, but the older children took their place—a good alternative.

Some mothers put aside a specific time for play every afternoon. Others arranged their babies' sleeping times so that they were awake in the evening when both parents could play with them. This arrangement means that each parent can give one child undivided attention and the twins will sleep more in the day, giving the mother time to keep abreast of household chores or to rest. The main disadvantage is that it can create difficulties if you want an evening out without them.

If one twin is asleep in the day you can use some of the time to give the awake baby your complete attention. Even five minutes of intimate play will be of enormous value to the baby. It is an opportunity for you to notice his or her behavior without the distraction of the other, and to adjust your timing and your responses to the child's mood, a chance to really communicate. Even if twins lose out on quantity of contact, there is no need for them to lose out on quality.

Mothers of singleton babies, even those with other children, usually do not even need to think about finding space for intimacy. With twins, take advantage of every moment you can get. And if such occasions do not arise, make a point of creating space for them. Sheila, who had a toddler as well as her twins to care for, succeeded in the following way from the time the twins were about five months old. "It was an effort and quite difficult to do," she said. She got the twins to have their daytime naps at different times, one in the morning and one in the afternoon, and thereby had an hour with each every day. If the toddler was around, he was involved in the play of whichever twin was awake. He had his special time on his own in the evening after the twins were in bed. Sheila deliberately prolonged his regular daytime nap to allow for this and occasionally to have each twin entirely on his own:

> "I can remember making a conscious decision to do this, mainly because they were developing so differently. Michael

had been ill and was so slow that he needed the time. Christopher was so good, there was so little free time left that he never got any . . . he was a very contented baby, and I was very aware that in fact, of the three of them, he was being left out because he was good, not so demanding as the toddler and not ill like the other one."

We are not suggesting that you attempt to emulate this model—it suited Sheila and she succeeded in getting it to work for her family. We have described it in some detail, however, in order to emphasize that it is often possible, with a little thought and planning, to make the space you might have thought was non-existent.

Entertaining two
A mother of a single baby usually plays with the child on her lap. With two or more it has to be different:

"Every afternoon from the time they were about six weeks old I used to sit them in their baby relax chairs (infant seats) and talk and play with them. It was always a boost for my morale to suddenly find myself a star performer. I remember these two pairs of very attentive eyes following a music box as I moved from side to side, and looking in amazement or laughing as I made noises or sang or bounced soft toys toward them."

If your twins were premature you may find yourself feeling frustrated in your efforts to entertain them.

A mother of six-week premature babies commented:

"I'd read the books about babies' development and knew that they need stimulation and are taking it all in even if they don't seem to respond. But it was hard going, confronted by these two solemn little dollops who just sat and stared. It seemed *such* a long time before they smiled and burbled."

Premature babies do take correspondingly longer to reach developmental milestones, and this is most obvious in the first weeks when parents are hungry for the first sociable smiles and sounds.

Walks and outings provide enjoyment for all and a period of

respite for you. When the babies are still lying in their carriage, the patterns of leaves and branches as they pass overhead is usually fascinating. When they are old enough to sit up, dogs, cats, horses, trucks, buses and of course people are endless sources of wonder and excitement, each baby often reinforcing the other's delight. Outings help give shape to the day and, especially in the early months, ensure that you and the babies regularly have some kind of contact with the outside world, something that can all too easily be forgotten with the many demands you have to meet.

Once they are old enough to crawl and sit unsupported, play and contact with two simultaneously is far easier. If you lie on the floor with them they can both enjoy pulling themselves up on you, leaning against you, pulling and prodding you and eventually scrambling over you. Several parents said they and their twins had all been able to thoroughly enjoy rough-and-tumble and other forms of physical play.

Play on their own
Play suggestions where you need not be involved and can take advantage of the babies' mutual companionship include any situation in which each child has access to its own toys but can also watch and enjoy the other's presence. Some mothers had two baby bouncers and could leave both twins safely and happily bouncing away while they attended to things elsewhere. A bouncer apiece, however, is not necessary. Several mothers have successfully combined the above activities, placing one twin in a bouncer and the other nearby in a chair with a supply of toys. When all the toys are lost or dropped, the seated twin is often content to watch the bouncer for a while before boredom sets in and the mother's attention is requested.

Changing and diapers

You will find yourself spending a considerable amount of time each day changing diapers, especially in the early months. First-time mothers of single babies sometimes tend to overdo diaper-changing. With twins you would be forever at it if you rushed to change them every time they were wet.

With more than one baby, casual arrangements for changing

are at best time-consuming, at worst chaotic. If it is reasonably well organized it can be a relaxing time for you and each baby to enjoy each other's company.

An established changing area where the necessary tissues, cotton wool, lotions and powder are easily reached enables other people to occasionally do the job for you with a minimum of fuss. Reluctant diaper-changers among fathers are much more likely to share the task when the setup is reasonably efficient. Gerry, "from the sort of background where males don't do much of this kind of thing," felt he was unlikely to have dealt with the diapers had there been only one baby. As it was, he and Christine worked on the principle that the one who noticed or smelled a diaper dealt with it and *was not allowed* to tell the other. Both admitted to sometimes turning a blind eye.

Where you choose to have the diaper-changing area will depend on the layout of your home and the strength of your back. Near a basin is ideal, but many bathrooms are just too small. You will need a reasonably sized surface, and space for the twin who is not being changed.

If you have had any back problems it is essential to choose a surface with the height that is most comfortable for you. With the amount of changing you will be doing this is fairly important anyway. Clare, who used a table, had a washable blanket on the floor nearby for the other:

> "After a feeding I used to take the diaper off the one who had finished first, clean him up, and then put him to kick on the floor. Then I'd do the same with the other. They loved it. There was the occasional accident when one sprayed himself or the other, but they didn't mind."

A large double bed has the advantage that at least in the early weeks the second twin can lie safely near you and be in touch with what is going on. Sheila, who had a toddler, always used a large mat on the floor. There was no danger of either twin falling if she had to chase after the toddler. And she was on a level with the older child and could involve him if he was in a good mood and keep an eye on him if he was not. Sometimes she used the playpen to put one twin in the middle safely out of his reach while she dealt with the other twin.

Cloth diapers

You may be surprised that on our basic list we recommend as many as four dozen cloth diapers for twins. Surely they are not going to need more than six or seven each day, you may think. Allowing for contingencies such as tummy upsets and even a short delay in getting the wash done, you will find this quantity to be a bare minimum, at least during the early months, unless you have a tumble dryer. One exceptionally well-organized mother managed on only two dozen but she did her diaper wash daily at 6:00 A.M. so it was out of the way before her twins woke up!

A conventional diaper pail is useless for the quantities you will be dealing with. A large plastic bucket will probably be adequate if you do the wash fairly regularly. For triplets, though, or even for twins if you don't want to be tied to too regular a schedule, the only conveniently sized receptacle is a large trash bin. Once the diapers are washed and dried, then folding them ready for use can save precious minutes at changing times.

Disposable diapers

If you decide to use disposable diapers, we suggest that you first experiment to find a type that suits you and your babies and then purchase a large carton at a time. At the outset it is worth trying to negotiate a reduction on the many bulk buys you will make. Shop for price which may vary greatly from one store to another.

Whether you decide to have cloth diapers or disposable, it is a tremendous help to have a supply of the latter to help you through the first couple of weeks at home while you are settling down to some kind of a routine. Bulk supplies are often advertised in baby magazines.

Disposable diapers are best disposed of by wrapping in plastic bags.

Standard cloth diapers and disposable diapers tend to swamp even the sturdiest of newborn babies. If your twins are premature or even just small, you may find it necessary to purchase smaller than standard diapers. Procter & Gamble supplies Pampers in a size for premature infants (up to 6 lb.). These can be ordered directly (see Appendix 3 for details).

Bathing

How often?

The twins we saw were bathed anything from weekly to daily:

> "Baths they didn't have. It was quite apparent early on that
> the one thing they disliked was being dunked in a bath of
> water. So they were bathed every week perhaps . . . I couldn't
> think when to fit it in. There wasn't any time."

Some twins were given a ritual dip twice a week, others saw
water on alternate days if their mothers could manage it. In
several families, time was in fact found for a daily bath.

To our surprise all the mothers with two or three older children were in this last category. None mentioned older children
helping, though sometimes they probably did. We can only sur-
mise that a daily bath ensured a space in the day when these
mothers could give their full attention to each twin. "It was one
of the few times I could enjoy handling them," said one. A twin
being changed can usually be left instantly to deal with an older
child's demands; a twin in a bath cannot be left instantly, and
the older children know it.

The only family in which both parents were working also
gave their firstborn twins a daily bath. Their baby bath was
large enough to take both twins at the same time with each
parent holding a twin. It was a time for the family to be together before the parents went to work and the babies to a
baby-sitter.

Together or separately?

The role of fathers was spontaneously mentioned by many of
the mothers we interviewed. Several chose to bathe their twins
in the evening so that he was there to help. If you bathe both
twins at the same time, i.e., one immediately after the other, as
most mothers did, a second pair of hands is almost essential.

Twins bathed at the same time inevitably have to wait longer
than singletons to be fed. If their hunger is making bath time a
misery, there are a number of tactics you can try out to over-
come it.

• Provide the waiting twin with a pacifier.

• Bathe only one twin on any one day, as a number of mothers did.

• There is a general belief that babies will throw up if bathed soon after feeding. Not all do. Yours may well be among the latter, particularly if you handle them gently.

• One mother who breast- and bottle-fed her twins alternately would bathe the one due to have the bottle first, put him down nearby with the bottle propped up, and then bathe and breast-feed the other.

If you do bathe both at the same session there is absolutely no need to change the water. Only half fill the bath for the first twin and have a jug of hot water ready for freshening it.

On the rare occasions when the water is dirty and needs to be changed and this is a chore, remember that you have the option of leaving the second twin unbathed that day.

When the babies are old enough to use an ordinary bathtub, they will need either a full size adult safety bath mat or two children's mats. When they are sitting steadily, they can be put in the tub together but should not be left alone together. Once the babies reached this stage most parents found bath time fun:

> "When they were big enough to sit up and enjoy water, bath time became the high spot of the day. Simon was often home in time to bathe them. There used to be shrieks of excitement coming from the bathroom as they splashed and played with the bath toys. We have some lovely photos of two damp happy babies and an almost equally damp father!"

Many parents enjoy sharing the occasional bath with their children. Twins can easily miss out on this and it is worth finding time every now and then, at a weekend perhaps, to enjoy the intimacy of a bath with one of the babies.

Clothes

Quick and easy dressing
Your main aim will be to make things as easy as possible for the babies and most of all for yourself. From the outset, do not try

to live up to the image of babies that we are constantly presented with in the media. For that extra special photograph your babies, too, can look just as pristine, fresh and bright if you want them to. But for most of the time, aim to give yourself the least work possible. As long as your babies are warm enough and are not pulled around too much when dressed, they will not mind what they wear.

We suggest that you have as many garments as possible and do not refuse offers of outgrown clothes. We also suggest that you cut down on the number of garments each baby wears. Bootees and mittens are a waste of time. Stretch suits and nightgowns take care of feet while jackets with hoods and turn-back cuffs, take care of ears and hands. While they are very small simply wrap them in a shawl or baby blanket to protect them from the cold. In the carriage each acts as a wonderful bumper-size hot-water bottle for the other.

When we asked mothers about clothes, virtually all felt stretch suits were the ideal basic garment for quick and easy dressing. You should move on to the next size before the suit gets too tight, as it could distort a baby's feet. There were mixed feelings about baby gowns. This seemed to depend on the type. While one mother discarded several beautiful gowns that needed careful ironing of frills, another swore by cotton jersey gowns with a drawstring at the hem. The latter are particularly suitable for very small babies who are swamped by even the smallest stretch suit. If the drawstrings come adrift in the wash or in use they can be replaced by light elastic, not so tight that it cannot fit comfortably round the babies' chests while you are changing them. One mother replaced the ties at the neck of her twins' gowns with Velcro for quick and easy fastening.

When it comes to fastenings, Velcro, snaps and zippers are in while hooks, slippery bows and tiny buttons are out. It helps, too, if you can possibly manage to have the openings on the same side of the baby, i.e., all either at the back or at the front. It goes almost without saying that garments should also be easy to care for. Think twice before buying anything that requires hand washing or ironing.

Finding clothes for tiny babies can be a problem. Most first size baby clothes fit an 8–10 lb. baby comfortably and it could be several months before a 4 lb. pair reach this size. French baby clothes tend to come in smaller sizes but are expensive. Several manufacturers are now producing a newborn size stretch suit, but even this may be too large. For more information, see Appendix 3, page 292.

Matching or different?

We consider the importance of parents, close friends and relations being able to distinguish the twins early on pages 123–124, and the significance of dressing older twins alike in "Twins as Individuals" on pages 234–236. You may nevertheless decide that while they are babies you wish to dress them alike all or some of the time. Some mothers who were basically opposed to dressing twins identically in fact did so in the early months. "I enjoyed them looking matching," said one. Another confessed, "I used to get a mild kick sometimes out of bathing them and then dressing them in the same clothes."

Identical gifts were one of the reasons given by mothers for dressing their twins identically, at least in the early days. There are ways around this if you are opposed to the idea. You can either allot both garments to one baby or let each wear them but on different days.

For those who choose to start out alike and then change, the question arises of when you do it. Twins show signs of taking note of each other at three months or even earlier. At this stage they are unlikely to be aware that they are dressed the same. Where confusion is not a problem, there is probably no harm in leaving them in identical clothes for a while longer if you enjoy doing so. It is a good idea, though, from about six or seven months to occasionally have them dressed differently. They will not protest or bother much at that age. If you leave it any later you may meet with considerable resistance. This will depend a lot on their natures and their feelings about each other but as it is impossible to predict what smiling, amenable seven-month-olds will be like a few months on, it is as well to prepare the way. Twins as young as ten months have protested vehemently at suddenly finding themselves dressed differently. A mother found the pressure of her one-year-old identical girls too much. "They used to look and they didn't like it. They had to have the same, so I used to change the one into what the other one had on," she said. At the age of six these girls were still dressed identically.

Practical considerations

Dressing twin children in matching outfits does require considerable effort and expense and has a number of practical disadvantages:

• You cannot take advantage of clothes that are passed on.
• You cannot pass garments from a larger to a smaller twin.
• If one garment is worn out or torn beyond repair you have to buy two new garments.
• Stores may have only one garment in the size you require.
• If one child wets or dirties his clothes you may have to change both.
• Outsiders are more likely to confuse the twins.

Advantages include:

• Having to find only one style that you like when shopping.
• When the toddlers are older it is easy to say, "Go and put on your green striped ones."

Health

In sickness . . .

If one baby has a cold the chances are that the other will get it and it is probably not worth making the very considerable effort necessary to keep them sufficiently apart to prevent this, especially if the first baby picked it up from you or another member of the family. With more serious illnesses, especially if one or both babies are delicate, you should consult your doctor.

When both are feeling ill it is futile to pretend to carry on as normal. You will exhaust yourself with holding and comforting them or listening to them whimpering and wailing if you do not. One suggestion we had was to get a large plastic undersheet for your own bed and to take yourself to bed with a twin on either side of you—at least for some of the day. Let any source of help take over or take the twins off for a walk to give you a brief respite.

Rosemary's girls had whooping cough as quite young babies. She was fortunate in having someone to take care of her toddler and house while she attended to them. She was still breast-feeding them:

> "As one threw up she would throw up over the other one, so I would have two babies to change. Then as soon as I got them both changed the one who hadn't just thrown up would throw up over the first one. . . . We had about six weeks when they were only throwing up milk and I was expected to produce a whole lot more because they had just thrown up. And everybody said the only time to feed them is immediately after they've been sick because that relaxes everything and they're more likely to take it and so every time they were sick after a feeding I had to sit down and start all over again. It was totally time-consuming—an endless sort of mopping up."

If you have no family or paid help to take over when both twins are ill over a long period, ask your health care provider for suggestions about obtaining the assistance you need. Once they are well again they will need a mother who has some energy left to look after them.

. . . and in health

Eventually, whether it is at a week, a fortnight or six weeks, you are at home with full responsibility for the health and welfare of both your twins. If there were complications at the birth, if your twins were premature or separated from you in special care you may hold on to some of those very real earlier anxieties and feel your babies are still delicate and vulnerable. First, reassure yourself that the hospital will not have released the babies until they were confident they were fit enough to leave. Then, if you have any lingering doubts about the health, the strength or the normality of either or both of your twins, you can put your mind at rest by discussing your concerns with the babies' pediatrician in the follow-up visits after your discharge from the hospital. Don't be afraid to ask any questions that you might have.

Premature babies

Babies born prematurely may appear to develop more slowly than babies born at term. If you deduct the number of weeks at which they were born, e.g., 34 weeks, from what might be considered term for a twin pregnancy, 38–39 weeks, then you can add the difference, 4–5 weeks, on to the usual times when babies reach developmental milestones. For example, the first smiles may not come until 8–10 weeks instead of the 4–6 weeks in a term baby. This lag in reaching milestones matters less and less as the babies get older and the "normal" age for reaching them has a wider and wider range, but they may seem quite significant in the early weeks.

Apart from making allowances for their rate of development there is no need to regard them as being different from term babies in any other way. They need the same confident—not overcautious—handling as any other baby, the same outings and opportunities for rough-and-tumble play and meeting other babies as they get older, and they will not benefit from being overprotected.

Premature babies will gain weight at their own rate and you cannot hurry it, only meet their demands for food. Some premies remain on the small side, others gain at a great rate. You will obviously make allowances for their prematurity when introducing fruit juice and, later, solids, but basically be guided by the babies themselves.

If your babies are severely premature and require a long time in intensive care before coming home, you might find it helpful to read *The Premature Baby Book,* by Helen Harrison with Ann Kositsky, R.N. (see Appendix 4, page 294). This comprehensive volume provides information and reassurance for parents of premature infants, both singletons and multiples.

Clinics and doctors' offices

"A struggle," "an absolute nightmare," "chaotic" was how a number of mothers described taking more than one baby to the clinic or doctor's office. First there was the limited time for them to get there, get two or three babies through the system and get back again before the next feeding. Then there were the difficulties of dealing with two in a system designed for one baby per mother:

"I went once with just the twins and it was chaos. It was a rainy day. I had to get someone to hold one while I ran to get the other. Then there was nowhere to put the one while the other was being weighed and examined. I don't take them nearly as often as I did with Tim because of the difficulties."

"I recall a doctor being very peeved because I had both twins in the office for their two-year checkup. She was annoyed because one looked at the other instead of getting on with arranging her little bricks. She seemed to expect me to have a baby-sitter for one and bring each on different days. She obviously hadn't a clue what it was to have twins."

The general tendency was for twin mothers to visit the clinic or doctor's office as little as possible. When they had to, bypassing one or two of the "rules" or making special arrangements reduced much of the "struggle" involved. Following is a list of strategies adopted by various mothers to take the pressure out of doctor and clinic visits.

• There is no need to undress the babies for weighing. If you want an exact weight, weigh their clothes at home the next time you change them.

• Find a shop with scales in your local shopping center.

• Ignore "no carriages" notices. A carriage will usually be accepted once it is known you have twins. If you are still not permitted to bring one in, insist on having a helper to hold one of the babies.

• If at all possible take a helper, especially on injection and checkup days when there will be a longer wait.

• Talk over the problem with the clinic nurse and make a special arrangement to have the twins seen promptly or before the clinic opens to others.

• Regular appointments with a pediatrician in private or small group practice are likely to be easier, although more costly, than visits to a large well-baby clinic for routine inoculations and checkups.

On the move

The kind of equipment that will be most useful for transporting your babies will depend very much on your life-style. If your expeditions are largely on foot, then a large carriage or solid double stroller with a shopping tray will be the most useful. If you use a car, then you need to concentrate on a safe means of transporting the babies in the car and need only a light stroller.

Carriages and strollers

Large twin carriages are very expensive and you may be able to find a secondhand one. Be sure to examine it carefully to make sure that it is sturdy and safe. The more compact twin carriages were voted least useful by mothers. They are seldom more than a few inches longer than a single carriage so that babies very soon become cramped and uncomfortable. Several mothers complained that the chassis did not appear to have been strengthened and soon sagged.

The most adaptable carriage we know, the Duo Dodger, has been designed by a mother of twins. It has an extra long carry-crib-style body on a sprung chassis with a good-size shopping tray underneath. When the babies get too big to lie together it can be adapted so that the babies are in reclining seats, and when they can sit up it becomes a stroller in which the babies sit facing each other, all for the cost of a conventional carriage. This carriage is made and sold in England, but it may be possible to find a store in the U.S. willing to order one for you.

A few mothers did not bother with a twin carriage at all. Until their babies were old enough to go in a stroller, they carried one baby in a sling and pushed the other in a lightweight single carriage for short local outings.

A compromise between carriage and stroller that a number of mothers favored was the solidly built stroller with a folding tow section that can start as a carriage and later convert to a stroller. A large stroller may not fit in the car, however, and if you frequently take your children somewhere where you will need a stroller, the lightweight folding variety may be more serviceable for your particular needs. Many manufacturers make these in a twin version.

Some parents mentioned the difficulty of maneuvering a double stroller or carriage through entrances to shops or buildings designed to take only a single carriage width. There are a few strollers that can seat the babies one behind the other or facing each other. Parents of singletons close together in age have found these to be helpful as well.

Your Mothers of Twins Club should be able to help you locate sources of needed products near you. Because new products are continuously being introduced, the best source of current information is the club that keeps up-to-date listings of such items.

Triplets and more

As far as most manufacturers are concerned, you have to stay at home if you are on your own with three or more small children. A large old-fashioned carriage will probably hold two babies at either end. The mother who designed the twin Duo Dodger carriage mentioned above can also produce it for four, taking either quads or triplets or twins plus a young toddler. Some parents, in desperation, improvise by fastening carriages or strollers together. If you resort to this, make sure the product you have created is sturdy and safe.

Traveling by car

If you travel in a car with your babies, they must, no matter how many of them there are, each be properly restrained in a car seat that meets federal safety standards. This is essential not only for the safety of your children but to comply with the law in most states. Infants are transported in rear-facing seats that fasten to the car by means of the seat belts. For triplets, you may have to have an extra seat belt installed in the backseat of your car to accommodate the infant seats. Older toddlers ride in a more upright position on seats that face forward. Some brands of car seat convert from infant to toddler use. Whichever seats you choose for your children, it's important to use them correctly and without exception. This is easier said than done for multiples, but there is no safe way for a small child to ride in an automobile without a car restraint, and after all the other things you've gone through why put your babies at risk now? Although some parents interviewed admitted to dangerous arrangements with unrestrained portable cribs in the backs of station wagons or even the front seats of sedans, we cannot recommend such arrangements, although we do understand the desperation that leads to them. Once your children weigh about 40 pounds each, they can use the adult seat belts. It's safer to transport children in the backseat.

For information on the latest models of car restraints for young children, write to Physicians for Automotive Safety, 50 Union Avenue, Irvington, N.J. 17111. Send a stamped, self-addressed envelope and $.35 handling charge.

For twin mothers who feel cheated at not being able to use a cycle when the babies are bigger, there is a tricycle with two child seats.

Public transportation

Traveling by bus or train with small babies in comfort and safety generally requires two adults. A few brave mothers made unaccompanied trips. It may be easier on your own to travel with one baby in a sling and one in a single stroller. Seeing parents struggling with babies, bags and buggies often seemed to bring out the best in other passengers.

Further afield

Several parents traveled abroad, mostly by plane. Bulkhead seats, where there is room for baskets provided by the airline are the best. Airlines are generally helpful, but you need to let them know your needs in advance. All parents stressed the importance of keeping the stroller on board with you in the cabin for use at the airport.

Whether you travel by car, boat, train or plane, the golden rule applies: always take more prepared meals and more diapers than you expect to need. Long delays can occur on the best-planned journeys.

Other recommended aids for traveling and visiting with several small children are lightweight folding camp cribs—especially those that can be used up to age three; folding chairs that clamp on to sturdy tabletops; fabric seats that secure babies to ordinary dining chairs and can be folded and carried in a handbag.

Shopping

Probably the most frequent outing you will have to make will be to the supermarket or grocery store. The problems you'll meet can be amusing, though shopping with one baby is bad enough; with two or three it can be a nightmare. Any mother who could did the bulk of her shopping without her numerous children in attendance, although some did learn to be quite adept at maneuvering two shopping carts through crowded supermarkets.

The problem of juvenile shoplifting is increased with multiples!

"It was chaos. They would get lost and be found pulling things off shelves and eating things. I remember a classic incident when I was checking out of a supermarket and I had the two of them with me. The ladies at the register were cooing and gurgling, "Oh aren't they cute and beautiful?" I said, "Yes, they are, but they're a real handful in the store. I have to frisk them because they steal." The assistants thought it was all so funny and were falling about laughing . . . and when I got them home I found they each had half a dozen toothbrushes down their fronts."

· 5 ·

Adjustments in the Family

Becoming the parents of twins

> "If you've got twins you may not admit it, but people who go on about having 'a baby' are not really in the same league. You do have a slight superiority complex."

That was how one father voiced the feeling that many parents admitted to having at one time or another. When things are going well and friends exclaim in admiring tones, "How do you cope?" or bemoan their problems with their mere one baby, then parents of twins and more may be forgiven for feeling a little smug. Of course there are also the times when the answer to "How do you cope?" may well be "Right now we don't!" And it may be difficult to force a smile at the "Aren't-you-lucky-getting-it-all-over-in-one-go" remarks that all parents of multiples encounter.

This chapter looks at some of the difficulties that parents, and particularly the mother, encounter when adjusting to taking care of twins in the early months. We focus on the mother because in virtually all the families we talked to, the main responsibility for the day-to-day care of the babies fell on her.

Relating to two at a time

Telling them apart
Once parents have come to terms with the astonishing fact that they have produced two (or more) babies they begin to look for ways to distinguish one baby from another. Telling them apart

is the start of developing a relationship with each baby as an individual. This inevitably takes time and it may take an especially long time with identical babies who show little difference in temperament. Research suggests, and common sense confirms, that it is much easier for parents to relate to their babies as individuals where clear differences exist between them. If your twins are very alike, it may therefore be quite some time before you stop thinking of them as "the twins" or "the babies" and begin to see each as a little person in his or her own right, whom you love for him or herself rather than as one half of a pair.

Parents who were in any doubt about their twins' identity usually waited to remove the hospital name tags that each baby has on wrist or ankle until they felt confident about distinguishing them. A few had nasty moments:

> "When we got home from the hospital we put them [identical girls] one at each end of the crib and then realized we couldn't remember which one we'd put at which end. We finally managed to identify them because Danielle still had her cord. That was the only time we ever got them muddled."

Although most parents could distinguish their babies' appearance quite quickly, several found it very difficult to distinguish their cries and could not tell them apart for many months. A few continued to confuse them for years.

Helping others to distinguish the babies may be a problem. It may not matter when they are very small whether someone you meet in the street can tell them apart, but it is important that grandparents, relatives and close friends can distinguish them.

If the babies are not easily identifiable, then you and others will naturally look for some other way to tell them apart. One of Jackie's twins developed a cyst over his right eye at five months and people other than his parents used this to identify him, which Jackie found upsetting. Another identical pair could be identified by the fact that one had a strawberry mark. Parents understandably will not want any of their children to be identified by a physical peculiarity, however slight.

Identity tags on bracelets or badges (unsafe on tiny babies) are not really satisfactory as they require someone to peer at a label before being able to make contact with the individual baby. Different hairstyles may be useful later, but are not relevant for small babies, so the only possible way left for immediately recognizing the babies is the way they are dressed.

If the twins are easily distinguished it may not matter if you want to dress them alike while they are small. When twins are very alike, dressing them identically is simply a further source of confusion. If each twin is always dressed in a particular range of colors or shades: Roger in reds, oranges, yellows, George in greens and blues, or Sarah always in pastel shades, Jane in darker ones, then, provided you are consistent, others can begin to recognize the babies and, more importantly, you can quickly identify each. An alternative might be large embroidered initials.

The twins themselves are unlikely in the early months to be aware of similarities or differences in dress. Babies do, however, begin forming their perceptions of their world and of themselves from a much earlier age than they are usually given credit for. If the people in their world are confused about their identity, they are bound to assimilate some of the confusion.

Preferences

Researchers have suggested that human beings have developed skills to deal with one offspring at a time, unlike many animals that cope quite efficiently with several. It is not surprising therefore to find that most parents experienced times when they felt they were more interested and responsive to one baby than to the other.

Some mothers had given the matter some thought:

> "After all, there are very few situations in life where anyone is expected to form two close relationships simultaneously. It's the same really as taking on two new lovers at the same time. How many people can do that?"

Most parents, however, made the generally unspoken assumption that they would be able to feel the same for both babies and that they somehow "ought" to love them equally and simultaneously. Some felt they did. Others were disturbed to find that their feelings were not constant and that for weeks or months they would feel more for one baby than for the other:

"Ben had a very mobile face and produced endearing expressions even when he was asleep and he was very responsive when he was awake. Daisy just lay there, sleeping nearly all the time, totally expressionless, and she had this funny domed head because of the way she was born. Both of us responded much more to him, we couldn't help it. Over the months I realized that it switched around. I would have weeks of finding that I was more involved with one baby than the other, then something would happen and I would switch back. At first I felt rather guilty—that I should love them both equally and fairly, but after a while I just accepted that that was how things were and maybe you can't love two babies equally at once. It didn't seem relevant as they got older and I'm not aware of it now."

Most parents found that, as the months went by, their attention would switch from one baby to another as they reached different stages of development or went through a minor crisis such as illness or teething troubles, and eventually these feelings ceased to be an issue.

Sometimes the disparity in feelings toward the babies is much greater and may last longer:

"Although I love both girls equally now, it wasn't like that to start with. I had Josie with me on the ward while Anna was in special care. I used to go and visit her dutifully but she was there for three weeks after I went home. When they told me I could take her home I wasn't really interested in her anymore. I just didn't feel anything much toward her. It is all a long time ago now but I still feel guilty and sad about all those months when I didn't really love her."

Mary felt that her relationship had been deeply affected by having only one baby to relate to for so many weeks and wished she had been given the opportunity to stay in the hospital with both babies.

Sometimes it was the very different needs of the two babies

that led to a mother feeling differently toward them. Frances had two little girls, one small and contented, the other larger and more demanding:

> "It got to the point where I was saying, 'It's always Lizzie . . . not you again.' She had really bad problems with colic and always seemed to be kicking and crying. So there was this problem of the demanding child who is driving you crazy and this lovely little one who is sweet and nice and you can't give any attention to. I did feel very guilty about how I felt, and talked to my husband about it and he was very helpful."

Most parents seemed to hold the sometimes apparently conflicting views that each baby should receive the individual attention that it needed and that each should be treated "fairly," i.e., have the same amount of time and attention. It was trying to reconcile these feelings that caused several mothers concern.

Gillian, a very maternal and experienced mother, used to feel that if one cried and received a lot of attention, then the other ought to be compensated for it: "I knew it was irrational. I thought to myself, how silly to wake a baby up to give it a cuddle."

Guilt about negative feelings toward one baby, or about the babies receiving unequal amounts of attention, was not uncommon. Such feelings are understandable but unproductive. If one baby demands more attention for a time, then you are meeting that baby's needs in giving it, and the other will not suffer as long as you remain aware of its needs and are able between you as parents to find some time for that one. If the imbalance continues for more than a few weeks or months, then you may need to check that it has not become an established pattern and that one baby is not constantly losing out. If so, then you can take steps to remedy the situation. Sometimes it requires only a small change in your routine to give the other baby more time.

With as many as four or five babies, it might take many months to get to know and relate to them all:

> "They were in incubators for a long time. I couldn't touch them for ages. It was just like taking four complete strangers

home. Having the first two at home wasn't too bad but the last two I resented. They were particularly obnoxious. When there were so many helpers at different times it was easy to avoid feeding them and avoid having much to do with them, which was awful really. I'd say, 'I'm not feeding that one. I'm going to bed.' And then I realized the only way to do it was to spend more time with them and make an effort to get on with them, which was what I just had to do in the end when I'd come more to terms with having them all in the first place."

Helping older children to adjust

Toddlers

No matter how well you prepare older children for the arrival of a new brother or sister, they are bound to experience some difficulty in adjusting to being replaced as the baby of the family. It would be unrealistic not to expect some expression of stress: the wanting to be a baby again, coming into their parents' bed, climbing into the babies' carriage, wanting a bottle, wanting to be back in diapers, soiling pants, wetting the bed. In families with older siblings, many had experienced one or two of these difficulties, but most of the children seemed to have coped with the arrival of the babies very well, much better than most parents had anticipated.

Several mothers commented that they felt their older child had accepted two babies more easily than one. "He saw that neither of the babies got a great deal of attention and I think this helped him accept that he got less, too."

Because they realized that being displaced by two babies could be a difficult experience for a toddler, most mothers had taken considerable trouble to prepare them for the babies' arrival, making arrangements well in advance for extra help and encouraging a closer relationship between the toddler and her father. But even Patricia, whose twins were diagnosed only a week before they were born, found her toddler was able to cope:

"He was very good. He had been expecting me to be away for one night and come back with one baby, and instead of that I was away for ten days and came back with two! I just had time before they were born to dash out and get a book on babies, which has pictures of twins in it, to try and explain what was happening."

Most mothers were concerned to make time in the day when their older child had some exclusive attention. Ruth went home without her babies and felt that in the circumstances it was a good thing, as it gave her time with her 18-month-old, Kate. She and Kate visited the babies together until they came home after two weeks. Ruth had special pens, paper and books that came out at feeding time, though even these could not occupy Kate happily when feeding the two babies took two hours:

"The most useful visitors were the ones that came, not to coo over the babies but to give Kate some attention, and I arranged for a schoolgirl to come regularly and take Kate to the park . . . I think that deciding my priorities was the vital thing . . . I felt that Kate must take priority sometimes. Five minutes concentrated attention is worth half an hour's partial attention, and if I felt that Kate really needed some time I would shut the doors between myself and the babies and let them scream for ten minutes. I have also encouraged her to be involved with the babies. She helps me give baths and wash their clothes. So far [after six months], we really haven't had any problems."

Sheila's little boy was just two when his twin brothers were born. Despite several periods of separation from his mother when first she and then the twins were ill, he coped very well: "I worried more about the separation than he did." Sheila had made a point of feeding the babies separately, partly so that she had a hand free for Peter. She also ensured that he had some time with her on his own each day. Although she was offered a place at a nursery soon after the twins were born, she waited until the twins were a year old before she sent him: "I didn't want him to feel that he was being shunted off to make way for the babies. When he did start he adjusted well and his kindness to smaller children was commented on."

A number of mothers mentioned the difficulties of dealing with the "oohing" and "aahing" over a twin carriage, while an ignored toddler stands by miserably: "It was all right at home but as soon as we went out everyone would stop to look in the carriage and say, 'Aren't you lucky to have two babies—do you help Mommy?' and so on. It really upset her and she became quite withdrawn for a while." Patricia avoided this problem by simply not taking the twins out when they were tiny. She would leave them with her mother-in-law and take her little boy with her on his own. If you can leave the twins behind at least sometimes, it will undoubtedly be good for the older child's ego.

Another difficulty in taking twins and a toddler out is that when the toddler adopts the common protest strategy of refusing to walk you cannot simply pop him or her into the other end of a carriage as you might with only one baby. The problem can be solved by investing in a really big old-fashioned secondhand carriage that will accommodate two babies at one end and an older child at the other, or is strong enough to take one of the special carriage seats designed for twin carriages and that sit the toddler sideways.

Inevitably there are situations where a mother has a difficult pregnancy, necessitating a long spell in the hospital, or where one or both twins are subsequently ill and need a great deal of attention and an older child has a very difficult time:

> "Joe had to stop being a baby all at once and grow up and cope with all sorts of things . . . "

> "I think Andrew suffered tremendously. Their first eighteen months I think really knocked him for a loop. He is still [aged five] not in control of his emotions. He gets upset easily. If a Lego brick falls off, it's tears and screams and the end of the world, and he has to be cuddled and given lots of love and reassurance. His emotions have been so near the surface, I'm sure because mine have."

Coping with a crisis period and its aftermath is hard on both mother and child. Use all the help you can get, so the older child still has some exclusive attention.

Older children
In some families the twins arrived to displace children who were already of school age. In the families we interviewed all but one of these older children were girls. In general they

coped well. They were old enough to feel fairly secure in their own position in the family and to be involved in caring for babies. Helen's daughter, Louisa, was four when the three babies arrived:

> "As there were three of them she did not have one nasty little baby to hate because I was cuddling it so much. I used to make a point of telling her that as they were three, she, Stephen and I would all have to be mothers. She rose splendidly to this challenge. It was a situation of them and us, and she was on Stephen's and my side."

Both younger and older children seemed to cope with the arrival of twins, provided it did not involve prolonged separation from their mother; it was later, as the twins grew older, that problems began to emerge for some older siblings. These are discussed in Chapter 7 on pages 198–203.

Mothers

Being a "good" mother
Mothering twins, triplets or more is different from mothering babies who come one at a time. If you can accept this rather than comparing yourself with a friend who has just had her firstborn singleton, or with your own previous experience of mothering a singleton, then you are likely to have a better image of yourself.

Not enough time for each
It is always easier to see what it is you cannot do because you have twins or more, than what you can do. One thing you cannot do is give each baby as much time and attention as you would had you had a single birth—though of course it is only the firstborn singleton who ever receives the parents' exclusive attention—subsequent children get a great deal less and generally still manage to thrive. Most mothers did feel strongly that "there was no way I could ever give each enough time" or "I felt I was trying to divide myself in two the whole time." But you may be able to see this lack of time as a positive advantage, as some mothers did:

"Somehow because there were two I worried less about each one individually—you can see how different they are in so many ways so you don't worry all the time about what is normal."

Another mother agreed:

"I might not have had as much time for them as I would have liked, but at least I didn't have the time to fuss over either of them doing the anxious 'Is she still breathing?' and 'Is this sniffle significant?' routine that I saw so many friends doing with their one baby."

Resentment

It is quite common for first-time mothers to feel resentful at the loss of freedom. With twice as much to do, life may seem very unfair:

"I couldn't help feeling sometimes as I stood knee-deep in diapers and bottles—why did this happen to me?"

Several mothers admitted to feelings of resentment at the loss of the rather special experience they had looked forward to with a first baby:

"I saw friends with their baby in a sling going off on a bus to do some shopping or visit a museum or just dropping around on a friend—just the way I had imagined myself doing it, and I felt it was unfair that I couldn't. I'd looked forward to the freedom of stopping work and having this nice time with my baby, and I felt cheated."

Such feelings are not of course incompatible with loving the babies, but mothers may feel that they are and be afraid to express them:

"I'd felt pretty apprehensive about having twins while I was pregnant, but I'd adjusted to the idea. When they were born I was so grateful that they were all right despite being six weeks premature . . . and then I really fell in love with them. But at the same time I still felt anger and resentment at having this double burden but I couldn't really talk about it. It seemed disloyal to the babies somehow, and anyhow friends with only one didn't understand. I did feel very martyred at times."

When you find yourself feeling sad, resentful or frustrated by the "double burden," talking to another mother of twins and sharing your feelings with your partner—he may be feeling similar emotions—are good ways of finding support. Your doctor might also listen sympathetically. Acknowledging these feelings frees you to deal with the practical difficulties of the situation.

Taking care of yourself

Your well-being comes first. Looking after yourself has to be your first priority. If you are ill, suffering from severe fatigue (as opposed to the inevitable "normal" level), not eating properly, then what may be a difficult and challenging time can become impossible. We know only too well how easy it is to say this and how difficult the advice may be to follow in practice, but it is largely a matter of attitude. If you really believe that your welfare is important, you will find ways of taking care of yourself and will be open to others taking care of you.

Jean felt strongly that her own good health was crucial to everyone's welfare:

> "I made a conscious effort to keep in good health. I ate well and regularly and rested every day. I felt that if I was fit mentally and physically I could stay on top of everything."

Ruth, who was breast-feeding her twins and already had an 18-month-old, was equally clear about her priorities:

> "I knew I had to be fit to cope. I had a rest every day either taking my toddler to bed with me or letting her play on the floor beside me."

One form of taking care of yourself is allowing someone else to mother you. Caring for more than one baby is one of the most demanding jobs anyone could undertake. It is physically and emotionally demanding. When you are giving so much to the babies, you need replenishing yourself. It can be very helpful to have someone around whose first question is not "How are the babies?" but "How are you?", someone who will occasionally attend to your own physical and emotional needs, someone to support you and perhaps take over when you feel overwhelmed by the insatiable demands of your babies. "Good" mothers often find it hard to accept mothering themselves but those who just bravely soldier on till they drop are no good to anyone. You will be in a much better position to care for your babies when you too are being cared for—and you may need to let this be known loud and clear!

Isolation

"I think it is vitally important to get out of the house, I really do. Because I think it's an insidious thing, feeling lonely and cut off. You don't realize you are, especially if you've got these little babies. There's actually a lot to do and also you don't realize you're lonely because there's all this extraordinary sound going on around you, but you do just get very lonely for another adult."

Many mothers found that there was so much to do that it was weeks or even months before they got out of the house or felt able to invite friends or relatives to visit. Loneliness and isolation are factors associated with postnatal depression so, while it is understandable that parents often feel they have no time for anything but the babies in the first few months, it is important to keep in touch with the outside world.

Even if entertaining friends or family is out of the question for a time, you can still ask them to come for a cup of coffee, share a take-out meal, or give you a hand with a meal or the babies.

As well as retaining old friends, most first-time mothers need to find new ones—other mothers who are experiencing the same hopes and worries. It is difficult to get to the places where you meet other mothers: the clinic, postnatal groups, parks, mother and baby clubs, but it is worth hurrying through a feeding and bundling the babies into a carriage to get out and meet some friendly faces.

The greatest mutual support can come from another mother of twins. If there is no Mothers of Twins Club in your neighborhood you can ask your doctor or perhaps someone at your local school or religious institution if they know of another mother of multiples living near you. If you see a mother in the street pushing a twin carriage, go and talk to her, she will probably be delighted:

> "It changed my life, the day that Carol knocked on my door and said that she lived around the corner. . . . I'd seen her pass the window once, pushing her two in a carriage, and nearly rushed out after her then, but I was feeding or something. It made such a difference having her to talk to. Until then I'd just been on my own at home with the two babies and I had begun to feel really lonely."

Getting away from it all
There came a point sooner or later in the first year when the babies needed less physical care and mothers began to emerge from the culture shock of total baby care and had time to wonder "What about me?"

> "You lose all sense of yourself if you don't get a little bit of space, and I wasn't getting any space at all. And it was all that I wanted, just to be somewhere where I couldn't hear them."

A few mothers worked at home while the babies were tiny, but this did not necessarily provide the space that they needed for themselves:

> "I thought by working freelance at home I would keep in touch with the old 'me,' but it was just another pressure, something else to be fitted in."

Some, perhaps not feeling that their need was legitimate, made space for themselves in a roundabout way:

> "Every Saturday morning I left them with my husband and went shopping, even when I didn't have anything to buy—just to be on my own."

Child care

The only satisfactory arrangement is to have a regular break when someone else takes care of the babies and you have some time that is just for you:

> "When they were three months old I realized that I desperately needed to have a break from time to time. I don't have any relatives who live close by so we paid Sally to come for four hours every Thursday. The first time I went out I remember a feeling of enormous release and relief. . . . She continued to come until the twins were at playgroup. It was a very high priority for me. We didn't have much cash to spare and I didn't have any new clothes for ages, but I had this time to myself when I could do what I liked when I liked."

A number of mothers relied on fathers who were on shift work or on their families to take care of the babies from time to time. One family even moved to be near a helpful granny. Another couple took the babies to their grandmother's every Friday night and collected them again on Saturday.

If you are not lucky enough to have this kind of help, then you may be able to pay someone to come for a few hours a week. Occasional day care in someone else's home is another alternative. Mothers coping on very limited budgets may be able to get some form of support to allow them to get away through their local social services department. If you have triplets or more, then the need for a break is all the more urgent.

While a reciprocal arrangement for child care with another mother is usually out of the question for supertwins, it is not necessarily impossible for twins. Nevertheless, many twin mothers are reluctant even to consider it: "There is this guilt feeling when you are exchanging twins for one," "I've been very loath to dump them on other people. I still am," "Although I get sick to death of them, I don't think I'd like anyone else to look after them." A natural hesitancy to hand small children over is often compounded for twin mothers by the anxiety that others will not be able to manage two, and also by the effort of getting it all organized. A regular arrangement disposes of much of the organizing. If you give others a chance you may find that, with a little practice, they learn to manage just as well as you:

"We started the swap when our babies were about nine months. I did feel at first that it was unfair that Nell had to take two of mine in exchange for just one of hers but then I thought, well, we're both getting what we want—a few hours a week without having to look after our babies. As I had two, one more didn't make much difference to me for a few hours—I think it may have been harder for her to start with but she soon got used to it and said she enjoyed watching the three of them interact. It was like our own personal playgroup but nicer. The children have been great friends ever since."

Whether you choose to work, play, have a drink with a friend or sleep during your time away from the twins, we suggest that you do it, if at all possible, out of the building they are in so you are out of earshot and can feel that the responsibility for them has been entirely handed over.

Baby-sitting
Parents sometimes had similar difficulties arranging baby-sitting to give themselves an evening out. If you have qualms or difficulty in finding anyone to take your lot on you could try hiring sitters in pairs!

Work
It is possible to continue working full time. Two of the mothers we saw chose to do so. Barbara, a single parent, had live-in help and Christine used to drop her two at a baby-sitter near her work. This arrangement enabled her to continue breast-feeding and to play with them during her lunch hour. Christine and Gerry, her husband, had a secondary arrangement on weekends. They paid a schoolgirl to come in and play with the twins for a couple of hours on Saturday mornings while they quickly got on with household tasks.

Only a very few of the mothers we saw did any part-time work outside the home in the first year, though several began to do so in the second year.

Postpartum depression
It would be surprising if caring for two or more babies did not occasionally produce spells of anxiety, feelings of exhaustion or

isolation, but for most mothers these pass. Sooner or later in the first year mothers begin to surface from the sea of diapers, the endless night feedings. Things begin to look brighter. When this does not happen—when the things seem uniformly gray and appear to be getting worse rather than better—a mother may be suffering from postpartum depression.

Postpartum depression is not easily defined, and it is not an illness like measles where you either have the spots or you do not. A few women suffer severely and receive medical treatment, but many suffer from moderate depression and simply wait for it to get better—which it eventually does.

In her book *Depression after Childbirth* (Oxford University Press, New York, 1981), Katharina Dalton describes the symptoms of postpartum depression: perpetual tiredness, feelings of gloom and despair that deepen as the day progresses and the mother feels that yet again she has failed to cope; irritability and sudden bursts of anger; fits of crying; eating binges leading to rapid weight gain; loss of interest in sex; a general loss of confidence; withdrawing from people. Even though such a mother is clearly "not herself" and experiences life as bleak and dismal, she may well not be aware that her condition is not normal. She comes to believe that what she is experiencing is just the way life is with small children.

Postpartum depression may begin within a few days or weeks of the babies' birth or not until much later in the first year. Usually it improves spontaneously, but it can last for several years. Of the mothers we talked to quite a number admitted to feelings of depression in the second half of the first year— "You don't really have time to notice it before then, do you?"— but only a few sought help:

> "I enjoyed the first six months despite the hard work. . . . I was engrossed in them from the time I got up until I went to bed. By about nine months that's when depression really began to strike. . . . There were days when I was feeling so bogged down I just couldn't cope. Things in the house irritated me—it wasn't as clean as it should be. . . . They were more into a routine so maybe I had more time to sit down and think 'What's happening to me?' I went to the doctor and he asked me about my concentration, nothing else, nothing about looking after twins. He prescribed Valium, which I

took for a few weeks and it helped get over that immediate period. But the depression continued on and off. . . .I felt this was my prison—I don't drive and had to rely on my husband to get to shops or a park. I didn't own up to the resentment then, but it gnawed away. I really only began to feel better when I started work again when the twins were nearly four."

A study carried out at the University of Surrey comparing symptoms of postpartum depression in mothers of firstborn twins with those of firstborn singletons found that the mothers of twins did exhibit more symptoms of mild depression.

Katharina Dalton, who has had great success with progesterone therapy for women suffering from severe postpartum depression, has not observed a higher incidence of multiples among her patients. However, the kinds of stresses that are associated with postpartum depression are more likely to be experienced by a twin mother. They include a difficult pregnancy, medical intervention in labor, separation from the baby after birth, a long stay in the hospital, anxiety over small babies, frequent visits to the hospital or clinic with the babies, isolation at home. Some or all of these combined with the fatigue from the sheer physical hard work involved in caring for and feeding two make a twin mother more vulnerable.

Getting help
Although the depression usually lifts spontaneously, there is no need for a mother to simply wait for things to get better if some of the stresses can be removed. Since the mother herself will almost certainly be unable to see her situation clearly or have the energy to change it, it will be up to her partner, a relative or close friend to help her to help herself.

The first thing may be to help the mother realize that she is depressed. The knowledge that she is suffering from a recognized condition following birth may help her to cope with her feelings. Her state of mind may, however, make her reject reasoning and logic. Helping her may require great tact and patience.

Then there are the practical aspects of her situation. Discuss these with her and make the necessary arrangements. If she is exhausted and obviously overwhelmed with physically caring for the babies, what kind of help can be arranged? Has she had a break from the babies to have some time for herself? Is she at home all day, isolated from former friends and other mothers?

Alleviating some of the stresses of her situation may not be enough. She may require some medical help, and the family doctor or obstetrician is the first person to turn to. It can be difficult for a family doctor to diagnose postpartum depression: it is still a condition about which there is a great deal of ignorance. Things may be made difficult by the woman herself who can "pull herself together" sufficiently to appear to be coping, and will often present the doctor with some quite trivial complaint. In such a situation it is helpful if someone else goes along with her to assist in explaining her difficulties.

Sedatives and tranquilizers may be prescribed and they can help some women through a difficult period, but often what is required is someone to listen:

> "My family doctor said five months was too late for postpartum depression. He didn't ask about how I had felt having undiagnosed twins or show any awareness of the stresses involved in caring for two. I took the pills he prescribed for just a week . . . but it was going back to the hospital where I had worked and talking to friends and colleagues that really helped me to feel better."

If your doctor cannot help you in this or any other situation where you are anxious, you should persist in seeking help elsewhere. It may even mean finding another doctor. The mother whose twins cried continually was finally helped two years later when she moved and found a more sympathetic doctor. No one should have to wait that long.

If your problems are really getting you down, a trained counselor who will listen to you and offer support can be very helpful. Look in the classified section of your telephone book for available agencies or individuals in your area, or ask your doctor or clergyman for recommendations. Your marriage need not be breaking up for you to consider a counselor who specializes in marriage difficulties. Postpartum depression and the burdens of rearing multiples can put a strain on even the best of relationships and it is a sign of strength, not weakness, to seek professional assistance where needed.

The person who can give a mother the most support is, of course, her partner. It can be very difficult dealing with a mother who cannot "snap out of it." Besides practical help, she needs constant reassurance that she is still loved despite what she perceives as her inadequacies, that she can be a good mother, and that things will get better. It may be hard for her partner himself to believe this. He too may be suffering from fatigue, even some degree of depression. But things do get better.

Fathers

"It's quite easy to cop out and be lazy with only one child and so miss out on the baby bit. I'm glad I had to get involved."

"It would have been very hard for Christine to have survived if I hadn't helped."

Fathers of multiples, whether they like it or not, are usually much more involved in their children right from the beginning. Mostly they did like it, and later reaped the rewards of having been close to their children from the earliest days.

Mothers were in no doubt that they needed the help:

"From the very word go he needs to become involved because there are two. It's a necessity almost, because when you first come home you can't do it on your own. It's virtually impossible."

And they saw the need to involve the father as a bonus, avoiding the exclusive relationship that mothers sometimes have with singletons:

"I was absolutely staggered by the amount of love I had for these babies and I said to myself, 'If I had one of these I wouldn't let anybody touch it, but because I can't do anything about it I'm letting everyone touch it.' It's really odd. It's a very natural instinct to hold a baby to oneself, whereas if you have no choice . . . I was really pleased by that, very pleased."

Fathers not only shared feeding, changing and comforting the babies when they were there but also took responsibility for specific daily tasks: laundry, bottle preparation, preparing the evening meal, doing the last feeding while the mother had an early night or, later, giving the twins breakfast while she caught up on a little sleep—thus leaving the mother more time and energy to tend to the babies during the day. Fathers who worked unusual hours were often able to take on an even larger share of child care. Tony was always at home in the mornings to help with the feeding and to take the older child to play school. Helen and Stephen had a flying start with their triplets because they conveniently arrived at the beginning of Stephen's long summer vacation.

Some mothers depended on the fathers' involvement and capabilities to allow them to keep in touch with their careers. A father of two sets of young twins, only two years apart, took all four on for a day every weekend while his wife slept after doing a night duty in a local hospital.

Fathers of multiples may find their involvement fulfilling but are prey to many of the pressures that mothers experience. Like mothers, they were often overtaken by fatigue: "It's so tiring and wearing," said Simon. Gerry commented, "You're so exhausted just coping with them and simply living that you don't get around to doing anything additional." In the early months Dave had to give up helping with the night feedings when he began falling asleep at work.

Many a father welcomed the respite of a day at work!

> "I used to long to be at the office, knowing I could sit in peace without them there. I used to come shooting home for the early evening feeding and I used to suddenly come to the end of the street and say to myself, 'I can't go home without a drink.' I have a drink sometimes anyway after work, but this was a different sort of drink. I'd shoot into the pub and have three very quick large drinks and then go home."

The necessity of sharing the care of multiples often brought about rapid changes in fathers' attitudes:

> "With Louisa, Stephen had a much more traditional role. He'd have lazy mornings, for example, while I'd feed and see

to Louisa. With the triplets, he got up every night to help me feed them. We did everything together. It's completely changed his attitude toward kids and caring for them."

More than anything, mothers welcomed—and needed—their partners' moral support, someone to take over when they were feeling worn out, someone to talk to when things were difficult, someone who really understood what caring for more than one baby means.

Parents' relationship

What has happened to us?
It is not just the mother who needs time away from the babies. Many couples suddenly look at each other sometime in the first year and wonder, what has happened to us? Some couples were aware from the start of the need to find time for themselves, others tended to put the children first and only later realized that they had no life for themselves:

> "Twins are more demanding and excluding. They take a greater toll than one child does. With the fatigue and emotional drain we reached a point of drifting along, merely existing. There had been no time to come to grips with and sort out feelings about being a mother, let alone think about us."

Almost all couples felt that it was worth making great efforts to get out together. Even if it is not possible to go out much, then some kind of routine whereby the babies are in bed fairly early in the evening does at least allow you to have some time together.

Not only their social life but also their sex life may suffer. A mother of twins is more likely to have the aftereffects of a difficult delivery to contend with. In the early days after the birth she may have a sore perineum and bruising. Even after these have healed there may remain a residual anxiety that making love will be painful, and this combined with fatigue can lead to loss of libido. In addition, the emotional space taken up by the babies may leave little energy for anything else.

It is important for the couple to talk together about what is happening, and it may be that all that can be done is to accept that that is the way things are at the moment and they will improve as the babies get older. An unsatisfactory sex life, in addition to the other stresses that the parents of twins may face, could be the last straw. If the situation becomes very tense you could seek help from your family doctor, a professional counselor, or perhaps just a close friend with whom you can both talk.

Contraception

With two or more babies to care for night and day, you may wonder if you will need to think about contraception ever again. There's no time or inclination to make love, so there's no risk. But the time will come. Most parents wtih two babies are concerned they do not conceive again in a hurry. A mother who forgot to take her pill one day talked of her fears:

> "I remember going back to bed after a night feeding. It was about four in the morning, I think, the time when any anxiety gets magnified. I suddenly remembered I hadn't taken my pill. I was sure I'd end up with triplets this time—five babies. It was a nightmare."

Fortunately this particular nightmare remained within the realms of fantasy. Less fortunate mothers have had two sets of twins within eleven months of each other.

As twin mothers are normally more fertile and conceive easily, it is particularly important to use a reliable method of contraception. But no method is perfect and a mother could find herself pregnant again while the babies are still very young. Some parents in such a situation would consider termination of the pregnancy to be the best course of action. Others go on and, probably, hope for a singleton the next time.

Following a multiple birth parents may consider vasectomy or sterilization. Doctors are, however, unlikely to agree readily to either on the grounds of the multiple birth alone. They are even less likely to do so if the decision is made during the first few months after the birth, while the parents are still adapting to the large increase in the family. A father of firstborn triplets was astounded and dismayed not to be given a vasectomy on demand soon after the babies came home. With this instant larger-than-average family, he could not possibly foresee ever wanting another baby. He was, however, in his early twenties and could presumably still be considered to be in a state of shock following the birth.

If you decide on or want to consider abortion, sterilization or vasectomy, it is very important for both parents to discuss the matter with either a sympathetic doctor or a counselor from the agency concerned. With more babies than you had planned, you may feel quite decided. And it may seem an unnecessary chore to discuss it any further. It is well worth doing, however, as it will give you the time you may be unable to find at home to consider thoroughly together what is a very important decision. A counselor is not there to set up arguments against what you feel you have decided but to help you think through all the pros and cons and to arrive at the decision you feel is right for you and your family.

·6·

Practical Management— Into the Toddler Years

Once your twins are mobile, a whole new set of factors comes into play. The world is a fascinating and exciting place for a toddler. He or she wants to explore it and experiment *now*. A twin, however, has to fit in with another small person who has the same urgent need to do things his or her own way. Getting the pair, or the threesome or foursome, to more or less coordinate their activities without too much friction, and allowing them opportunities to explore and experiment without sacrificing safety, calls for planning and ingenuity, and is best achieved, most mothers found, by maintaining some kind of routine. We hope the following suggestions will help you to plan ahead and also to try out different solutions when you are at your wits' end.

Safety

Creating a safe environment for your small twins to play in without your having to constantly keep an eye on them and intervene is a high priority.

Playpens
Only one mother reported that her playpen was really useful as a play area for the pair together. She had a large old-fashioned square one with its own floor, and her identical girls would play in it happily for hours. A few mothers found this type of pen useful in the garden in warmer weather but one of them lamented, "They seemed to chew each other and fight when they

were in there." Another used hers only once, as her normally friendly identical boys treated it as a boxing ring. Yet another said the only occasions her boy-girl pair enjoyed being in it was when she joined them and it became a game.

For some twins a brief spell in the pen was a novelty they enjoyed. A few mothers found the pen invaluable for occasionally separating twins who persisted in interfering with each other's activities. With bars between them each could get on in peace for a while.

While it is fairly obvious that you cannot bank on your twins accepting their playpen as a congenial play area, having one is still worth considering. One mother used hers for propping the twins, each in opposite corners, before they could sit on their own. Others used the pen successfully as a downstairs sleeping area for one or both. Playpens can also be converted into a toy repository at night. Many used their so-called playpens primarily as a safety pen—a place where they could quickly put one or both twins while their attention was distracted by the doorbell, a phone call or a flooding bathroom, for example. Only a few of the mothers we saw did not use a playpen at all.

A play area
The most practical solution to keeping tabs on two or more active crawlers or toddlers seems to be to have at least one room or area where they can play and explore and, should the need arise, be left in safety—a giant playpen. Twins are a bonus in this respect. Because they have the company of each other, they will sometimes tolerate their mother's absence more readily.

Ideally, the room for play will be the one where you spend a lot of time—or adjacent to it. The children will want your company much of the time. At every stage it is important for their future language development that they have as many opportunities of hearing their mother speak as any singleton would. Not many parents will have a room that can be devoted entirely to the babies, but it is worth seeing how you could modify a living room so that in the daytime it can be largely given over to your crawlers or toddlers.

The basic furnishing requirements for their play area will be as much floor space as possible and a large bean bag, sofa or enough cushions to accommodate you and several children comfortably for looking at books and for cuddles. If space permits, a mattress will give the children a bouncing area as well.

One of the greatest potential hazards in your twins' play area will be the twins themselves. Some play peacefully alongside each other for hours. Many do not. A rising one-year-old will experiment by bashing anything in sight—after all, her twin's big toe or head might produce a different noise from the usual pegs. An older sibling can usually perceive the potential danger and is mobile enough to get out of the way. A twin cannot. While you do not want to stifle one twin's impulse to explore, you do not want the other to get hurt! It is helpful to both children if the parents have determined at the outset how they are going to handle this kind of situation. One possible course is to divert the "experimenter" to strike at legitimate targets and hope that will satisfy her curiosity. If she approaches her twin again, a firm no may be enough. If it is not, remove the hammer and put it out of sight. At this age she will soon find something else to interest her. While they are too young to protect themselves from assault and particularly before they understand the vulnerability of various parts of the body, the eyes in particular, all sharp, pointed and hard tools should be kept out of reach. Some mothers would include even pencils and children's scissors in this category, at least until they are fairly sure the children are beyond poking an eye or stabbing a tummy.

Safety in the home
"It was like being under siege" was how a mother of triplets described the exploratory toddler stage, which does sometimes seem as if it will never end.

With a single child, even if the mother is temporarily out of sight, she is usually aware of the child's whereabouts and very "tuned in" to any silence that might occur. As any experienced mother knows, silences often mean forbidden and therefore potentially dangerous territory is being explored. A parent of twins will inevitably be less in touch with the individual whereabouts of her children. One source of noise will blot out any ominous silences that may serve as a warning signal. Also there will be occasions, for example an upset over a spill or a cut finger, when all your attention will be concentrated on one twin and the other has a chance to slip off unnoticed. You will need to make any room the twins have access to as accident-proof as possible.

Be on the alert, too, for cooperation that could lead to danger. Two or three may have the strength to push a bed or table to reach an open window or forbidden shelf. Even quite young twins have been known to escape from playpens and to reach high door handles by one kneeling to provide a stepladder for the other. Gillian, probably the most experienced mother among those we interviewed, said of her girl twins, "They concentrate longer than most two-year-olds because they work together and their destructive powers are infinitely greater."

Where there are two or more small children in the house, a number of useful measures were suggested by parents in addition to the normal safety precautions:

• *Baths.* Stay in the bathroom while your twins are in the bath, even when they can sit very steadily. One may knock the other off balance.

• *Harnesses.* Some mothers had several harnesses that they left permanently attached to high chairs, carriages and strollers. One or two left their twins in harnesses throughout the day so they could quickly clip them in whenever necessary.

• *Stairs.* Many of the parents we saw had safety gates at both the top and the bottom of their stairs. Do not use a detachable type of gate at the top of a flight of stairs. The joint weight of twins could easily dislodge it, and all would come tumbling down. You may need to use gates for longer than you would with a single crawler or toddler as it is all too easy for one to knock the other off balance, whether by accident or design. If you have a short flight of stairs (two, three or four steps), then giving the twins the freedom to practice on those will allow them to learn good stair behavior before they graduate to a half or full flight unattended.

• *Windows.* Make sure all windows above ground floor level, even those that are fairly high up, have safety catches or bars.

• *Doors.* Doors are a menace, particularly during the stage of great interest in opening and closing them. While it is unlikely that one child will catch his or her own fingers in the jamb, even a moderate shove can crush the twin's if the other child happens to be exploring this fascinating peephole. Where it is inconvenient to keep doors closed, either tie or hook them open. The same applies to flaps on stoves or other appliances and cupboard doors: remove the handles or have some device to tie, stick or jam them in a closed position.

• *Dangerous and precious objects.* Keep poisons such as medicines and cleaning fluids doubly secure, on a high shelf in a locked cupboard or in safety cabinets that are well out of reach. A pair of identical boys succeeded in getting hold of a bottle of aspirin off a high chest of drawers. Both were taken to the hospital to have their stomachs pumped out.

Several families made access to knives, china and other potentially harmful items virtually impossible by removing drawer and cupboard handles, or by installing child-proof catches.

Very few families were able to leave any breakable or valuable possessions within the twins' reach. If you are anxious to protect certain areas in your home from assault, a hook and eye near the top of a door is easy to install and quick to use. In fact, it is quite a good idea to have several of these around the house so that whole areas can be quickly and easily sealed off. Older siblings need to be able to protect their areas without having to refer to you all the time.

• *Ironing, machine sewing.* One possibility is to put yourself in a playpen, fence off a corner or put yourself on the far side of a safety gate near the play area. Several mothers just did not do these activities while their children were up and around.

• *Furniture.* Loose-standing bookshelves and cupboards that can tolerate the assault of one child may topple easily if two decide to scale them simultaneously. Check your furniture and where necessary attach it firmly to the wall, or put it away temporarily.

• *Kitchen.* A number of parents used a guardrail around the stove. A couple of mothers kept their twins out of the kitchen altogether for safety reasons. Another had a lock on the door so that the twins could not go in unless she was there. If you have the space, prolong the use of high chairs as long as possi-

ble so you can put both children out of harm's way while dealing with difficult situations such as sweeping up broken glass.

Among the twins we saw, three had had burns serious
enough to be treated in the hospital. Two had pulled electric
kettles on themselves by tugging at the cord.

• *Garden.* Keep fertilizers and weed killers as well as garden
tools locked away. Eliminate any ornamental ponds even if they
have an apparently safe cover. A pair of sturdy, cooperative
two-year-olds can move considerable weights. Or one can crawl
under while the other holds up a corner. When visiting, take
special care. One mother, who was particularly cautious about
water, recalled one evening seeing movement near a pond in
the dusk. It was one of the twins for whom water had a special
fascination. The mother had been aware of childish chatter
with their grandmother upstairs and had assumed that both
twins were there—a clear instance of the background noise of
one masking the absence of the other.

Twins should not be left unattended in a garden or yard
unless the gate leading to the street is absolutely secure and the
fence high enough so that one cannot assist the other over
the top.

If safety precautions are in the twins' interests, they are also in
your own. Creating as safe an environment as possible will enable you to relax and not be constantly checking and chiding.

Accidents

A totally safe environment is not really possible no matter how
hard you try to achieve one. Accidents will happen no matter
how safe you make your home. They will almost invariably
happen to only one child at a time. A mother who had to rush
her two-year-old son to the hospital to have a lip stitched em-
phasized the importance of having a good relationship with the
neighbors. She really appreciated being able to leave the other
twin happily and give all of her attention to the distressed one
during their long wait in the emergency room.

Another good reason for leaving the noninjured twin behind
is the possibility that the trauma of observing the anxiety and
the treatment may leave a deeper impression on him or her
than on the one who is receiving all the attention. The injured

child is likely to be far more aware of his physical hurt than of his mother's anxiety.

Safety in the street

While twins will usually not be able to enjoy the freedom of walking along a sidewalk until they are older than singletons, it is a pity for them to miss out on the experience altogether while they are anxious to explore. Only one or two mothers used reins with any success. Others gave up after getting tied up in knots or having one or both go on strike because they could not go the way they wanted. Allowing the twins to get out of a stroller only one at a time will usually only be tolerated when the other is particularly obliging or asleep. Mothers often began by letting both out onto the sidewalk for short spells on quiet streets.

It is only through experiencing walking along a street and their mother's response to its dangers that children learn to be cautious. Because there are two and the lesson is repeated more often, twins often learn to be street-conscious and therefore reliable about not stepping off the curb before singletons do.

Twin mothers at least have a hand for each. It was a mother of triplets who reported the only accident among families we interviewed involving a child running into the street:

> "When they were about four, Katie got knocked over because she was the child whose hand I couldn't hold; she was supposed to be holding on to another child but she let go. She waited until a car passed, then rushed out—but there was a second car. Fortunately, she was OK."

Another triplet mother had a friend who offered to make her a false hand to attach to her coat! You can insist that a third and fourth child hold on to your coat. They will then be able to sense your movements, and you will notice if they let go.

Play

Through play a toddler learns all about his or her environment, how to live in it and how to relate to the people in it. As in the early days, it may still be necessary to make a point of regularly putting the many other demands on your time completely aside to be with your twins and enjoy their company, playing with them, talking with them, looking at books and singing with them. Even if they are good company for each other, both need you much more than they need each other— for love, for ideas, for language development, to help when a toy or puzzle frustrates.

In this section we deal with the toys and activities that mothers found particularly useful for occupying two or three small children relatively peacefully.

Large toys and outdoor activities

Several found a good size sandpit a boon. "It was fantastic," said one. "It kept them quiet a whole summer." Paddling pools can be fun, but they need constant supervision. If one or both twins are alarmed by splashing, giving each a plastic bowl of water will be less frightening.

The one backyard toy that mothers would not have was a swing—they are just too dangerous with more than one toddler around. A family that had a swing on a climbing frame removed it and replaced it with a rope ladder, which was very successful. There was little risk of a serious accident and the twins could both be on it at the same time. A possible substitute for a swing, if you happen to have a large tree, is a car tire suspended from a rope. It is virtually impossible to swing very far out on one of these, and if a child is struck by it he or she is likely to suffer no more than a bruise.

One family bought a seesaw believing it would encourage cooperative play. They were disappointed! A large wagon or cart tough enough to take one child while the other pulls it can involve two children simultaneously and may well provide an early incentive for taking turns. A rocking horse before the age of 2 to 2½ is likely to bruise fingers and toes repeatedly. A rocking boat, which needs two children to make it function well, is preferable.

A good toy for the yard in summer—and indoors in the winter if you have the space—is a small inflatable bouncing mat or trampoline with a handrail, specially designed for children under five. If there is a firm rule that you get off when you cannot jump anymore, taking turns becomes fairly frequent. A few minutes' constant jumping is about as much as any small child can take. In bad weather it provides contained yet vigorous indoor exercise. Such equipment has a fairly long life span—that is, it can be enjoyed from the ages of about 1½ to 5. A mattress on the floor is a satisfactory alternative.

For children who enjoy punching their twin, providing an inanimate object to punch may divert some of the blows. An inflatable plastic figure that is weighted at the bottom is an ideal toddler-size victim. A big soft toy or a large ball suspended from a doorway are good alternatives.

Suggestions for physical activity where the mother can be simultaneously involved with both included dancing, rhyming games such as ring-around-a-rosy, hide-and-seek, or ball play with a ball apiece. One mother swung both children as they ran around her, holding each firmly with a hand.

Outings

Even more than in the first year, outings were a highlight welcomed by both mothers and twins. Enclosed parks and toddler playgrounds, away from water and swings, allowed mothers to relax for a few moments while the children played. Some parks have an enclosed area with play equipment for children under five. Many sports clubs and YMCAs have a "baby bounce"— gymnastic equipment set up for children under five where they can bounce, jump, tumble, run, hang upside down and generally work off any surplus energy in safety. If you belong to a sports or health club check out the facilities available for small children. Ask your pediatrician for suggestions about available facilities.

Indoor toys and activities

Indoor toys that twins played well with, together or side by side, included bricks, construction toys, puzzles and play people, as long as there were enough pieces to ensure the children were not quickly thwarted. This may well mean that for the most popular construction sets they need at least half as many pieces again, or preferably twice the number of pieces a single child would. Jackie's two-year-old boys played with their train set happily for hours, but it was large enough for each child to keep to his own end and not get in the other's way.

Other recommended indoor activities included drawing, painting, gluing, cutting, waterplay and dough. For each of these, your twins will need their own basic tools and materials if you wish to avoid constant interference and squabbling. Children only gradually learn to share, and to expect them to do so when they are absorbed in any of these creative activities is asking for tension and trouble. For cutting and gluing, for example, each will need a pair of children's scissors and a paste brush, though it might be possible to share a glue pot. A mother of triplets said she found herself running painting and cutting sessions like a class. Each of the triplets was expected to join in, or at least be there, and to clear up his or her own mess. Provide each with his or her own cloth to clean up the mess and that, too, may prove to be a trouble-free activity. One mother used to put her twins in an empty bathtub to contain them for painting sessions.

Single children often spend hours at the sink next to their mother. If you find your twins do not have much opportunity to play with water, and this is likely as it is usually too great a hassle to allow two interfering pairs of hands to be with you at the sink, then do try to manage time for it even if it is only very occasional. You will need lots of newspaper on the floor, a plastic apron or overall and a firm chair for each, an assortment of small jugs and cups, spoons and strainers. Place a twin on each side of the full sink and you may have anything from a half hour to a whole hour's peace. Allowing ample time for play at bath times or putting them in the tub just for play will also make up for any lost opportunities for water play.

Dough provides a wonderful activity for any child. It will often keep twins, even the warring ones, happily occupied side by side, possibly for longer stretches of time than anything else. They can pummel, poke, pound and squeeze the dough, and it is hoped, work off any aggression they feel toward each other, besides enjoying the many other activities it offers.

To make enough dough for two small children, put 2 cups plain flour, ⅔ cup salt, 1 tablespoon cream of tartar, 2 tablespoons cooking oil, 2 cups water and coloring (optional) in a saucepan. Stir over a moderate heat. At first it will become lumpy. When it has thickened, remove from the heat—it may still be lumpy. When cool enough, knead the mixture to a smooth dough. Kept in an airtight container, it will last at least a couple of weeks.

One of the most successful of all indoor activities is looking at picture books and reading. Most twins are used to sharing a lap and are willing to be there with you and the books for as long as you are. For many mothers it was the best way of reducing tension, as it provided an occupation and a cuddle for both simultaneously. With more than two children, finding a comfortable arrangement is more difficult. A mother of quads with a toddler close in age had three astride the arms of an armchair and two on her lap. The earlier the children get used to whatever position you decide to adopt the better, as a pattern will be established for you all to quickly settle down and get on with reading. If you leave it till they start shoving and competing with each other for your attention, you are likely to spend much more energy sorting them out than in getting on with looking at pictures or reading. Many parents found a large bean bag a particularly cosy way for all to be comfortable during reading times. A sofa or bean bag in front of the television has the added advantage of allowing you to snatch an occasional catnap with the children snuggled against you.

Better or worse with two?

Limitations
"It's tough being a twin," one mother commented when talking of play. It can be argued that all children, except for only children and firstborns, for a period, have to share their mother. True, but demands vary with age and what is possible with one toddler may be well-nigh impossible with two when it comes to certain activities such as joining mother at the sink, freedom to go their own way in the park, freedom to get out of a stroller and explore an icy puddle on the pavement:

> "It's often a matter of time. It's too much bother to get two out and let them wander around. . . . I'm very aware that I don't mind putting William's [younger sibling] waterproof dungarees on, and letting him go. Luke and Rachel would have been shut inside because that would have been too difficult."

Your resources are obviously limited, and where this puts limitations on your twins' play experience, it is a fact of twinship that you have no alternative but to accept. Having twins or supertwins unfortunately does not magically turn the mother into a supermom. However, if you are aware of the limitations, you can ensure the twins do not miss out altogether on important play and exploration experiences. We have already suggested a way of providing occasional organized water play. When you are with another adult or an older child, this is the time to take them swimming or to give free rein on a sidewalk or in the park or near a pond. The experiences will inevitably happen less spontaneously than with singletons but at least the children will have them.

Often it was the twins themselves who created the limitations:

> "They interfered constantly with each other because as one of the twins set up an interesting situation for himself, the other one would come over and want to know what was going on and so destroy that situation. And that left them kind of permanently at a loose end because they could never actually get their own thing going without the other interfering. And I think partly out of the frustration and feeling it's almost not

worth trying because he'll come and knock it over, they did an awful lot of fighting rather than getting into playing."

When one twin is consistently being molested and is unable to do anything without interference, occasional spells in a playpen or alternatively in a high chair might give him a chance to concentrate and complete a construction or puzzle. Even better, particularly if the molesting is an attention-seeking ploy, would be for you to put yourself between them on the floor and let the molester turn his energies toward you, or involve him in playing with something else and so leave the other to get on. All easier said than done but worth a try.

A number of parents experienced difficulty in playing with both twins together. A father had this to say:

> "When you're playing with them, you find you can't do it with the two of them at once. There's no way. I haven't really consciously followed it through but I'm sure that what happens is that one of them probably, whether consciously or not, deliberately creates a distraction and will actually destroy the activity. It's usually Rosie, I think. She realizes that he is the one who's really getting into it. We've got this toy with a screwdriver and nuts and bolts, and it's just impossible to actually share that activity with both of them. You either do it with one of them or you do it all and let them play with the result, which is very frustrating."

Bonuses

Several parents found, as they had so often been promised, that their twins were indeed very good company for each other. Those that got on well together engaged in long periods of cooperative and imaginative play.

Some parents found that they joined their twins in play more readily than they did with a singleton:

> "Somehow there being two of them seems to make it worthwhile to join them on the floor and join in with whatever they're doing, or to mix paints for both of them to use."

> "Tina [singleton] tends to join me in my activities. With Barry and Alexander I used to join them—and really enjoy it. I remember once being a passenger in a bus with two very attentive conductors to care for me."

Ownership

When it comes to ownership or sharing toys, parents may find themselves behaving quite differently from the way they originally intended. Many, at the outset, felt that toys should not be duplicated but very few in fact stuck to this in the face of pressure from their twins or triplets:

> "Graham is a very good socialist. He said this is wonderful. Now we've got three children all starting off together so everything is going to be communal, everything must be shared, toys, clothing, everything will be common property. By about eighteen months, really, everything in the house had an owner, though they did play with each other's things. It was very innate, the feeling of property."

> "We originally thought they would benefit by a greater variety of toys but in reality they get more pleasure from having the same things."

During the second year, individual possessions begin to be important to children as part of their newfound individuality. "Mine" is one of the earliest words. Twins will often use "our" before "my." Being aware of their own possessions may well be a vital step toward the process of each twin developing his or her own identity. We feel that twins should be allowed to possess in the way that is most comfortable for them. It may well be that knowing his twin has an identical object makes the child's ownership more secure, as there will not be any expectations from him to share it at an age when he is not mature enough to do so.

The need to have the same toys at an early stage usually gives way to individual preferences once the children are more sure of themselves and are able to choose without reference to their twin.

Apart from anything else, there is the more practical consideration of what you can tolerate. If different little cars are going to be the cause of endless misery and squabbling, is it worth it? A sign scratched underneath or different colors will provide quick and easy identification if necessary. This is more for the parents' benefit. The twins will usually know whose is whose.

The general pattern, then, in the families we saw was for certain items, usually important large toys, whether they were doll carriages or doll beds, tricycles or large trucks, to be duplicated. We do feel that each child should have one of each, the same or similar, of any large toy that is used for long periods of play. To expect small children to wait patiently to put a doll in the one and only bed or to ride the one and only vehicle with pedals is asking too much of them, and will make life unnecessarily difficult for yourself.

With smaller toys families varied from having all to none duplicated, with most coming somewhere in between, the extent of the duplication usually being dictated by the twins' behavior. A few mothers did point out that duplication does not necessarily avoid friction. If children need to use possessions to provoke, they will find a way of doing so. However, for most, some duplicating did make life easier.

Even if your twins do choose to duplicate, there will still be situations where they have to take turns. One mother found a simple solution that worked very well with her twins:

> "They did find sharing difficult, particularly using my kitchen tools for dough play. Instead of getting on, they'd squabble interminably over who was to have this and that. My trying to sort it out only made matters worse as each would feel I was favoring the other. Then one day I had a brainstorm. I tried the kitchen timer. It worked like a dream. They seemed to see it as an impartial referee. The moment the ping went, they would hand over the prized tool and then help me reset the timer for their turn."

If you have fond hopes that learning to share will be easier for twins, be prepared to have them dashed. Being able to share valued possessions depends on a child's confidence in himself as a person and on his confidence in his right of control over what is his. Having a sibling of the same age around all the time will mean a twin's possessions are constantly under threat. It may, therefore, take him longer to gain the self-assurance that makes sharing possible. Some twins may feel more at ease sharing with visiting children. On the other hand, twins who are close enough to cope fairly easily with sharing and joint ownership may jointly experience difficulties in extending this sharing to others.

Fighting

No parents felt that they had completely solved the problem of dealing with fights. Some conflict is inevitable, but there are tactics that may help to reduce some of the tension.

Preventive measures
Sometimes fighting may be the result of the twins or triplets spending too much time together:

> "We always fought. It carried on in lessons. In class we'd be pinching each other's legs and scratching, and it would get more and more out of control."

Twins who fight when they sit together at school or at home can be separated, and this in itself may be enough to reduce the level of tension. Providing their own room for each of a five-year-old pair transformed their relationship: "They've been different children. I don't know why we didn't do it before." If this is not possible, then ensuring that they can each have a corner of the kitchen or living room that is theirs may help. Or perhaps their bedroom can be formally divided. As they get older, if you do not do it they probably will: "We had an imaginary line down the middle of the room and each got furious if the other crossed it." Time apart from each other can also help to improve difficult relationships even in quite young twins: "We are all—myself and the children—so much better tempered after one of them has been out to a friend's house."

If the squabbles are about possessions and taking turns where turn-taking is inevitable, then you may be able to introduce some acceptable rules. Duplication of important possessions may also help if you have been expecting too much of their ability to share.

Fighting may be a way of seeking attention. A mother who is too busy or too tired to give attention to her well-behaved twins has to take notice when they are screaming and fighting.

Providing them with interesting activities and joining them in play is an antidote to this kind of fighting. Do you have the energy to do this some of the time? If not, perhaps you need to have more time for yourself (see pages 206–209.)

Biting was mentioned by several mothers as a particular problem with small twins, especially around the age of two. Occasionally separating them by putting one or both in high chairs or on stools on the opposite sides of a table with an interesting activity will give you a period of respite from constant surveillance. If they are willing to use pacifiers, you may be able to divert some of the chewing in that direction—or try giving each his own rubber bone from a pet shop! No parent, alas, had a magic remedy for putting a stop to biting. It is a very trying stage, but they do grow out of it in the end.

Calling a halt
Once a squabble is under way parents have to decide whether or not to intervene. Most children under two can be fairly easily distracted and many parents found that offering an exciting activity or just a quiet time looking at a book could defuse the situation. Several mothers kept bubble mixture handy, as watching and trying to catch bubbles never failed to restore peace when things got out of hand. A change of scene, such as a walk around the block or, in bad weather, going to a different room will often bring an end to the current bout of squabbling. A mother of triplets made a point of taking hers off to the park on difficult afternoons. She found she needed to be very firm about getting them there—"No matter if I take one of them shouting, screaming and yelling all the way, I take them"—but it paid in the end. One mother recommended "being funny"—a bit of clowning can turn the snarls into laughs and break the tension.

Some mothers dealt with fighting by getting their twins to turn their aggression toward them:

> "I join them on the floor and soon the fighting turns into rough-and-tumble play with me. It doesn't make them upset and they are not then doing anybody any harm. I feel physical contact acts as a control for them. Somebody else is with them and is patently stronger than they are and in control."

"Rather than try and sort things out, I sometimes just remove what they are squabbling over and walk away knowing full well they'll both turn their anger on me, and they do. They go for me, and then they soon forget their quarrel with each other and the incident is forgotten."

Apportioning blame may be neither easy nor appropriate.

"I used to try to get to the bottom of things but it usually led to more ill feeling—'He started it,' 'She kicked me.' In the end they both got angry with me as well as with each other. So I just separate them and try not to make any kind of judgment unless one is obviously in the wrong."

Letting them fight it out
As the twins got older, distraction was not so easy and parents were more inclined to leave the children to sort their quarrel out for themselves, but they knew when it was time to intervene:

"If only one is crying they are all right, if both cry there's a problem."

"Whether I interfere or not depends on the tone of the cry . . . if they obviously aren't going to resolve the problem, I separate them until they cool down."

Parents of triplets and more seemed to survive by becoming as impervious as they could to fighting beginning at an early stage. A mother of triplets had a break from them every afternoon when she left them in their room regardless of the squeals and yells that emerged. A mother of small quads usually left her lot to sort it out for themselves, too:

"There's no way I can settle all of them and if you sit down and try to placate one, the others all just cling around and they all end up pushing and trying to get more and more attention and it just makes it worse. . . . I suppose it just hardens you really, having four. It doesn't upset me at all when I know it's only temper and they're fighting."

Enough is enough
While most parents accepted that a certain amount of fighting

is to be expected, for some it reached a level of frequency and intensity that began to make life intolerable:

> "When they [triplets], were five they were driving me demented, quarreling all the time. I really felt I couldn't cope and said, 'We've got to go to family therapy and get all this sorted out.' Graham said, 'Nonsense,' and he went storming off to them and said the fighting had to stop—next time there was a fight he would deal with it his way. Within a week everything was fine. We were a happy family again."

If the children know that excessive fighting will always be firmly dealt with, it will help them contain the situation. Fighting, like anything else, can become a habit.

Presents and parties

Whether you give your twins like or unlike presents will depend on you and their current attitude toward duplication. For some twins, identical presents are a letdown:

> "I never really enjoyed Christmas. We always got the same things. I'd sit and watch my sister opening a present, and all the excitement was gone."

After about the age of three or four they will enjoy being involved in the choice, and having a certain amount of say may well prove to be an impetus toward choosing differently if they have hitherto insisted on having the same thing.

When they each choose, the value is irrelevant—that is as long as it is within your limits! It is usually not until they are about five that children begin to understand what things cost. Janet told of a trip to a local toy shop to choose a gift for each of her boys, then aged three:

> "Nick got this big crane lorry and James chose a little van that he wanted. The price difference was enormous, and I somehow felt guilty about it and stupidly suggested he get something else as well. They were both rather confused and no wonder. Each had chosen the one thing he really wanted and was satisfied with that and here I was suggesting that one of them get something else."

Twins often feel very strongly about having to share presents or cards:

> "I do remember I used to resent presents if we had to share them. I remember one ghastly Christmas when we were about six or seven. My father had got this present for us, and he obviously thought it was the most wonderful thing in the world. We opened it. It was a white football. You've never seen two such fed-up little kids in your life. We had to share it. It wasn't mine. It wasn't his. It was between us."

You may want to treat the twins to something you might otherwise not be able to afford by giving it to them jointly. This is fine until they reach the stage of being aware of and enjoying their own possessions and presents. Even then, they may be happy to have a joint present if they each have a small personal gift as well. In one family where the parents wanted to give each of the twins something special that was also expensive, they arranged for the parents to buy one and the grandparents the other.

Where it is possible, let friends and family know how you and the twins feel about individual presents—and about birthday cards. Cards addressed to "the twins" ought to be outlawed.

If you have the energy and inclination to give your twins a party apiece they will no doubt enjoy having a double celebration, though a three- or four-year-old twin may find it an unbearable strain to stand back while the other opens his or her presents! The general tendency seems to be that twins share a birthday party in the early years. Once they are established at school and have their own friends, they may prefer to separate their birthday celebrations by choosing their own treat or party.

For a small child, the high point of a birthday is having "Happy Birthday" sung and blowing out candles. All attention is focused on him- or herself. It is a magic moment—not one to be shared.

Playgroup or nursery school offers a golden opportunity for each to be a very special person in his or her own right if they take their cake or sweets in on different days.

Visiting

"When we visited, it was so difficult to keep an eye on them all [triplets]. They would systematically go to work to destroy a room and it was difficult to stop them from making headway."

"It's like an invasion when you arrive with twins. It's a take-over bid. They take over. And so we tend not to go and see people. It's very unrelaxed."

"When you've got four young children, you know who your friends are."

Taking two or three or four young explorers visiting seemed to be a universal problem. The difficulties, unfortunately, often limited the amount of visiting families felt capable of undertaking. The children usually had a whale of a time. The parents did not, and staggered home vowing never to visit anyone ever again.

But parents need to keep up with friends. And a mother needs other adult company during the day. And the children need to get to know children other than their brothers and sisters, and adults other than their parents. How can this happen without parents getting totally exhausted every time?

When visiting as a family, warn friends of your twins' demands in advance. Ask to be in a room where precious objects are well out of reach and you will be off to a good start. If you know them well you can try asking outright if they will take charge for half an hour or so while you are there to give you a break from constantly keeping an eye on them. Many adults are diffident about watching other people's children when their parents are there. They may be delighted to take up the challenge when you put it to them. Failing that, parents can take turns at being in charge so that each can have a brief respite from that role.

Rather than rush home when things start getting out of hand, suggest a walk or a stair-climbing practice organized by dads or give each of them a piece of Scotch tape to shake off their fingers or . . . It is difficult. When the children are at their worst, parents may need to remind each other that they can at least see their own friends in the evening when the marauders are out of the way.

Friends

In the early years twins tend to meet other children of their own age less frequently than singletons do. The mother is under pressure; and they have each other, so the need appears to be less. "Mine were more isolated because there were two. They had each other for company."

When twins play well together it is tempting to let them continue and not go to the trouble of exposing them to the pressures, and pleasures, of making relationships with other children of the same age. But meeting other children helps them learn to cope with unfamiliar, and sometimes difficult, social situations. If they have had little contact with other small children before joining a group at a day-care center, playgroup or nursery school, they may be totally bewildered by the cut-and-thrust behavior of their peers. They will turn to their twin for comfort and support—a tremendous advantage for them as long as they do not continue to rely too heavily on this support for every new social situation they meet. This can set a pattern that may continue into adolescence and beyond. Mariam told us of her experience when she and her fraternal sister, Leilah, first came to London as students. They shared an apartment for five years:

> "It made us isolated because we had each other and it meant that we didn't have to make any kind of attempt to make any contact with people in London. I'm sure that had a very detrimental effect on the way we studied, the way we made friends, what we decided to do, for me anyway. Leilah was studying medicine, but I was studying the arts. I was unsure of what I wanted to do and I think that if I'd been on my own I might have tried out more interesting things. I would have been stimulated by other people much more instead of cutting myself off."

Difficulties

Mothers of twins are usually only too aware that it is important for the children to have contact with other children, but the obstacles are very real and occur frequently enough to discourage bothering to do anything about it.

Anne's identical boys reacted very strongly to other children visiting. They regarded it as an invasion of their territory and reacted accordingly, attacking and driving the visiting child away:

> "On the rare occasions when another child of the same age did come, I used to have to put her in a high chair so they couldn't reach her—pinching, bullying, hitting, pushing—a pincer movement. I remember watching them. There was this little girl and they scissored her. She was terrified, and with good reason. I just didn't have other children in the house because there was no attempt made to play at all. It was just a matter of establishing power and evicting the stranger."

Helen's triplets who met very few peers in the early years, tended to treat a visiting child as a baby, as an object. Hardly surprisingly, the child's response was to sit silently and not want to visit again. Until they went to school the triplets' friends were limited to one or two "strong-stomached kids," the youngest of large families.

An adult triplet recalled the difficulties of establishing friendships when he was a child:

> "From our point of view it was difficult because the chances were that all three of us were being introduced to an individual at the same time. Therefore if attention or affection was being sought, it might well be two- or threefold. For the individual who had just met us, the reaction to being confronted with three children all at once was one of surprise. They themselves didn't know how to react and therefore any affections or communications were guarded and limited."

Even twins who enjoyed the company of other children sometimes proved to overwhelm not only the children but the children's mothers. Clare felt other mothers regarded her boys "with some trepidation." Sheila was fully aware that her three boys had less contact than she felt they should have: "I'd have loved to have known another mother of twins who would have been quite happy to have me and them." Diana would leave two or three quads at home with a baby-sitter while she took the other one or two and her older singleton to visit friends.

Solutions?

In putting forward a few suggestions for coping with launching your young twins into society, we are well aware that they may not work. A pair of determined toddlers with a deep understanding between them is a powerful force indeed. If you get nowhere with your efforts, leave it and try again a month or two later. It may seem an eternity, but in the end they will mature.

First, the powerful unit. Twins intent on molesting visitors in order to protect their territory may be less aggressive if they make their early social contacts on neutral ground away from home. The same strategy is worth a try for those whose joint exuberance overwhelms outsiders. Suggestions:

• Meet friends and their children in a park or playground before letting them loose on the fearful duo in your home.

• In bad weather take them to a playgroup, or some other meeting place. Better still, take them to your local Mothers of Twins Club. If there is none in your area, think about starting one.

• Try to get them into a playgroup early—visiting even only one day a week will help them adjust to other children.

In cases where the "territory" that is being defended is the twins' close relationship, the obvious way of giving them the opportunity to make real contact with other children is to separate them. Having a child in to play with one of your twins while the other goes out with a parent or to see another friend takes some negotiating and organizing, but it is well worth the effort.

Making their own friends

Having their own friends helps twins to express their individuality. All of the adult twins we interviewed valued their friendships as part of their existence apart from their twin, or triplets.

When there is an opportunity for one twin to go off on an outing, or out to play on his or her own, without the other, take advantage of it. This will give them the opportunity to establish their own friendships. It will also help them to realize that they can both function without backup from each other.

Christopher, one of Sheila's boys, was much more extroverted, sociable and popular than his twin, Michael. He was frequently invited out for tea and dinner, and Michael was not:

> "In fact, in the early days I think it was me that felt they ought to invite the two. Which was strange considering I've always treated them so separately, but I felt so sorry for Michael. I did sometimes ask people to invite Michael on his own. Otherwise, I make the point of always doing something special together when we get home, just the two of us. We make cakes or whatever he wants to do, and that time is his."

Sheila also talked with him to help him accept the disappointments and said he would make his own friends later. Having an older brother helped to make it easier, too. Sheila would point out that he had not been invited either. Once Michael was at school he began slowly but surely to make his own friends.

One or two in to play?
Some mothers found inviting only one child to play with both twins a burden as one of the trio often tended to get left out. Dawn reported one of her girls being distressed and not knowing how to cope when a single visitor attached herself to the other twin, leaving her on her own. One way of dealing with this is to take all three children out. Several parents found that inviting children in twos was the easiest way of having friends in. A father did complain that there were problems with the "home team" fighting the "away team," but on the whole this arrangement usually proved to be less stressful for all than just having one visitor.

Parents of warring twins often found that visiting children, whether single or in pairs, brought calm to the afternoon's play. Within-pair aggression did not necessarily turn toward outsiders. Nira's five-year-old boys fought each other but neither ever hit or bit another child. An adult male twin we spoke to said his identical twin was the only person he had ever fought with physically.

Imaginary friends

It is not uncommon for singletons in their early years to invent an imaginary friend to keep them company and to take the blame for all kinds of misdemeanors. Twins, it might be thought, have no need of an imaginary companion. In some families, however, one or both twins did have an imaginary friend.

One mother related how her deaf twin, Yuan, would have long conversations with, laugh, cry and smack an unseen person. Lin, his hearing twin, would occasionally behave in the same way, but, the mother felt, only in imitation.

Mark, one of an identical pair, had a very useful friend called Charlie who needed cookies as well as fulfilling other functions. Simon, his twin, accepted Mark's Charlie but never had his own imaginary friend.

James and Nick, fraternal twin brothers, shared their friend:

> "Oh yes, Ippoli was around on and off for quite a long time. He was about the only thing they shared amicably apart from their real friends. That's probably significant. I don't know which one invented him, but he was there all right. After he'd been around for a while he produced a friend or a cousin called Renault, who lived around the corner from Ippoli. Renault was never quite as important as Ippoli. He tended to belong to James, who's keen on cars."

Dressing and clothes

Most toddlers enjoy exerting their newfound independence in getting dressed. Either they want to do it themselves or they do not want to get changed at all. It is a difficult stage for any mother. Two going through it simultaneously can reduce you to a limp rag if you allow it to. Time is short enough as it is without having to spend an hour or more cajoling, coercing and chasing just to get them dressed. If you can occupy yourself with other things to take the heat out of the chase, you might be able to slip on a garment at a time as they pass by or play. It will still take time but will leave you feeling less frustrated.

Suggested tactics for riveting a toddler's attention long enough for you to do a speedy dressing job or diaper change include: an account of what has happened that day; naming colors on a string of beads; interesting pictures, photographs or postcards; nursery rhymes, or deliberately distorting a well-known nursery rhyme, e.g., "Georgie Porgie, yogurt and pie, kissed the boys and made them laugh."

As with singletons, twins should be given every opportunity to try dressing themselves when they begin to show an interest. Your patience "helping" two at this stage may be stretched to the limit, but it is worth persevering, as the sooner they can do it themselves the better for all concerned and most of all for you, the mother. When it comes to getting them undressed there is a bonus in that twins can help each other pull things off long before they can do it for themselves.

Most toddlers are less bothered about having their own clothes than are older children. Among the twins we saw, there was a tendency for earlier sharing to give way to individual ownership at around two or three years of age. Even then, however, either because it was convenient or because the twins did not mind, things like socks, tights, T-shirts and pants were still shared. We found only one set of twins who still shared clothes up to the age of four or five. But in this family individual ownership of both toys and clothes was discouraged when they were younger, and the pattern continued. A mother of identical girls, who had been dressed alike throughout, said they knew all their own clothes even though only coats and hats had names on. She could not distinguish them and had no idea how her twins did, but it was obviously important to them. All in all, apart from an occasional tiff over a particular garment, ownership of clothes seems to be a relatively trouble-free area.

New clothes and shoes were much more likely to cause problems. It seems you either steer completely clear of trouble by buying double every time (a potentially expensive approach) or you resist. One mother, whose twins minded, made a point of getting the other a small item such as a pair of socks at the same time. If you are likely to have scenes in shops and feel you might succumb under the pressure, it may be better not to take the twins if at all possible, and in the case of shoes, you may be able to arrange to go with only the one who needs to be fitted.

Avoid any shoes with complicated or fiddly fastenings. A mother who found herself dealing with eight buckles every time the shoes had to come on and off swore she would never make the mistake again!

Sleep

Many toddlers go through a stage when they are unhappy about going to bed, most commonly around the age of two. Their very desire for independence some of the time makes them reluctant to be separated from their mother at other times, especially at bedtime. Twins and more are no different from singletons in this respect. The problem for their parents is in dealing with one or two reluctant sleepers who may want individual attention or who may reinforce each other's anxieties.

Though several parents encountered some kind of problem at this stage, a good number experienced very few bedtime difficulties at all. One or two suggested that having multiples had contributed to their insisting on good sleep patterns being established and maintained. The importance of having their own time meant they dealt firmly with any attempt to invade their evenings: "The days are theirs. The evenings are ours," "After a day with those two I need some space to myself. Evenings are definitely grown-up times."

Daytime naps
Before the end of their second year, a number of twins had developed different needs for sleep. Some mothers saw this as a reason for separating them; others felt that both had to compromise in order to have any kind of predictable routine and left them together for naps, allowing the one who slept least to wake the other at the end of a nap. A considerable number of mothers prolonged the daytime nap "just to give me a breather," as one put it. "Pacifiers were a great boon in getting

them to drop off when they could probably have managed without a nap—though I couldn't," said another.

Bedtime and waking at night

Whether twins disturbed each other at night was hard to establish. One mother who had her boys in separate but adjoining rooms until they were three years old felt that it had made bedtimes and any night disturbances much easier to handle:

> "Before he was two, Robin used to wake and cry at night quite often. Sometimes by the time I arrived to deal with him, I could hear Tom in the next room talking and moving in his crib—I'm sure if he'd seen me with Robin he would have wanted attention too. . . . It was also much easier to deal with their different bedtime needs; Robin seemed to need his bottle longer than Tom did. I used to give it to him in his room after we'd said good night to Tom—again, I'm sure if Tom had seen it he would have wanted one too."

Other parents felt that their twins settled better through being together, or, if they did wake at night, their being together made little difference:

> "We had a dreadful time around age two. They both hated being put into their cribs at bedtime and screamed. We didn't deal with it very well; we were always deciding that we would be firm and try leaving them to yell it out and settle by themselves, but in the end one of us couldn't bear it and would go in and it would start all over again. Separating them didn't seem to make any difference. They made so much noise that they could hear each other anyhow. They also woke during the night. Then it was a bonus to have them together. We didn't want to start having them two at a time in our bed so we took turns going upstairs to sleep with them on a mattress on the floor with one snuggled up on either side. That way at least we all got some sleep. It all sorted itself out by the time they were two and a half. We let them have beds of their own and just sat with them till they went to sleep."

Seeking help

Most sleeping difficulties resolved themselves during the third year. Dealing with two or more toddlers through a difficult stage is very trying but not impossible. It is very different, however, dealing with babies who never begin to sleep through the night and continue the pattern into toddler years. Where this happens, parents may need to seek help.

A number of parents had asked their doctor for a mild sedative at some stage for one of the babies, often when they were teething. Most were reluctant to use them for long, but many found them helpful when used over a few nights to restore a child's regular sleep pattern.

Very occasionally a doctor will prescribe a stronger sedative. Veronica, whose little girls had always been restless and miserable (her experience is described on pages 102–103 in the section on "Crying"), began to see a doctor fairly early:

> "One day I carried both of them screaming to my doctor, who just said, 'There's nothing wrong with them—they're just two demanding babies.' He said, 'I can't give them anything.' I said, 'Well, then, for Christ's sake give me something because I'm going mad.' But he didn't give me anything and he didn't suggest anything else either."

Eventually, when the twins were two, Veronica and her husband moved in order to be nearer her mother. Only then did she see a doctor who understood the extent of her difficulties:

> "He was super. He said, 'You just can't go on like this. I don't know how you've managed for two years. You need sleep.' He said, 'We don't like giving sedatives but in a case like this, when they're very high-strung, very demanding babies, they need something—as long as we don't overdo the dose and you do try to get them off it.' One needed a little more sedative than the other. The doctor used to have us back about once a month to check on the amount I was giving them."

Within six months they were off the sedatives and sleeping through the night, and Veronica at last had the energy to enjoy her twins.

We came across only one other instance where waking at night was a serious long-term problem. Sandra's little girls slept reasonably for the first three months, but after that her difficulties began:

"I was lucky and had a lot of help with the babies—maybe that was what started it, there was always someone there to attend to them whenever they whimpered. By fourteen months it was terrible. They each had to be nursed off to sleep and then put in the crib. After an hour or so, one or the other would be up beginning a game of musical beds that went on all night. My mother or aunt or me would always be up with one of them. Each would be awake for an hour or so before dropping off again. If I was lucky, I slept in the same bed as my husband once a week. It came close to finishing our marriage."

Sandra's doctor sent her with the little girls to a sleep clinic at a children's hospital:

"The doctor there was marvelous. They did endless tests to see if the girls were all right, checked to see if they had problems with nightmares—I kept charts of their waking patterns and what we did when they woke. Eventually he said to me, 'I don't think there's anything wrong—you have two bright little girls who have got you running around entertaining them all night.' He was prepared to come and spend a night with us to observe them, but asked us first to try for five days leaving them when they cried. He said, 'They are old enough to understand what bedtime is. When they cry, go in to show them you haven't abandoned them, and then pop in every fifteen minutes while they cry, but don't pick them up.' Other people had suggested that to me but I couldn't have done it if this doctor hadn't asked me. He had been so helpful that I had to try it. So we did it for five nights. The first two nights were dreadful. I felt heartbroken, listening to them cry. They went on for an hour and a half with us just looking in now and then. On the third day it was one hour, the next half an hour and on the fifth night just a protesting 'Mom.' And they've slept at night ever since."

Worn down by fatigue it is easy to come to see a difficult situation as the norm and feel that you simply have to tolerate it, as both Sandra and Veronica did for a long time. Very few parents function well without adequate sleep (though their children may!), so help with serious sleep problems can dramatically change your relationship with your toddlers and the whole family.

Using a potty

Doing a double load of diapers may seem a time-consuming chore you are more than anxious to get rid of at the earliest possible moment. If you use disposables, the cost of a double supply can lead to hope for early toilet training. This feeling is very understandable, but beware of letting it push you into pressuring the twins before they are ready. Unless they have reached the point where they are ready, willing and able to cooperate, you will only find yourself spending much more time and energy over encouraging them to use the potty correctly than you would carrying on with the diapers. Lorraine, who started when her identical girls were about one year old, reported that at about 18 months one would be "clean" a few days and then as the other was getting clean the first would revert. This went on till they were coming up to age three:

> "I got Linda clean and I couldn't get Danielle clean at all. And Linda did it for me in an afternoon. She got her sister clean. She said to me, 'I'll do it, Mom' and she did. She took her by the hand to the potty, got her to sit down a few times, told her off and so on. Ever since then, they've never had any accidents."

Toilet training is one of the areas where parents are all too ready to be tempted into measuring their child's development against others'. There is nothing to be gained by comparing your twins' progress with that of singletons you know, or even for that matter with other twins if you happen to know any.

As a general rule, children begin to use a potty or toilet reasonably well somewhere between their second and third birthday. A few of them, mainly girls, twin or singleton, accomplish this a little earlier and a number, mainly boys, a little later. It may be reassuring for you to know that the twins we saw fell comfortably into the pattern broadly outlined above. This, of course, applies to the daytime. Control at night usually comes later.

If it is important not to compare your twins with other children, it is even more important not to compare their progress with each other. Identical twins, with their presumably identi-

cal rate of physical maturation, are most likely to have inter-
twin comparisons made of them, if not by their parents, then
by others. Any child-care manual will point out that physical
maturity is not the only prerequisite for learning to use a potty
appropriately. The child must also be willing. A mother with
identical boys reported a difference of many months in her
twins being reasonably competent. She felt Richard's acquiring
control had been a discouragement for Nicholas, who had compared himself unfavorably and then chosen, consciously or unconsciously, to opt out.

A mother of fraternal boys found that the lack of success of
the slower of the pair rebounded on the one who was already
competent. She started introducing her boys to the potty simultaneously. Christopher took to it quite quickly. Michael was a
little slower and took three or four weeks longer, by which time
Christopher had deliberately begun to wet himself again. With
hindsight she felt it would have been wiser to have dealt with
them one at a time, particularly as Christopher seemed to be
the more capable.

That twins are aware of each other's performance is clear.
That they care from a young age is well illustrated by the following incident:

> "They were about twenty-two months old. We weren't trying
> to train them but their potty chairs were around and we had
> explained what they were for. It was all very casual. One day
> Tom by chance crapped in his potty chair and we let him
> know how pleased we were. A few minutes later Robin ap-
> peared holding his potty chair. We hadn't actually been
> aware of where he was while all this was going on with Tom.
> Anyway, in his potty chair were the most awful-looking
> greenish stools. For a moment I thought he must have some
> dreadful disease. When we looked more closely it turned out
> to be plasticine. He had quietly gone off, rolled a few pieces,
> brought it back and placed it next to Tom's."

It is only natural for parents to show pleasure and encourage
a child when he does what is expected of him. But if one twin is
ahead in this sensitive area of development, it is very important
to play down expressions of pleasure, particularly when the
other twin is within earshot, even if he does appear to be totally

unconcerned. Occasionally, learning to use a potty may take only a day or so. More often it can take a few weeks or even months for a child to be reliable. Each time the achieving child is praised the other may take it as a reproach that may in turn create unnecessary tension and set him back considerably. We are not saying it is unwise to express any pleasure, but rather that it should be low-key, and once they know what is expected there is no need for any more than a quiet comment, much as you would when they wash their own hands or brush their own hair.

Awareness of each other's progress can be counterproductive for twins. Several mothers, on the other hand, found it very helpful. One twin's success provided positive encouragement for the other. For Jean, it was "the easiest thing in the world" to get her girls to use their potties, much easier than it had been with her older boy. Potties had been around because of him, and Jean had explained to the twins what they were for. She reports that when she decided to try in earnest they each learned in a day. On the first day Sharon started using her potty properly and went on doing so throughout the day with her mother expressing pleasure at her success. All the while Sarah was watching and the next day she did the same. Jean went out and bought a dozen pairs of attractive colored pants and, apart from the occasional accident, there was no looking back. Jean felt that an important contributory factor to the ease with which this was accomplished was the visit of a very helpful aunt who dealt with other household matters, leaving Jean to concentrate on the twins.

Dry at night
Although Jean's twins were "dry" by day virtually simultaneously, there was a whole year's difference in their gaining control through the night. This is not particularly surprising as other factors come into play. It is perhaps more surprising that for most of the twins we saw there was not much more than a few months' difference in gaining bladder control through the night.

A mother of fraternal boys reported a difference of a year and a half. Alexander started waking with a dry diaper just before his third birthday while Barry was still frequently wetting his bed well into his fifth year. There were several fairly obvious reasons for this wide variation. Barry tended to drink more than Alexander. He slept much more deeply. Emotionally, too, Barry was the more volatile and liable to be easily upset. No fuss was made, and once he was dry at night he was just as reliable as his brother.

Among the twins we saw, where one twin had her diaper removed before the other because she was dry at night, the other usually objected to continuing to wear one. There are two options for parents when faced with this dilemma. Either you concede and prepare yourself for a change of sheets every morning for a few days or weeks if you are lucky, or many months if you are not. Or you resist gently, explaining how different people grow at different rates and that it won't be long before she, too, can put diapers aside. You may prefer to experiment with the first option for a short while, but keep it short if you have any intention of putting the child back into diapers again. If you feel that constant wet beds will get you down, do keep the one twin in diapers. A little tussle over getting the diapers on at this stage is preferable to a long period of tension later on.

Private or public?

There are some children who like to be private when using a toilet, particularly when defecating. Communal potty times are probably fairly stressful for these children. If one of your twins shows signs of wanting to be alone, you can try leaving a potty for him behind a sofa or chair so that he can disappear quietly to use it and still be in the same room as you and his twin. If he is already using a quiet corner fairly regularly, try leaving a potty for him there without making any comment. Keeping quiet for days, or even weeks, is very hard work, but it often does the trick.

If your twins like to do everything together, you may have an awkward time when they transfer from the potty to the adult toilet unless you have the unlikely fortune to have the two close to each other. We can only suggest that you keep a potty next to the toilet for such contingencies. If both of your twins are boys, they will be able to share, but steel yourself for cries of "He wet my hand/pullover/trousers/socks/shoes." A far more likely difficulty than the use of the lavatory, however, is flushing the toilet, a fascinating activity for any child around two years of age. Lucky is the mother of twins who does not experience screams, tears and tantrums over this.

Apart from flushing the toilet, showing your twins how to use the bathroom is unlikely to present any undue problems as long as you remain sensitive to their individual needs and remember that these may differ considerably. In general, then, until they show signs of being ready, don't try. If one twin responds, persevere with her with a minimum of fuss, and leave the other for the time being.

·7·

Twins and the Family

Parents and twins

On being parents of multiple toddlers

"It was like starting all over again, rearranging the house, readjusting to these lively individuals who were zooming off all over the place and interacting like crazy. And they seemed to demand so much more in the way of attention. I got quite dizzy with it all at times."

The real impact of adding two or three or four lively personalities to your family will make itself well and truly felt when your twins get themselves up and about around their first birthday. A first-time mother finds herself handling not the one close relationship she anticipated, but three, hers with each twin and that of the twins themselves. A mother of triplets finds herself dealing with six relationships. And so on as illustrated on page 199.

At around age one they begin to explore their environment—with a vengeance, or so it seems. Twins have a remarkable knack of wanting to explore in different directions. And so it should be—they are individuals eager to learn what they want, when they want, and how they want. Encouraging each to do this independently without coming to grief undoubtedly imposes a strain on the parents. There will be many more "nos," many more snap decisions to make, many more tears of frustration to deal with simply because each twin will not be able to enjoy as much freedom as a single toddler. The difficulties will sometimes mean a parent curtails or puts a stop to "exploratory" activities for the child's self-protection:

"When they were about a year old, I took them to the beach once or twice. They'd get out and one would toddle one way and one the other and I would spend all afternoon running, getting one, bringing him back, running and getting the other. It was so limiting that I just didn't do it anymore. Just things like that, rather simple things, just going out and sitting on a beach was impossible."

Then at around age two, the "terrible twos"—the phrase takes on a new meaning with twins—each will be testing separateness from you, and probably from each other as well. At the same time each will be feeling very vulnerable about this newfound separateness and may come running back to your lap for security and comfort, wanting it for himself or herself alone. Earlier it was often possible to bypass potential trouble by distracting them. Now they resist any such attempt. It is tantrum time. It is clawing and biting time. It is passionate-struggles-over-possessions time. It is clinging-to-mom time. It is needing a lot of attention, patience and love time.

The ease with which parents navigate the potentially stormy seas of the toddler years will depend to a large extent on the personalities of their twins. Like any other children, some are easygoing, some anxious, most are a mixture. Dealing with the demands of two small people who are beginning to move toward a new independence, to explore the world and impose their separate wills upon it, is bound to be exhausting at times and lead to what has been described as "parental task overload." If the twins are basically equable and get on well together, then the task will at least seem possible; if they are constantly fighting each other, then the task may become a burden that seems intolerable at times:

"There were certainly some dreadful times but also many good ones. We were lucky, I suppose, that they got on well. . . . They were often enchanting, all sunshine and smiles. At last I felt I was reaping the benefit of having two. They would play together often for an hour at a time on their tricycles in the sandpit or mostly pushing their strollers around. I would rig up some kind of house for them and they would disappear under the blanket or whatever and be busy arranging dolls, teacups and saucepans, muttering away to themselves."

"When they were two, the fighting was awful. There were times when we couldn't be out of the room for even a minute before one would be at the other, hitting, biting or scratching. The bruises on their backs were worthy of the front page of the *News of the World*. It was a tremendous strain and still is. It's improved with time, but you never know when there's going to be a vicious outburst and that tension is always around."

The rewards

Having preschool twins is very hard work. But it has its rewards, too. Toddlers are delightful and often quaint and funny when they come in pairs. Parents found a deep pleasure in just watching their twins.

Simon:

"They looked so attractive with their little round limbs . . . still cuddly but also becoming very lithe and coordinated. They were like two little monkeys chattering away as they climbed and explored together."

Anne:

"Watching their relationship has given me quite a lot of joy. They are very, very close. And they do have a very nice relationship. It's very caring given that they fight . . . and all the rest. Just watching them interact, the sensitivity to each other is very nice to see, and sometimes they're just like two little old men. They sit there and gossip, and that's nice."

Clare:

"They both had a thing about spare wheels. It seemed as if they felt a wheel not attached to a car had lost its mom. We once saw one propped against a wall. One of them said, 'Dear, dear' and pointed it out. It was somehow very funny to see these two little things seriously tut-tutting and expressing their dismay to each other in their stroller."

Many parents found the way their twins developed to be a constant source of interest, learning and fascination.

Annie:

"When I saw how upset some mothers get when their little darling is hit on the head the first time or when he goes around bashing everyone in sight, I realized it was quite an advantage to have twins. The basher and the bashed were both mine, so there was no embarrassment. . . . We learned one hell of a lot about aggression and about the victim role."

Kate:

"That's very exciting to me, to find very extensive characters developing without really much to do with me, as if they're there already really. . . . I think we were very much more aware because there were two."

Philip:

"It's changed a lot of my ideas about the conflict between genetics and environment. They've been so different from such an early age, whereas if you'd only had one you'd feel a lot more was actually your influence and the effect of the environment around them, but because they develop so separately, so differently, I'm having to change my thinking considerably."

It is a pity to become so preoccupied with the pressures that the pleasures get forgotten. But the pressures are very real. Awareness of the stresses and pitfalls inherent in caring for more than one willful, demanding, loving small child will, we hope, enable parents to deal with difficulties as they arise.

Too little time and attention
The area mothers tended to feel worst about was not being able to give their twins or triplets the time and attention they'd have liked or that the children demanded:

"There is this sense of letting the children down."

"I constantly feel I can't give enough time and attention. I'm aware of the things I did with Philip, and I'm just not doing them with the twins."

"When they [triplets] were tiny babies it was OK because they used to just sit on my knee. When they're older they want to fight for attention. There's such a strong motivation for them. They all want my attention in terms of listening, looking, touching, being with them exclusively. I find that really hard to do."

A recent study in Canada by Hugh Lytton of the University of Calgary looked at the interaction between parents and small children (boys aged 25 to 35 months). In the sample there were 46 sets of twins (19 identical and 29 fraternal) and 44 singletons, all of whom had a sibling. The families were observed in their homes over a period of time. Not surprisingly, Lytton found the experience of twins in their families was very *different*. "In terms of the immediate harsh reality, it simply doubles the demands on mother's and father's time, effort and patience." We would say that, depending on the quality of the twins' relationship, the demands may be more than doubled.

If the stress of twins is considerable for two-parent families, it may be even more so for a single parent, who will at times feel the need of another supportive adult. But a family with three relationships is less complex. A single mother alone with her twins may well find them a good deal easier to handle than a mother whose attention is divided between husband and children. Lytton found that some of the twin children of single parents received more attention and spoke more competently than twins in two-parent families. He concluded that "some mothers compensate quite effectively for the absence of a father even under the extra stress twins impose."

Lytton's survey explores both the feelings of affection expressed between children and their parents and also the way they respond (or don't!) to parental requests.

Expressing affection
A mother's responsiveness and sensitivity to her child helps him to build a secure relationship with her. From this secure base he is able to be more confident in his explorations of his surroundings and his relationships with other people, and so move toward separating himself from his mother. Lytton found that twin mothers "cannot afford to show the same appropriate sensitivity to their children's demands that singleton mothers show."

A twin, he observed, is more likely to be ignored more often by his mother or to receive a negative response, e.g., an outright "no" or told not to be a nuisance. This in turn is likely to make him more demanding of her affection and attention to reassure himself:

"They had me around seeing to them virtually all the time. But that still wasn't enough for Barry. . . . He found being a twin very difficult. He's a very physically affectionate child and wanted lots from me. I gave him as much as I could, and it still wasn't enough. He became very clingy and temperamental. From the outset Alexander seemed to cope better with being a twin. He was more self-contained. He seemed to need less. He seemed to be equally affectionate with both David and me."

Father's role

Lytton noticed that a significantly larger proportion of twin children than singletons had a close relationship with their father, turning to him, he suggests, to compensate for reduced attention from their mother. (It is likely, too, that fathers are reaping the rewards of their deeper involvement with their children when they were babies.)

The mother of Alexander and Barry talked of her concern that:

"Alexander might become David's child while Barry became mine. I remember feeling quite anxious about needing to keep in touch with him as well as with Barry. David and I talked about it and we worked out a plan that David would make a point of being with Barry and doing things with him like singing with him and reading to him. And it worked."

Sarah, whose twins were undiagnosed, found it very difficult to come to terms with having two babies at once. She was very aware of wanting to give them individual attention. From an early stage, she felt that she identified with the baby who seemed most like her toddler. She finds the other little girl, Emma, slower and more predictable: "I get impatient with her." However, Sarah's husband James feels more of a bond with Emma: "She's very stubborn, which I admire because the rest of the family lacks this quality." Sarah and James do not see Emma's role in the family as a "problem," they simply recognize the situation and do not feel that they can change it.

In families with older siblings there were several instances where the father related to and did things with the older sibling while the mother dealt with the twins:

"Joe felt very isolated from me and turned to Dave to get his needs met. Dave has become almost mother and father for Joe, and I am to some extent the twins' province. Joe has a much more tactile relationship with Dave. He's quite demonstrative with Dave and apt to be quite babyish with him, but there's very little of that with me."

Do I love them both?

By the second year most mothers have adjusted to the fact that they will at times feel more for one twin than for the other. Prolonged periods of difficult behavior by one twin can again raise serious doubts about whether a mother is capable of loving them both. Is Esau's behavior awful because I favor Jacob? Or do I feel more for Jacob and sometimes even hate Esau because his behavior gets me down so much? Some twins do polarize their behavior over a long period. Then suddenly the "goody" reaches a new stage and becomes a "baddy." It is highly likely the former "baddy" will calm down and be the "goody" for a while. And you can take a breath of relief and know your relationship with him can be positive and warm.

The more children there are, the more difficult it may become to show them affection.

A mother of triplets found she was sometimes overwhelmed by their emotional demands:

"I got to the stage where I found myself so surrounded by children that I found it hard to get into that thing of being very affectionate with them, to cuddle them as much as they probably wanted and needed to be cuddled. There were so many of them that it seemed like a hopeless task. I found it hard to shut off from the practical task of looking after them, which had become such a massive thing. There seemed to be little space left for emotional caring. It demanded a lot of effort."

A mother of quads found that she felt estranged from one of them in the second year:

"It was hard. It would have been easier for me at the time to reject him completely, but I knew that if I did I'd be in for dreadful problems later. I couldn't bear the thought of any of them growing up saying they didn't get on well with their mother. That made me come to my senses. I decided I would do everything for him, and I got over it in a few weeks."

What's to be done?

How can parents handle the harsh and sometimes painful realities of not being able to meet their young children's demands to the extent they would like?

• Try as far as possible to respond to their individual demands. If one needs more affectionate attention than the other(s) over a period of time or throughout the early years, then give it, so long as you do not neglect the other(s).

Some children, particularly among larger multiples, may fall into a pattern of not seeking attention because the others are doing it more effectively. Sue and Graham dealt with this by taking their undemanding triplet away on vacation with them, leaving the other two with a grandparent.

Children may sometimes ask for attention in indirect ways:

"Lawrence was pretty demanding from the start in a very straightforward way. Sophie was more placid, so she tended to get less attention. Then, when she was about two, she went through this awful phase of attacking the babies and smaller children of visiting friends. She was quite vicious sometimes. I realized that it was a demand for her share of attention, but it was quite hard to give it in a loving way when she was being so horrid."

• Make opportunities for being with each child on her own so you can give her exclusive attention. It is not just the amount of time that a parent spends with a child but a willingness to be close and tune in to the child, even if it is for a shorter period, that fosters her attachment.

Many of our parents had evolved specific policies so that each could have individual time with each twin; e.g., one parent and twin going off to a grandparent or an outing or shopping while the others stayed at home. Or one twin or two triplets attending playgroup while the mother had just one at home. One mother took advantage of a prolonged visit from her mother to take each of her year-old twins out on his own for the day, leaving the other in his grandmother's care.

Parents reaped the rewards as well as their children. "It's lovely having just one," "It's so peaceful being with one, so relaxing. I love my children individually, not so much as twins," "It's fantastic. They often blossom when they're on their own," "They're so different apart."

• Let your children find compensation in their own way if they need to, perhaps by forming a "special" relationship with another adult, older sibling or even their own pet.

Wendy valued enormously the interest a pair of her elderly aunts took in her twins. They were able to give Jason and Kevin the undivided attention and interest that she felt she did not have time for. Hazel felt it was very important for her girls each to have her own godparents and she fostered special links with them. When a godfather died, his 18-year-old son took on the special role. Helen and Stephen had several friends with no children of their own whom they encouraged to "borrow a child." The adult friend would take one of the triplets out on his own for a picnic or other treat.

• A research finding quoted by Lytton may give encouragement to parents who are anxious that their twins are not receiving enough attention in the early years. "What matters for healthy psychological development is not so much parents' actual early affection but whether a child perceives himself to be valued at any particular time in his life. The special climate that envelops the child is important. A caring climate does matter; caring includes being sensitive to the child's own nature."

Value each child for herself and it will be that much easier for her to tolerate having a constant competitor for her parents' love and affection.

• Do not be too disappointed if one or both do not quite match up to your friends' children when it comes to behavior and maturity. Just accept the fact that they might be a little more demanding, more dependent and more "babyish." They have good reason for needing mothering a little longer than their singleton peers.

Slower language development, too, may cause them to be dependent a little longer than they might have been as singletons. In *A Primer of Infant Development,* T. G. R. Bower states that "Separation anxiety declines once the child starts to talk—and declines step by step with his mastery of language and his ability to communicate with others in his environment." In the early days of speech the mother often acts as interpreter for her children. Those multiple children who are a little slower to talk will need their interpreter for longer.

• If you have long-term doubts and anxieties about behavior or your relationship with any of the children, share them with your partner, your Mothers of Twins Club, your doctor or a friend. Perhaps all he needs is a little extra individual time, or perhaps the family needs outside help.

Setting limits
Whether you call it encouraging reasonable behavior, setting limits or discipline, getting your children to do what you want poses many a problem for parents in the toddler years. And it is particularly so for parents who want their children to be free to develop in their own way with a minimum of restrictions. The experience for twins and triplets will again be very different in this area.

Dos and don'ts
Lytton found that mothers of singletons tend to use suggestions, reasoning, "let me help you," to get their children to do what they want more frequently than twin mothers, who tend to resort much more often to prohibitions: "No," "Don't do that," "Leave her alone" and so on:

> "It really struck me when each had a week away and I had one and then the other, that, whereas one will fit in quite happily and you can let them do almost anything around the house, when there are two you have to make great rules all the time, 'Don't touch this,' 'Don't go in that room,' 'Don't do that.' There's only rules because if they play with sticks someone will get poked or. . . . There's a whole load of rules that come into having two at that stage."

Lytton also observed that a parent's "repetition of a request, command or suggestion did not increase the likelihood that the children would respond." Your twins, hearing many more "dos" and "don'ts," are more likely than singletons to switch off or assume that the request or command is directed at the other and not react. So it's a double bind. For reasons of safety, you need to issue many more than double the number of commands and prohibitions and yet, the more they hear, the less likely they are to respond. We can only suggest that beginning very early you make it clear whom you are addressing; "Romulus, come back. Remus, come back" is clearer and sharper than "Come back, both of you."

According to Lytton, twins are more likely than singletons to be upset by reprimands, verbal or physical. These often seemed to have the effect of making them less rather than more obedient:

> "My worst moment, I think, was when they were about four. We were getting ready for nursery school—hassle over this, hassle over that. I was getting to the end of my tether and shut myself in the bathroom for a few moments of peace. Basically, I don't believe in smacking but recently I'd found I was resorting to it out of desperation. So I shut myself in the bathroom to calm down. They both went straight downstairs and got a hammer each. The next thing I knew they were both trying to bash the bathroom door down with these heavy hammers—the marks, incidentally, are still there. I came out, took the hammers, smacked the pair of them and went and sat on my bed feeling utterly hopeless. By then I was in tears. Sure enough I was followed. When they saw I was crying, Robin showed concern, but Tom took one look and said, 'Ah-ha.' I'll never forget the triumph in his voice!"

That twin parents tend to be less positive in their approach was again not surprising. What was surprising, and perhaps needs to be borne in mind if you think your twins are getting a raw deal, is Lytton's finding that the most common reaction of all parents, twin or singleton, to their child's doing what they ask of him, is to make no response at all. This was followed in frequency by a neutral response and then by issuing another request or suggestion. "Positive responses are only the fourth most likely reaction to occur for both mother and father. This would include such actions as smiling at the child, praising him, playing with him, or cuddling him."

Keep in mind that each of your twins or triplets needs recognition and approval for what he or she, as an individual, has done to please you because he or she loves you. Try as far as possible to acknowledge their efforts individually: "Well done, Romulus. Well done, Remus," with a hug and a smile for each. All children are thirsty for praise, smiles and cuddles of acknowledgment—something that can all too easily get forgotten when parents are befuddled by fatigue and too many demands.

Being consistent

Lytton also found that singleton mothers were more consistent in enforcing rules and expectations. There are any number of situations that prevent parents of twins from being as consistent as they would like to be:

> "If one was misbehaving and I'd put him outside the kitchen, the other would then become very aggrieved and say, 'But he's crying. Let him in.' And if I didn't he would go and open the door and let him in himself. What do you do? I was not going to enter a battle of wills with the second just because he wanted to help his brother."

> "When it comes to getting them to take responsibility for when they've done wrong, handing out punishment, what do I do? They both just deny the crime. Unless I've actually with my own eyes seen for certain that one is totally responsible for something I don't believe in punishing both, so they tend to get away with it. I find it a very, very difficult issue. How does one decide between the relative fairness and unfairness of either punishing them both or letting them both go free? I just don't know."

A mother spoke of the pressures of going through a difficult phase with one and then the other taking over where the first leaves off:

> "I reckon I've been pretty patient, all told, but there've been times when I've been pushed to the limit—and over the top. I seemed to have enough patience to cope with one toddler, but it sometimes used to give out when one picked up where the other left off. For example, for weeks or maybe even months James used to freak out if he was given a broken cookie—or even one with a minor blemish. My patience was wearing pretty thin by the time he began to grow out of that

phase, but I lasted the course. Then Nick started on the same thing and I just couldn't take any more, so he got it in the neck, poor child. I see that as a really hard thing when you've got twins."

Some order in the chaos

"It would be easier to let them run riot, but I don't." All children need the security of knowing there are limits to what they can do, limits to what will be tolerated by their parents. The boundaries will vary from family to family. A few suggestions follow to help you keep some order in those early years.

• Keep yourself fit and alert. A mother who is tired somehow fumbles through the day and is often unable to make decisions appropriately—and the number of decisions is legion when there is more than one toddler around. When she is well, she is able to anticipate potential disasters and gently steer the children past some of them. She also has the energy to enjoy being with them and doing things with them, and difficulties are less likely to arise.

• Provide them with stimulation: set up play materials and games. Don't forget to play with them, and arrange for them to play with friends, together and separately.

• If both parents communicate their expectations for their twins' behavior and come to some kind of agreement with each other, the twins will be much clearer about what they can and cannot do in their family.

• Avoid clumping them together or making any comparisons.

• Respond to their behavior, good or bad, individually.

• Some parents, particularly those with higher multiples or three or more closely-spaced under-fives, had a well-defined system for dealing with misdemeanors. Some children were sent to their room for a few minutes starting at a very early age. Others, one, two, three or four of them, might find themselves "on the mat"—not the same one but different ones scattered around the house.

• Knowing that it is harder to be consistent when you are dealing with two or three small children, limit the number of rules you make to the absolute minimum and you will stand a better chance of keeping to them. Give children as safe an environment as possible (see Chapter 6) and there need be far fewer "dos" and "don'ts."

• Rules protect the rights of each member of the family. Don't be afraid of making them if you need to. A mother who coped with triplets without any extra help had this to say:

> "If I feel like having a rule, just like that—'This is now a rule'—then I always stick to it because usually they're the rules that protect me. As far as I can see, those are the most important ones."

• A routine is still important. Helen and Stephen depended on it with their triplets:

> "Routine was our life. It's only really been since they were about four that we've begun to realize that we don't have to go on like that forever. We got to the stage where it almost became automatic to us. I've felt that, if we weren't in our routine, disaster would follow. If ever we were out particularly late or meals weren't organized or we tried to take them anywhere different it was awful and it's only recently that we find we can do things in a more relaxed way. We found routine essential and this was the thing that other people didn't realize, I think—how much you had to treat it like a job."

• If you find they are completely out of hand—and amoral into the bargain—don't despair! Lytton found that singletons tend to internalize rules more readily than twins, probably because parents can and do give them closer attention. Your twins may take a little longer to learn to take responsibility for their own actions.

• Remember, too, that parents are not the only influence for shaping the lives and social behavior of their children. Contact with friends, outsiders and teachers will help in the process, especially if they are occasionally without their twin.

Independence v. peace
In addition to encouraging their children to behave in a reasonable way, parents also want to foster their independence. A twin parent, perhaps more than any, is anxious to promote her

children's natural drive toward independence and so relieve
her of some of the load. For some this may proceed as
smoothly as for single children. For others the particular pressures of two or more of the same age being reared together
may delay the process for one or both of them.

Lytton's study concluded that factors conducive to a child becoming independent include a mother's encouragement of the
process by expecting and demanding mature standards of behavior and her consistency in enforcing rules. These factors, as
we have seen, are likely to occur less regularly with multiple
children.

"The mother should also grant the child freedom to take ini-
tiatives in his own way and to make his own decisions." Here
again parents will inevitably be thwarted to some degree as the
experience of multiples is so different. Not only do they need
to strive to separate from their twin as well as from their parents, but parents will be able to offer them fewer choices and
fewer opportunities to explore. And there are situations where
it becomes just too complicated to involve them in sharing
grown-up tasks. Kate's experience was typical:

> "It's very difficult. For a start they're very competitive. I'll say,
> 'Could you do so and so.' And one will say no, and the other
> will say no. Or one will do it and the other one will want to do
> it and then they'll have an argument about it. You can't ever
> seem to get it right."

Finding the delicate balance between allowing choices and
making the day as smooth as possible is quite an art.

Fairness
Fairness is an issue that many parents reported as being of increasing concern to them and their young twins. All of the
adult twins we talked to felt quite strongly about it:

> "You probably have to be more careful about being fair with
> twins than you would be with children of different ages who
> can appreciate that they have different needs and it doesn't
> matter so much if one is shown favor sometimes and not the
> other . . . but we were very quick to notice it."

> "When we were at junior school, there was an outing to France with the school and so many wanted to go that they drew names out of a hat. . . . They picked one of us but not the other and then decided they couldn't let one go separately, so neither of us went. I remember feeling there was something very unfair about that."

The kind of situation that Malcolm described above is one that some parents of twins dread. It is understandable that in the circumstances both twins must have felt the situation was unfair, but if one twin had gone on the trip what kind of outcry would there have been from the other, and how would parents deal with it? The kind of thing that could be said to brothers of different ages—"You had your turn last year, now it's his turn" or to the younger: "It's his turn now, but when you're older you'll have yours"—is often not applicable to twins.

While children's early feelings will derive partly from their parents' attitudes, they must also come from their own feelings of rivalry and competition for their parents', and especially their mother's, time and attention. Issues about fairness can easily get out of hand and children can begin to manipulate parental anxiety:

> "I don't feel under any compulsion to buy Elizabeth and Joe [older sibs] a treat at the same time. I feel quite happy about getting Joe a packet of chips and not Elizabeth and vice versa. I just dread the reactions when I try to do that with the twins because it would just lead to such a scene, and so much fighting and jealousy and tantrums that I chicken out. I think that is the answer to that one. I do treat them the same because I can't cope with the consequences of doing otherwise. . . . In making a decision whether to give one of them something, it's an all-or-nothing thing. I either give it to them both or I don't give it to them at all."

Another mother found herself having to buy an identical garment for both girls regardless of whether they both needed it.

Many parents felt, however, that "you can carry fairness too far."

"If one needs a pair of shoes I'm not going to buy another pair just to make it even. They have to accept that it all evens out at some time or other and that is just a fact of life."

With three or more to deal with at once, absolute equality of treatment is even less realistic, as this mother found:

"I keep saying to them, 'Look, I can't be fair, I can't be fair. If you're going to do anything interesting in life you can't constantly be being fair.' I try to be as fair as I can. I keep some sort of mental check on what's going on and I think it all works out in the end."

There are genuine dilemmas about meeting the individual needs of your children while still making it clear that they are valued and loved equally. Children are very quick to catch on to any uncertainty in their parents. It is often difficult not to succumb to cries of "It's not fair" rather than see that cry for what it often is, i.e., "Am I special? Am I important? Do you love me, too?" It is an area where parents' toughness and resilience is tested time and again and· where it is all too easy to give in in spite of good intentions.

Even though you may find it expedient to sometimes give way "for the sake of peace," a firm underlying attitude that they are each valued for themselves rather than as part of a unit will help them cope with what they perceive as "unfairness." This may have to be spelled out repeatedly while they are growing up.

Sometimes exaggerating "sameness" helps children see the ridiculousness of expecting absolutely equal treatment, for example, "When Dum falls over and hurts himself, do you want me to push you over so you can be the same, Dee?" is likely to elicit a knowing grin of understanding. Or suggest that for a period of time one does exactly what the other does—a good game with a clear message.

But it all starts before words can be used to explain. Seeing them and responding to them as different people with different needs right from the beginning sets a pattern, so that later on a special treat for one causes the other just to grumble rather than be plunged into the depths of despair.

Siblings

The advent of a single baby creates quite an upheaval in a family's structure. Twins or more, especially once they begin to be mobile and become individuals in their own right, demand a colossal readjustment. No one is likely to feel this more profoundly than an older single child. A little forethought and consideration for his or her needs during the second leg of this invasion on his life can go a long way toward helping the older child to cope.

How does it seem to an older sibling ("Sid," in our diagram) when two or more people join his family? He has been existing very comfortably with much attention from both of his parents, a family with three relationships. The arrival of one baby would double the number of relationships to six. The arrival of twins more than triples the number to ten. Triplets arrive, and the number of relationships is multiplied by five to 15. Quads takes the total to 21, seven times the number he has been accustomed to. A live-in help for the quads will bring the number to 28. Wow!

In the early months the babies took his mom's and dad's time and attention. He hated that, but they gave him time and attention, too, so he gradually learned to accept the intruders, especially as they were out of the way asleep in their cribs a good deal of the time. Now they are about a year old, demanding, intrusive, destructive, horribly charming and literally swarming all over the place. Sid needs protection.

Siblings need protection

First and foremost, protect his relationship with you by finding some time, however short, for him alone. Sheila managed this by ensuring that her twins' nap time coincided with Peter's return from nursery school. He also had time on his own with both parents after the twins were in bed at night. Louisa, who had younger triplet siblings to contend with, had time at night, too. She also went off shopping with her mother every Saturday morning and, over the first four years, joined her parents on outings and camping weekends while relatives took on the triplets. Anne, realizing that she could not make separate time

Family relationships

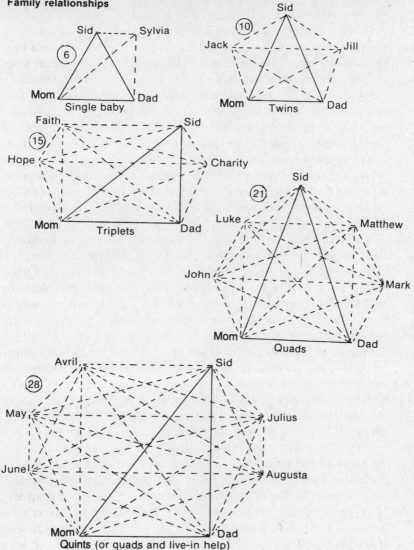

A family of Mom, Dad and Sid has three relationships (indicated by unbroken line). The dotted lines illustrate how the number of relationships within the family increases with the addition of one more baby on its own, twins, triplets, quads and quints (or quads and a live-in help). The total number of relationships is circled.

for the twins and two older siblings, gave them all time together on a large bean bag. Every afternoon after school they were there for an hour and a half when she was able to give each attention and cuddles individually as they came and went.

Then, protect his privacy. If he finds the toddlers burdensome, arrange for him to have some time away from them, at playgroup or nursery school or with friends. Joe, a child who suffered badly during the pregnancy and following the birth of his premature twin brothers, was able to build up his self-confidence again, his mother felt, when he went to nursery school when they were one. Later she sent the twins to a different school." Joe's space was so invaded anyway that at school it's quite important that his life should be free of the twins," she said.

The older sibling's possessions may also need protection. Ensure that there is a safe place for them, ideally in the child's own room, where he or she can retreat with a friend to play. When he or she wants to be near you, a sturdy table or work surface that the twins cannot reach will enable him or her to draw and make constructions without having them instantly demolished.

Finally, protect the older child from missing out on attention from adults, something doting grandmothers or aunts may need to be reminded of. Twin children will go on attracting attention long after people have stopped noticing singletons of the same age. The more alike they appear, the more attention they will receive, so protecting their older siblings is yet another sound reason for dressing the twins differently.

Lytton noted that twins had a considerably greater impact on the older siblings' existence than a single younger brother did. The siblings in the study were from one to three years older. "Not only did the twins, because of their more urgent needs, demand and get far more of the parents' attention than the older child, but by the time they were two and a half, they also tended to form a pair together who played and acted together, excluding the older child in the process. In these cases, the older child, perceiving himself to be isolated or downgraded by the twins, would develop intense feelings of rivalry. He would become the classic 'difficult child,' interfering with the interlopers and their play or throwing temper tantrums. While we showed earlier that twins were the recipients of less speech and fewer demonstrations of affection by parents than singletons— and, no doubt, received less than the older sibling himself received when he was the only child—when three young children compete for parents' attention and time, it is the older singleton who has the hardest time of it."

One of the mothers put it in a nutshell:

> "The twins dominate the family. They are the single most important influence. They are more indulged—by everyone—partly because they are the babies of the family, partly because they have immense charm, and partly because they can bring joint pressure to bear, particularly on the other two children."

Sibling/twin relationships

Among the families we saw, although there were several instances of older siblings being overwhelmed and feeling pushed out by the twins' exuberance, there was little evidence of twins deliberately "ganging up" to exclude them. The tendency seemed to be rather that an older child would share a special relationship with one of the twins:

> "Martha developed faster than Emma and soon became Philip's [20 months older] bosom pal. They became very close and Emma used to play on her own. This has continued."

Patricia felt her older child, Ruth, did not seem able to cope with the two of them and so shared a special relationship with each twin in turn.

Joe used to be terrified of his newly mobile twin brothers. He would be paralyzed at their approach and allow them to molest him. In time he resolved the situation by joining them as "gang leader." "He incites them to do things he'd never do himself and then blames them. It is very much a case of 'if you can't beat them, join them.'" As the twins matured Joe also enjoyed a special relationship with each in turn, but he definitely spent more time with Nicholas, who was more adventurous physically and more adept at drawing.

Older children

Although the arrival of twins is likely to affect most deeply a child of about two years of age, siblings who are older may feel the pressures as well. The worst period for them, too, seems to be when the twins are in the toddler stage. Susie's daughter, Fiona, was upset when the twins arrived when she was six but felt it even more when they were two. Susie commented, "They want to be one on either side of me very often and she wants to be next to me as well, and pushes one out and then there's an awful scene." Fiona, then aged nine, was frequently bewailing, with some justification: "You always give the boys much more attention than you do to me. You never do anything with me anymore."

Elizabeth was eight and Joe two when the twins arrived in their family. Although she focused her anger principally on Joe, it was undoubtedly the impact of twins joining him that was overwhelming, especially when all were mobile. She, and later Joe, compensated for the invasion by finding and establishing relationships outside their home. Their mother encouraged this, "out of a sense of inadequacy" she said. "It was not that I wanted to get rid of them but it was a way of their getting the attention I couldn't give them."

Some older girls reacted more favorably to having twins. Annette, five years older than the twins, was described as a "little mother." Sarah, four and a half at the birth and seven at the time of the interview, was marvelous with her toddler twin sisters. Louisa was four years older than her triplet siblings. Her mother said, "I always count Louisa as one of the adults. She very much plays that role." The tendency for older girls to assume some of the parenting was noticed, too, in a recent twin study (by Jim Stevenson) that has yet to be published. While each member of the family gains from such cooperative interest, it is important to remember that an older girl still needs to have her own childhood needs met.

A few of the siblings seemed to resent the fact that they had to do things alone. When Peter was joined at school by his brothers, who were two years younger, he began to have difficulties going into a full classroom on his own. Louisa, referred to above, found it quite hard to make friends. She thought the triplets were very lucky and complained, "Everywhere they go they've got each other."

The preliminary analysis of a recent twin study in Australia summarizes the attitudes of older brothers and sisters toward their younger twins thus:

• Most like having twins in the family and consider they get on well with the twins, but they would not like to be twins themselves.

• Girls are more likely than boys to have a close relationship with one of the twins.

• Compared with girls, more boys feel less important than the twins and consider the parents fuss over the twins too much.

• One big plus about having twins in the family is that the children's friends like them.

Younger siblings
The age of the twins in the families we saw ranged from three months to six years. Hardly any had younger siblings. The Australian study, too, found a dearth of younger siblings. Parents' caution at having any more children close to the twins ensures that subsequent children are protected from the "crowding" and lack of time and attention that is the lot of children who are closely spaced.

A single child coming a few years after twins is in many respects a privileged being. The mother is likely to find a lot of pleasure in the relationship:

> "It was so lovely to have this easy relationship. There were moments when I could tune in to her totally—no interruptions, no fear of interruptions, no hurrying the moment on in case we weren't ready when the other one woke up . . ."

A singleton after a gap enjoys many of the advantages of an only child yet has older brothers or sisters to play with and amuse him or her. When there is a reasonable gap, the fact that they are twins is unlikely to have much bearing on the single child's development. An incidental finding by Stevenson in his study of older London twins was that there was a tendency for a younger sibling coming many years after twins, i.e., when the twins are old enough to assume parental roles, to be smothered and overprotected. The likelihood, for some reason, appears greater in families of twins than in other families. No reasons are suggested but it may be that the twins vie to give attention.

A younger sibling arriving while the twins are still young will, like the twins, have a limited amount of attention. Do all you can to encourage a single baby to adjust to being in a baby sling. You will then still have two hands free in the first year for the twins and the baby will be getting the physical contact and attention he or she needs. Later, the baby, like Sid the older sibling, may need some protection if his or her needs are being crowded out by the demands of a powerful pair of twins. But is quite likely that the younger child will find his or her own way of getting the needed attention.

A great advantage for the mother at the time of the second birth is that the twins will already be used to sharing her lap and attention. Eleanor said, "I think in fact the twinness pays off in that they've never had you exclusively, they've never had that intense, special attention that one child can have." The baby is an intruder nevertheless, and, like singletons, the twins will benefit by careful preparation for the baby's arrival and sensitive handling while they adjust to the newcomer and the changes she brings. Make sure the twins' rights are not ignored, just as you would for a single child. Include them in caring for the baby just as you would a single child—a double dose of baby lotion will not do the baby any harm.

Two small children are much noisier than one. Put the baby in a quiet place for any daytime naps so the twins can play without constant demands for quiet, which is a strain for them and you.

A second set of twins after a reasonable gap will have many advantages over the older pair. Their parents will be expert in handling two at a time, and they will each have an older brother or sister to help care for them. When a second set of twins follows more closely, it will at times be like having quads, especially once the second pair are up on their feet:

"I find life hectic at times getting four ready to go out. I tend to forget and pair the twins and treat them as a unit. Then I have to stand back and say to myself, 'Hold on, you've got four individuals.'"

Keeping a balance

While there is competition for attention, a singleton often has little chance over a well-coordinated duo. Furthermore, individual twins will from the earliest days normally have developed strategies for ensuring that they receive attention. An older single sibling will have had little experience with attention-getting strategies until he or she becomes completely outnumbered with the arrival of twins. Unless the older child is fairly robust, he or she may withdraw from the competition much of the time or become, as the Canadian study found, "the classical 'difficult child.'"

Staying in tune with what is going on with each child in the family is a tall order for parents when there are so many of them. However, we suggest parents do all they can to find time to consider the needs of each child, giving particular attention to seeing that the twinship is kept in perspective and that the pressure group of the twins does not take over to the detriment of other members of the family.

Mother's needs

The preschool years are perhaps the most demanding time for any mother, demanding of her attention, her patience, her emotions, her adaptability, her whole self. Twin mothers sometimes found it was an advantage to have not one but two small children to care for:

> "When they were about fifteen months old I could actually leave them with their toys in their room for up to three quarters of an hour—enough time for me to enjoy a lunch in peace while they enjoyed puttering about. . . . One wouldn't have stayed for that long on his own."

In spite of this, most mothers found that caring for two or more took a lot out of them.

Caring for yourself

A good break from multiple children regularly is essential for a mother's health, well-being and survival as an individual. You owe it to yourself—and to your twins. When a mother can fulfill at least a few of her own needs, she is that much better equipped to fulfill the needs of her children. Just as for small babies, so for toddlers, the quality of her attention is much more important than the quantity.

Among the families we saw, the experiences ranged from no real breaks at all till the twins were of nursery school age to the mother returning to a full-time job a few weeks after the birth. Whatever their experience, all felt mothers needed some respite—a chance to escape, to recharge her batteries, to keep in touch with herself. Some had not recognized the need until they were exhausted.

If you have not yet made some kind of regular arrangement to give yourself a break, do so before you get caught up in what a mother called the "perpetual toddler stage."

When you have your regular break, or, better still, several breaks, use them for something you really enjoy, something that allows you to be you:

> "When I first had time to myself I didn't really know how to use it well. It was such a relief to be able to do things without being investigated and 'helped' to distraction, that I'd catch up on household bills, mending and so on. It was only through talking with a friend that I realized I wasn't really having a break from house and children. I'd been so tuned in to doing things for others that I'd almost forgotten how to switch off and enjoy just being me. From then on I made a rule that my time off was just for me, and I got so much more out of it."

When her twins were in their second year Jackie first sold cosmetics from home and then embarked on an open university course. She made the point that, besides the interest, the demands of the course took priority over her role as mother at certain times of the week. If you are the kind of mother who can easily be persuaded that one or both of the twins need you when it is your time off, it may be necessary for you to be in demand somewhere else to ensure that you do get away regularly, e.g., meeting a friend, taking up a course, or a part-time or voluntary work commitment:

> "When the triplets were three I went back to college. I thought at that stage it was just because I needed to upgrade the degree a bit. And in retrospect I think it was probably because it helped me get away from the children. And although I felt dreadful going off at half past five in the evening I felt better by the time I got to the station and I felt absolutely wonderful by the time I got to college."

Saying good-bye to them

How do you take leave of your children when they are reluctant to see you go? It can be very distressing to have two or more clutching and wailing as you go out of the door.

Once the children have had a chance to begin to know and trust the person who will be baby-sitting them, let the sitter take them off on an outing in a stroller the first time or two—good-byes are easier when they, rather than you, are going off somewhere exciting.

A strategy that often helps young children cope with the pain of their mother's departure is to let them know in advance, about 20–30 minutes before you go, what is going to happen. They may then protest, weep and wail, but you are still there to provide comfort. When the time of departure comes, they have done their protesting and grieving. They, or at least some of them, may then quietly accept that you are going and turn their energies to enjoying their time with their sitter.

Though you cannot bank on its being the case for your children, leaving older multiples is sometimes a good deal easier than leaving a single child.

Children are not the only ones to feel sad about separation. Mothers who are very tuned in to their children sometimes feel bereft when they are not there. Adjusting to the shorter losses of your twins' absence is a good preparation for when they go to school all day. A mother of singleton children gently eases out of her role of being a full-time mother. Two or three lively four-to-five year-olds suddenly off your hands for most of the

208 || The Parents' Guide to Raising Twins

day takes some readjusting to, particularly if they are the last in your family. Take care of yourself by making preparations well in advance for when they go to school full time.

The pressures
Some mothers, mainly those who had had little or no help, found caring for twins or more a great strain:

> "The really hard bit came between eighteen months and three years. I got worn down by the constant watching, the constant squabbling and fighting, the decision making. It was relentless. That's a bit exaggerated, I suppose. There were good bits. It's just that my main memory of that period is of slowly being worn down till I was nothing, just a caretaker, an appendage. I was a wife, a mother, but me, the individual me, had been swallowed up. I remember feeling very low the summer before they were three . . ."

> "The thing that springs to mind is the noise. That doesn't seem to get any better. In fact it gets worse. They just compete relentlessly. They shout each other down. And it means that the general pitch of verbal racket in this house is just awful. I don't know how our neighbors stand it. The school has commented on it. They are almost incapable of talking. They shout all the time. And then you add Joe shouting on top of them and it's horrible. And then in order to get myself across to them, I shout at them. So we're all shouting. I think the most frequent event in this family is me screaming at full blast, 'Stop shouting' which is an irony because I'm shouting loudest of all. And that, I think, has got me down most of all."

> "It was give, give, give all day long. I was on my own because Stephen was back at work and I felt very isolated. I couldn't even go out, really, and visit friends. It was just not worth the effort. I tried that once or twice but I got back so tired. I'd go out and have a coffee but all the time I'd be up and down pulling them off, pushing them off, seeing to their drinks, wiping up the mess they'd made. Up and down, up and down. Then I'd have to push and drag all three of them home and that was awful. They used to just hate it, so I gave up doing that."

Many mothers we saw felt isolated from mothers of singletons who would express concern in passing but had no real understanding of the complexities and pressures of living with and dealing with more than one toddler: "I'd feel I was moaning when I tried to explain"; "No one seemed to understand how torn I sometimes felt." For many mothers a local Mothers of Twins Club or another mother to share her feelings with provided moral support. Knowing another mother of multiples often allowed daytime visiting on a more relaxed basis, too.

The cumulative pressures can cause a mother to become depressed:

> "As time wore on I found that I sometimes withdrew from giving them attention when I quite easily could have done so. I'd find any excuse to detach myself from them. It was usually to get something done in the house, a task I could do mechanically. I suppose I needed to switch off emotionally. I felt it was OK to do that occasionally and by God I need it occasionally. But then it . . . became a way of life, a way of functioning. Sometimes when I was with them I'd try to escape whenever I could. Their emotional demands and the constant squabbling were too much."

If, in spite of a regular break and attempts to remedy difficult situations, you feel weighed down by the experience and this goes on over a period of time, then it is important to take action and speak with your doctor or a social worker. There is no shame in seeking help in coping with this exceedingly demanding job. The sooner you do something about it the sooner you will be able to enjoy your children again.

The advantages

> "It was the hardest job I've ever done, harder even than teaching adolescents all day, and at times I was quite worn out. But when I was on top of things it was deeply satisfying in many ways just being with these two loving, funny, ever-so-serious little people."

Being a mother of multiple children, though hard, is a very special way of being a mother: "It's nice and it's not a thing that many have a chance to experience—it is quite unique"; "It's been marvelous"; "In spite of the sweat and blood I remember a glowing feeling."

Several mothers found their experiences a source of inspiration. A number embarked on new occupations. We, the authors, began to think of a pamphlet that has now become a book. Another wrote articles on twins for a magazine when her girls were about seven months old. She took her own photos for the articles, discovered she did it rather well and has begun to take photos of children professionally. Yet another went out and did further study to obtain a psychology degree at college and is now doing research on twins.

Others have set up and become very involved in their local Mothers of Twins Club or even the state and national organizations.

For many a real bonus is the immediate bond they share with others: "I always get a lift when I meet another mother of twins. It doesn't matter who they are, there's an immediate feeling of rapport." "I feel terribly pleased when I meet other triplets. It's a great thing. I think it's awfully special."

Parents together

"Do you feel that having twins/triplets has affected your relationship?" we asked parents.

Positive effects
Dawn, with firstborn girls, felt that it had brought her and her husband much closer and that the marriage was richer for having had twins, probably, she thought because her husband had not been excluded—a not uncommon problem with singletons:

> "The thing that was nice, too, was that having had two straightway, you've always got one each. If I was cuddling one, Andrew would cuddle the other. There's this nice togetherness somehow."

Some parents spoke of a positive effect in spite of or maybe because of the strain they had both experienced and come through.

Philip (boy/girl twins):

> "Emotionally I think it's been an enormous strain, but we do share an understanding with each other about what we're up

against. I think that over the years we've probably developed a much deeper understanding of each other than we would have if we hadn't had twins."

Helen (second-born triplets):

"Yes, it has had an effect on our relationship, but it's not necessarily destructive. Because we've been through this ordeal together, it's a bit like spending a few years in prison together. You come out and you've got things in common. We've got this in common and it's a big thing between us, the children and what we've done with them. So, in some ways it's been very good for our relationship."

Negative effects
A number of parents found that the impact of twins had had little or no effect on their relationship. The majority, however, had experienced difficulties of one kind or another. For a few it had been very stressful. For a couple who already had two children when the twins arrived, it was all but the last straw to break their relationship:

"It's put an awful strain on everything. What might have been cracks in our relationship became chasms. You just have to demand of each other more than you can give. It's asked too much of us and we've asked too much of each other."

When her twins were about 18 months to 2 years old, another mother felt that she and her husband drifted apart:

"I don't think it's had any long-term effect but at the time I think it was a tremendous strain. I found it was a tremendous shock to find that here I was with three children when two years before I hadn't had any. . . . There was so much noise and so much chaos around the place. My husband had been used to his home being a haven. I'm a fairly organized, fairly managing type of person so the one child didn't make very much difference. The other two did."

Often the change of life-style was so dramatic that parents had no space to sort out their new roles and responsibilities and still have a little time to themselves. One or other parent may feel "I'm doing all the work," and resentments can build up: "I expect my husband to be more considerate. I always feel they ought to be taken off my hands as soon as he comes home. I realize that perhaps that's not always reasonable."

Kate and Philip's account describes the conflicting pressures that were felt by many of the parents we spoke to.

Kate:

"It's been a strain. . . . Both of us are not terribly keen on domestic things. We never have been. I was so untidy and untogether before the twins and quite happy with it, and now I'm very conscious of domestic things all the time. I don't particularly like being like that, but I've just had to be."

Philip:

"And I think on my side it's been very difficult for me. I've felt when I was at home that I was doing very much my share of the domestic chores. But on the other hand Kate was feeling that there was still more I could do."

Kate:

"We've got better about it now. I feel the problem is trying to get a balance where you both are doing a fair share of everything and it's very difficult because it's too easy to see your own side and not someone else's, especially when you're tired and irritable."

Several parents talked of stressful weekends. Where fathers were out at work during the week and mother in sole charge of the twins, roles were clear. Conflict arose on weekends, where the expectations and needs of both were not being met:

"Weekends were often the worst time. I know I often used to think it would be a letup for me, but often somehow it was more complicated fitting Gordon in to our, or rather my, pattern. We ended up competing for space—not openly but each trying to sneak off for a few moments of peace and then feeling resentful when we had to go back to trying to sort the muddles out. It was messy and neither of us liked it, but somehow we let it go on happening."

Sharing caring

It was the parents who got their heads together to plan strategies for coping with the twins who best withstood the onslaught of multiple children on their relationship. Being clear about their individual roles and contributions toward the task of caring for their children meant that energy was not wasted in confusion and that there was some left for their own relationship and their needs as individuals.

It is possible, for example, for *each* parent to have an hour or two to herself or himself on a weekend, or a breathing space in the week. Rather than sneaking it and feeling guilty about it, make plans to allow it to happen so that each can really benefit from the break and not feel that the burden is one-sided.

If you find yourselves caught up in a tangle of fatigue, confusion and mutual resentment, it is still not too late to set up a system for stating each other's needs and negotiating to get at least some of them met.

Some couples found they needed to fix a definite time in advance to get together to discuss any problems. Some removed themselves from the scene of action in order to come to grips with what was going on:

> "I always found it easier to talk if we went out somewhere, even just to a pub. . . . There's no reason why we couldn't talk at home, but somehow when you're both tired you tend to lapse into a stupified silence in front of the television."

Time for Everyone

The checklist below may be of help when you consider the needs of each member of the family.

Parents

Have I got enough time for myself?
   in the evenings
   during the week
   or weekends

If not, what can we do to change this?

Have we got time to be together without the children?
   in the evenings
   or weekends

If not, what can we do to change this?

When did we last go out and enjoy ourselves?

What are we going to do about it?

Would we like to see more of friends?

What arrangements can we make?

Am I resentful about something you have/have not done?

If yes, what can we do about it?

Have I got enough support?

How can you give me more?

Children
Have I had time this past week with X, Y and Z on her/his own?

If not, how can we arrange for me to get that time?

Is X, Y or Z withdrawing or not making demands because he or she feels left out?

How can I give him or her extra attention?

Are the twins taking over to such an extent that the others are being left out?

What can we do to change this?

Are the twins being lumped together?

What can we do to change this?

Am I being particularly ratty with one of the twins?

How can I find a time to enjoy being with her/him?

Do I know why?

How can I find more time for myself?

When I'm with the children, am I withdrawing from them?

What activities can I enjoy doing with them?

The Family
Is there a time of the day/week when things are often chaotic?

How can we/I change this?

When are the good times?

How can we make this happen more often?

Family planning

Nowadays, with easily available contraception, there is a generally high expectation that we can control the size and to a certain extent the spacing of our families. Twins and higher multiples, even if parents welcome them, knock any notion of planning sideways. The only planned twins are adopted twins.

For many of the parents we saw, twins put an end to childbearing. Either they had as many as or more children than they wanted or they were not prepared to risk another twin pregnancy. A couple with a very lively pair of mixed-sex twins, then approaching up to three years of age confessed to "the terror of having another set of twins!"

In some instances where the twins were born first, parents who had only planned to have two children went on to have a third because they felt that the pressures of caring for two at once had not permitted the gentler, more leisurely, more intimate and in many ways fuller experience of caring for one baby.

A further reason for having a third child was that having only each other was a limiting experience for the twins. Another child in the family is likely to dilute the "twinness," a benefit, parents felt, particularly for those who are inclined to measure their performance and their worth by comparison with their co-twin. Another sibling also ensures the twins grow up with an awareness of the differing needs of differing ages. A father commented, "Just having twins would be like having a rather complicated only child."

Twins a second time around?
Once you have had twins are you likely to have them again? If so, is there any known way you can prevent it, or at least reduce the odds?

The answer to the first question depends on the type of twins you have. Chapter 1 explains how the conception of identical twins is believed to be a random occurrence. Parents of identical twins are therefore as likely or unlikely as the general population to have twins of any kind again.

Once parents have had fraternal twins, however, their odds

for having twins again are considerably increased. A woman who has ovulated two or more times in one cycle is more likely than most to do so again. Race, maternal age (the number of births a woman has already had), and a history of twins in the family, can all have some bearing on any woman's likelihood of conceiving fraternal twins. But having actually had twins is by far the most important factor. Such a mother is at least twice (though some authorities would say three or four times) as likely to have twins again. That is, if you are Anglo Saxon, your chances are reduced from about 1 in 100 to about 1 in 50 or less, and if you are Yoruba, from 1 in 22 to about 1 in 11. The other factors mentioned above must also be taken into consideration. For example, if your grandmother and sister had twins, and you are 37, the odds are likely to be a good deal higher than 1 in 50. Conversely, if there is no family history and you are in your twenties and the twins were your first pregnancy, the odds are likely to be a good deal lower.

Once you have had non-identical triplets (without using a fertility drug), your chances of having twins in a subsequent pregnancy are likely to be increased ninefold, and sixteenfold if you have had non-identical quads.

It is possible that double ovulation may take place with a gap of as much as two or three days. Should this occur, fertilization of one of the eggs might, in theory, be avoided by having intercourse without contraceptive protection only once in any one cycle—if you time it right!

While there is conflicting evidence on the effect of the pill on twinning, snippets of information from this study and that and the experience of the mothers we saw suggest that there is an increased risk of having twins, both identical and fraternal, if conception occurs within two or three months of coming off the pill.

Spacing following twins

Whether they planned to have more children or not, we asked the mothers we saw what age gap they recommended for a pregnancy following twins. Almost without exception they gave three years as an absolute minimum, while several felt the gap should be five years. Jean, who had a two-year-old son when her twin girls arrived, said she would have given him an extra year had she been able to choose. After twins, she recommended at least four or five years. She, like many others, recognized the needs of small children for their mother's time and attention. Anne made the point that twins' needs are drawn out because they get significantly less than singletons throughout the early years.

A recent study in the United States based on feedback from children on their relationship with their parents concluded that, where children were born four or more years apart, their relationship with their parents was happier than with closer spacing. There was less argument, less punishment, and parents were seen as being far more reasonable and supportive. It was found that a two-year gap made for the worst parent-child relationship of all, probably—the study suggests—because the parents experience no respite between one stage of development and the next. No sooner had one child learned to walk, talk and use the toilet (for example) than the next needs help to acquire these skills. (In addition, of course, two is the age at which children tend to feel insecure and in need of extra attention.)

By and large the mothers we interviewed felt they needed time to recover from bearing and caring for two, and that the twins should be at a playgroup or nursery school or preferably in kindergarten, before they had another child. Eleanor, whose singleton arrived when her twins were just three, spoke of the difficulties of attending to a pair of toddlers while pregnant. It was a strain lifting two and pushing both in a buggy. Dawn, a mother of fraternal girls who would have welcomed twins again, pointed to the increased risk of a second set as a good reason for waiting till the twins are at school all day.

We asked mothers if they would choose to have twins again and were surprised to find a common factor in the few who would have been happy to repeat the experience. Except for one with a boy/girl pair, they all had girl pairs!

Adoption

Parents of adopted multiple children will often be better prepared than others. They will have self-selected themselves for the task and will usually have had the benefit of discussion with each other and counseling with the agency's social worker before actually taking it on. Nevertheless, as for any other parents of twins, there will be moments when they will wonder what they have let themselves in for:

> "I remember once Danny went on and on crying and I couldn't settle him and I had to see to Jack. For a moment I thought, what have I done? What upheaval have I brought on myself? Have I ruined our lives? I think you have to be very, very aware that the bond grows and is not immediately there. And actually it's the traumas that help solidify the love."

A real bonus in adopting twins is that each baby has a blood relative in the family. A mother who expressed some anxiety that her adopted children might rebel against her in the future felt reassured by the fact that "they've got each other always."

Some parents feel that taking on twins or triplets, "a family at one fell swoop," allows them to bypass the anxieties and stresses of going through the process of adoption a second time.

If your local Mothers of Twins Club is unable to put you in touch with other parents who have adopted twins or triplets, write to the National Organization of Mothers of Twins Clubs, 5402 Amberwood Lane, Rockville, MD 20853, and ask for the names of parents who have adopted and are willing to share their experiences with you.

Looking back

> "We were a family all in one go. . . . We've had such happy times."

> "I've never resented them. I've never felt they stopped me doing things or wished there weren't three of them. . . . I've always adored them although they've driven me mad at times."

One mother, a twin herself, said, "It's lovely. I've enjoyed it all so much," and proved it by adopting a second set of twins.

Even those who had a hard time found satisfaction. "We've

survived twins together," said Christine. Anne talked of getting "quite a kick out of the fact that I've survived. It was such a shocking experience for me that I feel quite proud of all of us, that we're still together."

We give the last word to Helen, who survived triplets and found it a very positive experience:

> "Although it's been monstrous in many ways, it's also brought lots of things into my life that wouldn't have been there otherwise. In some ways it's been a very liberating experience insofar as it's been such a concentrated experience. It's been like a sort of huge great encounter group in a way. . . . It's been the most powerful thing that's ever happened to me, really. So in that sense it's really changed me, perhaps in a way that maybe I wouldn't otherwise have changed."

·8·

Twins Together and as Individuals

In form and feature, face and limb,
I grew so like my brother
That folks got taking me for him
And each for one another.
It puzzl'd all our kith and kin,
It reach'd an awful pitch;
For one of us was born a twin
And not a soul knew which.

One day (to make the matter worse),
Before our names were fix'd,
As we were being wash'd by nurse,
We got completely mix'd;
And thus, you see, by Fate's decree,
(Or rather nurse's whim),
My brother John got christen'd me,
And I got christen'd him.

This fatal likeness even dogg'd
My footsteps when at school,
And I was always getting flogg'd—
For John turn'd out a fool.
I put this question hopelessly
To every one I knew,—
What would you do, if you were me,
To prove that you were you?

Our close resemblance turn'd the tide
  Of my domestic life;
For somehow my intended bride
  Became my brother's wife.
In short, year after year the same
  Absurd mistakes went on;
And when I died—the neighbours came
  And buried brother John!

Henry Sambroke Leigh

Society's attitudes

A mixed blessing

Society has always been fascinated by multiple births. Twins have featured in the mythology and history of many cultures. The relationship for some was close and cooperative, as with Castor and Pollux, whose devotion won for them a place in the heavens where, according to legend, they reign as the twin stars in the constellation Gemini. For others it was combative, as with Romulus and Remus, whose rivalry ended in fratricide—not an encouraging example!

Throughout the world twins have been regarded sometimes with reverence but mostly with fear. The threat posed by the mysterious appearance of two babies where one is the norm has been seen in many forms. Many tribes, notably among North American Indians, have associated the birth of twins with fertility. Sometimes their influence was seen as favorable, but more commonly it evoked elaborate ceremonies to ward off drought, famine and disaster.

For some cultures the birth of twins was evidence of their mother's unfaithfulness, as it was assumed the second twin was fathered either by another man or by a spirit. In others, multiple births were seen as a "litter," degrading and animal-like. The penalties in such societies have ranged from purification rites for the mother, through temporary or permanent banishment of mother and babies, to the killing of one or both twins and possibly their mother.

In societies where seniority was of great importance in the

social structure, anxiety focused on the possibility of conflict between the twins. There are many legends about the struggle for power between first- and secondborn twins. Some tribes dealt with this by giving the twins special fixed names to denote seniority, others gave the secondborn no name, and others simply killed the secondborn.

Some of the most elaborate rites associated with twins are still found among the Yoruba in Nigeria, who have the highest rate of twinning in the world. They carve small figures to represent the twins, and should one die, the mother and later the surviving twin carries the image with him, caring for it and revering it.

In some parts of Europe there were beliefs about the healing powers of twins; in others they were associated with fertility. There were theories about what caused twinning, such as eating a double fruit or drinking from a particular well. In medieval times twins were also thought to have two fathers.

An understanding of the reproductive processes and the biology of twinning has taken the fear and strangeness out of a multiple birth in Western societies—or almost. Some of the primitive responses seem to linger on:

> "I've sometimes been made to feel as if I were a real freak—workmen in the street have done a kind of nudge-wink routine and called out, 'Want another, then?' and one woman went past looking at them in the stroller and muttering 'Disgusting.'"

Some parents still admit to feeling a passing qualm about producing "a litter." And there are still difficulties in the relationship between the first- and secondborn and their respective roles in the family structure.

Contemporary attitudes

Our primitive fears have in general acquired what Marjorie Leonard (a twin researcher) has called a "cultural sugar-coating." "How lovely," "how sweet," "what fun," are likely responses to twins. However, there is still generally little awareness of what having or being twins entails, and there are some widely held myths.

Many people do not know that twins (or more) can be identical or fraternal, or what these different relationships imply. Many a mother of a boy/girl pair has been asked, "Are they identical?" Some people believe that, as in cattle, the girl of a boy/girl pair will be infertile.

Twins are often seen as a unit. Some people expect them to display opposite and complementary characteristics. Others expect identical twins, especially, to be alike in every respect both physically and mentally. They are frequently assumed to be each other's best friends and to be able to communicate telepathically. The more alike the twins are, the more everyone is fascinated by them. At its most extreme the identical syndrome is undoubtedly disturbing and freaky:

> "Identical twins Greta and Freda Chaplin were given suspended prison sentences by York magistrates yesterday for hounding a 56-year-old lorry driver.

> "The court heard that doctors were baffled by the 37-year-old women, who speak in unison and have had a lifelong obsession for the lorry driver . . .

> "Sentence was deferred until yesterday when the two appeared in court dressed alike, each wearing a pink mitten on one hand and a brown woolen glove on the other." (*The Guardian*, November 5, 1980)

It is this aspect of twinness that is featured in the press, together with the stories of separated twins who meet after 30 years wearing identical colored jackets, smoking the same brand of cigarettes, having married wives with the same names and having three children of similar ages, drive the same make of car and so on.

These accounts naturally color society's attitudes and expectations about twins—not always to the benefit of twins themselves or their parents.

There is no doubt that society looks for similarities. The confusion between twins is a popular comic device in the theater, and children's stories featuring twins usually portray them as a fun-loving pair who delight in the confusion they cause, fooling their friends and teachers. While twins may occasionally enjoy such confusion, in general their concern is to have their identity and individuality recognized.

Twins together

What is twinness?

The essential twinness of twins has not been satisfactorily analyzed either by twins themselves or researchers. Increasingly, it appears that there is no mystic bond between twins. A few twins have recounted telepathic experiences, but so have other close members of a family (telepathy between twins is currently being researched). However, the relationship between twins *is* very special: simply to spend 24 hours a day in the company of a brother or sister throughout early childhood (as many twins do) is a unique situation. Identical twins sharing the same genes are bound to have aspects of their physical and mental characteristics in common. Just how much they have in common has been the subject of most studies of twins.

Twin studies

Twins have been widely used in studies, mostly by researchers seeking to establish the relative influences of heredity and environment. In the past the bland assumption was often made that since twins shared a common environment, differences between them must have a genetic basis. Researchers failed to take account of the fact that the co-twin was probably the most important feature of each twin's life and that the attitude of parents—the way they differentiated one twin from the other and behaved toward each—could make the environment of each very different. Even before birth one twin may have a more favorable environment, especially in the case of identical twins. And the birth experience of each twin and his or her experience in the neonatal period may also differ radically.

The research most widely publicized in recent years has been carried out at the University of Minnesota. It has again attempted to look at the nature-nurture debate by bringing together twins (most of whom were identical) who were separated at birth and brought up by different families, often in ignorance of the fact that they ever had a twin. By looking at just how alike these twins were both in a whole range of mental and physical tests in the laboratory and in the circumstances of their lives, it is hoped that we will gain an insight into just how far their shared genetic makeup has influenced their lives. The study has produced incredible tales of coincidence and parallels in the lives of twins that are examined in detail in Peter Watson's book, *Twins*. Identical twins in the Minnesota and other studies have shown close parallels in their rate of intellectual development as well as in their patterns of growth and state of health.

A promising development in recent years, particularly for those of us who are directly involved with twins, is an increase in studies of the twin situation itself. Many of these more recent studies have begun to draw attention to the differences of a twin child's upbringing as compared with a singleton's. Caring for more than one child at a time will inevitably call for a different style of parenting. "It's a completely different ball game," in the words of an adult triplet.

There is scope for much more research into the way parents respond differently to twins and adopt different child-rearing practices when dealing with them, and into the effect each twin has on the other.

How close are twins?

What kinds of relationships do twins actually have? Parents of twins and more do not need academic studies to tell them that like any other brothers and sisters some twins get on well and are very close, while at the other extreme some are constantly feuding.

Closeness seemed to be most apparent in the degree of understanding a young twin would show when the other was in distress. From an early age many twins offered each other wordless comfort when one was upset:

> "When they were about two my mother-in-law took them to the zoo. Daisy poked her finger into a parrot's cage and got it nipped. She was very upset and kept wailing on and off. As they were coming home she started up again. My mother-in-law stopped the car and tried to comfort her but she wouldn't stop. Then Ben, who had been watching all this anxiously, apparently just reached out and took her hand and it did the trick. She was still sitting cuddled up to him holding his hand when they arrived home."

The feuding may also be an expression of a closeness that at times becomes oppressive:

"My two are not very close. They fight a lot. They try to be as different as possible. The 'bond' if you can call it that, seems like an elastic band that is usually taut and tense, pulling in opposite directions, and occasionally it's looser and easier, but in spite of their going their different ways there is undeniably something that somehow binds them to each other—for better or worse!"

Some twins may develop such an exceptional degree of understanding and acceptance of the other that it can be a protection against adapting to the demands of the outside world, thus setting themselves apart as a unit:

"They cooperate in mischief and fib-telling. They endorse each other's behavior so if one is doing something or both are doing something that isn't approved of, they can switch into each other and out of the external world, so the disapproval doesn't touch them because the other one is approving. . . . They can always shift responsibility on to the unit because other people confuse them, and I don't see how they can possibly grow up knowing where 'my' responsibility stops and 'his' starts unless they are separated. I think this is a very, very basic confusion, and because they confuse other people, that confusion persists."

The closeness of twins' relationships may be quite strongly influenced by the type of twin they are. An extensive study carried out by Helen Koch in Chicago over 20 years ago and reported in her book, *Twins and Twin Relations,* examined the way twins' relationships were affected by their sex and their zygosity (identical/fraternal). She found that different types tended to display common characteristics.

Identical
Identical twins had a closer relationship than fraternal twins. Identical girls were closer than identical boys and tended to be very outgoing and gregarious. Boys tended to be quieter and less sociable. She found no evidence that the degree of close-

ness had any bearing on either the twins' levels of intelligence or their sociability. None of the twins she saw lacked friends.

Fraternal, same sex
Both boys and girls were less close to each other than identicals, with boys having the most rivalrous relationship. Although boys were often at odds with each other, they seemed to have an easier relationship with their parents than singletons of a similar age. Fraternal girls were the most vivacious and outgoing group of twins.

Fraternal, opposite sex
Not surprisingly, perhaps, boy/girl pairs were generally least close. The girl tended to dominate the relationship as she got older and matured faster. She was more sociable than the boy but less so than girls in same sex pairs. They displayed less rivalry with their co-twin than singletons with an opposite-sex sibling close in age.

Helen Koch's findings are, of course, generalizations. The experience of both the parents and the adult twins we spoke to did, by and large, correspond with her overall picture. There are, of course, other factors besides the type of twin they are that will affect your children.

The following descriptions of their relationship by adult twins reflect a wide variety of responses to the situation:

Pam (identical girl):
"It was a very happy childhood . . . we've always been close. I'd find it very hard to live without her. I've thought about moving away and of course I'd cope, but it would be really difficult—like one of my kids going away or my husband—worse maybe. . . . Carol is the first person I turn to . . . I expect her to understand exactly what I mean without having to say too much."

Carol (her co-twin):
"We were each other's best friends. It was a very confiding, loyal relationship. . . . We live together more happily than

anyone else I've ever lived with. We just know what fits—when to keep out of each other's way, when to get in it. It's very natural and easy."

Malcolm (fraternal boys):

"I was quite pleased to be a twin, but I never felt there was any special link because we were twins. . . . I do remember one day when we were about seven, my sister had thrown a dart in his back and I remember crying all the way to school for him—I wouldn't have felt the same about the older two."

Miriam (fraternal girls):

"I didn't *feel* very close, though I think we were right up to adulthood—she was a sort of intrinsic part of me. But I felt that she was public enemy number one."

Colin (fraternal boys):

"It certainly feels a good thing. I like telling people I'm a twin. I like talking about my twin. I find I delight in him and the fact that we have a relationship that is different from that of just brothers. . . . It was he who got me through boarding school. I had a very tempestuous career, I was always in trouble, refusing to go along with things I didn't agree with and making myself unpopular. He never criticized me . . . I don't mean he championed me . . . but it gave me support, his just being there."

Marilyn (boy/girl):

"We gave each other support in different ways. I was more outgoing and confident socially—I was the one who asked for the sweets in the sweet shop. But he was better academically. I couldn't bear being in trouble for getting things wrong and relied on him for answers, especially in math."

There are as many kinds of twin relationships as there are pairs of twins!

Multiples

With triplets, quads and quints, each child is a member of a group rather than a pair. Though some multiples may group themselves into pairs, they do have the option of regrouping for certain activities or when they are fed up with the pair, and so they may avoid the intensity of the "twin" relationship. A mother of triplets who had come across a number of twins in her work felt there was an advantage in having triplets rather than twins:

> "Although it was physically a hassle, the one nice thing about triplets is that with ours there's a sort of interplay, a change of relationships so there isn't always that perfect little unit of two children. In some ways, I've thought that may make them more independent than twins. Three is an uneven number and as with all uneven numbers it's constantly changing. . . . I think our combination of triplets is the easiest—a boy and two girls—especially because the boy is very extroverted. He and one of the girls are closer than the two girls. They share a room but the girls usually go to the same activity. I feel they've got more individual space than they possibly might have had if there'd only been two. I'm sure with lots of twins that's not a problem but with some it is."

If multiples do not have opportunities to express their individuality the pressures may be very great. Mike, an adult triplet, felt all three in his trio had had difficulties. He and Phil were identical and Tony was very different. Their mother, out of necessity Mike felt, has treated them much the same. They were all dressed "like peas in a pod" till they began to establish their own choice when they were ten:

> "It was extremely difficult for us with my parents' lack of awareness of the problems we were subjected to. It was always Mike and Phil, Phil and Mike, can't tell the difference you look so alike, don't you have this telepathy business. Nobody could think Mike without Phil and vice versa. . . . The importance of individuality is paramount so that despite being identical twins, the emotional feelings between myself and my twin are remarkably little, almost nil. There is very little love lost, and very little contact now between any of us.

> "The pressures on Tony were even greater than they were on Phil and myself as the twins of the group because he was always the odd one out. He was never as big physically as us which stood him in bad stead. He was of a totally different make-up and by virtue of being the majority, myself and Phil were always held in higher esteem than he was, which made life very difficult for him."

War and peace?

> *Tweedledum and Tweedledee*
> *Agreed to have a battle.*
> *Tweedledum said Tweedledee*
> *Had spoil'd his nice new rattle.*
> *Just then flew by a monstrous crow*
> *As big as a tar barrel.*
> *It frighten'd both the heroes so*
> *They quite forgot their quarrel.*

Did Lewis Carroll ever baby-sit for twins, we wonder?

No matter how fond of each other twins are, they all fight sometimes, and some twins fight a good deal of the time. For parents and children, it can be one of the most difficult aspects of a twin relationship—not that fighting is confined to twins. Helen Koch suggested that, in general, singletons had a more rivalrous relationship than twins. But this is of little comfort if yours are a pair constantly at war.

Something that may be a particular problem for parents of multiples is the intensity with which the children fight. We have not seen this discussed in any study of twins, but enough adult twins and parents of twins mentioned it to make us wonder whether twins do fight more ferociously than singleton siblings do. Pat and Carol, who were very close, both commented on the ferocity with which they fought as children. Kenneth, also an identical twin, recalled:

> "I wasn't a fighter at school, but we used to fight terribly. I remember friends just standing there and watching Derek and me bashing each other's heads on the floor, almost killing each other . . . then they walked off and left us, they were so stunned by it."

John, not himself a twin, remembered twin friends at school:

> "Their quarrels seemed to reach an intensity that I never experienced with my own brothers and sisters. They seemed to know exactly what each other's most sensitive areas were and how to be most hurtful."

Eleanor's boy/girl pair did not fight often but when they did:

"They seem to totally let rip in a way neither does with their younger brother—they really hurt each other."

Shared experiences

Something that is special to a twin relationship or perhaps to that of very closely spaced singletons is finding themselves so bound up in some of each other's experiences that both are equally affected by a mishap to one:

> "We were in a greengrocer's in a busy street and Nick tugged at my dress and said, "Where's James?" No sign of him anywhere. I grabbed Nick and panted up and down the pavement trying to find him. It was a broiling hot day and my cheeks were red with heat and panic. Eventually we found him at the other side of the block surrounded by a huddle of strangers. He was quite tearful but soon cheered up with an ice pop. . . . Several weeks later it slowly dawned on me that Nick was much more affected by the incident than James. He wouldn't leave my side when we were out and got worked up if James so much as slipped a few feet away. Of course it was he, not James, who had experienced my fear."

> "Jason got his head stuck under a shelf, but it was Kevin who screamed and screamed."

> "When Luke pulled the bookcase over on top of himself and cut his lip open he seemed to cope quite well with the trip to the hospital and being stitched up, but Rachel was clearly quite upset and went on and on afterward pointing to where the blood had been on the floor and saying '[Ri]bena, 'bena.'"

In such situations the twin who observes the incident needs just as much comfort and help in understanding it as the child it has happened to.

When they are small many twins seem to feel a need to share each other's experiences and demand a repetition of an arrangement where they have gone their separate ways—but with roles reversed. The fraternal twins in the following example were three years old:

> "If, say, David has spent the afternoon with their friend Douglas and I have had Paul at home and we've made jam tarts, they will want to know exactly what the other has done and demand a repeat performance. Paul will want to visit

> Douglas while David makes tarts with me. And it must be tarts, no matter how many we have in the cake tin. They seem to need to catch up on each other's experiences."

Sometimes you may be prepared to organize a repeat performance of the experience and sometimes not. Sooner or later the twins have to accept that they are different people and they will have different experiences, however "unfair" this may seem. The younger they begin to accept this the easier it will be for them. Even those who choose to go up the aisle together in a double wedding will presumably be going their separate ways after the reception!

Blame and shame
We asked parents how one twin responded to the other's being reprimanded. Quite frequently, especially when they were over three years, there was no response. "This idea that one twin will come to the other's rescue doesn't seem to work in my case," said Jean of her non-identical girls who had a good relationship with each other. But overt support and comfort for the other twin was quite common, too. Hazel's girls would tell her off—"How dare you speak to my sister like that."

A fairly frequent response—and one that parents found hard to stomach—was "glee," "smug self-righteousness," "the other revels in it."

Occasionally the other will do something to gain approval, almost as if he feels responsible for his twin's misdemeanor or as if he feels he too is at the receiving end of his mother's wrath even though it may be directed at only the one.

Or the other will repeat the performance:

> "They do encourage each other. Rosie uses it as a way of attention-seeking as well because if Leo does something that you initially tell him off for and then try to explain why you're telling him off, Rosie will then do exactly the same thing to get attention. I assume that's why she's doing it."

Too much togetherness
However happy small twins are to be together all the time, if they come to rely too much on their twinship for receiving at-

tention and making friends it may be at the expense of developing their own personalities and of developing strategies for coping with the outside world:

> "You're quite special being a twin and you're a novelty and you get a lot of attention. You realize afterward you only get a lot of attention when you're a twin, when there's the two of you there. So when the two of you are not there, when it's just you, you're just another little boy and it's a strange thing that one moment you're quite a celebrity with the *two* of you and the next you are nothing."

Twin girls are particularly at risk here as society still encourages girls to rely largely on their appearance for social success. It is hardly surprising that it is twin girls, both identical and fraternal, who are dressed alike far more often and for longer than twin boys. Furthermore, as Helen Koch found, they tend to be dressed more attractively than normal so that society is bound to notice them. Koch reports the following: "One of our pairs of identical twin girls who were visited when they were teenagers regaled us with a long account of their effort to discontinue the practice of dressing alike. They finally gave up the effort and returned to dressing alike partly because they believed the quantity of favorable attention they received had fallen off markedly from what they were accustomed to getting." It is sad that these girls had not developed the confidence to "go it alone" on the threshold of their adulthood.

Constant togetherness may not only inhibit individual development but also make it very difficult when the twins do finally come to separate:

> " . . . I didn't really develop at all until I went to college and we were separated. Until then I was half of this twin act and desperately trying to be completely me."

> "We were together until we left school. It was very traumatic being separated then, much more difficult than leaving home and my parents; to some extent I think I'm still going through it."

> "Our parents were very good about treating us as individuals within the family context. . . . At boarding school we were in different streams but shared a bedroom. We weren't sepa-

rated until we were seventeen, and that was very difficult. It took me about five years to develop a direction as an adult. Looking back, I felt a lot of grief though I didn't realize it at the time."

Patterns of coping and behaving are established in the early years. The older the children get, the more difficult it becomes to break out of the patterns. If each of your twins can begin to rely on his own personality and presentation of himself in the preschool years, he will be that much better equipped to deal with society through school and into adulthood.

Parents who have enjoyed stressing the twinness of their twins may find it quite hard to play it down as the twins get older. Why should it be so satisfying to be identified as parents of twins? One mother felt she had an answer:

"The other day, I was waiting to collect my two from school when I noticed a mother with her two young twins in a stroller. As always there were people around her asking about the babies, making a fuss over them and I felt a stab of—well, jealousy. I thought, what about me, I've got twins, too. I realized that no matter how much you play down the twin thing, you do have a certain status as a mother of twins. You can't help feeling special as you push your two around attracting attention, and often admiration. It's quite hard to give that up and just be an ordinary mom in the playground."

Twins as individuals

It is understandable that parents feeling that the twin relationship is a very special one should want to emphasize the twinness of their twins, but in the last analysis each twin is an individual, and while twins who are brought up together will have every opportunity to experience and enjoy their twinness, what they may not have is sufficient opportunity to develop their individuality.

Becoming an individual
Twins, triplets, quads and quints are two, three, four or five separate individuals who need to grow up into adults who are

able to stand on their own feet. They have as much right to fulfill their potential as any singleton child. Society may see them primarily in terms of their relationship with each other, but to the twin, he or she is first and foremost him- or herself. The process of becoming an individual may however be more difficult for a twin.

It may be even more so for a supertwin who is paired within the group. Esther Goshen-Gottestein, in her work on twins and supertwins in Israel, noted a tendency for mothers of triplets with an identical pair to see the identicals as a unit and treat them as such. Mothers of quads tended to divide them into two sets of twins and then differentiate each set according to appearance or personality, much as twins are sometimes distinguished from each other.

Who am I?

All infants pass through various stages in which they learn to separate themselves from their mother. First they have to learn the physical boundaries of their own bodies, differentiating between themselves and the rest of the world, including their mother. This is usually accomplished before nine months, and by the end of the first year they can tell the difference between themselves and others in pictures. Twins have to learn to differentiate themselves, not only from their mother but also from each other. In the early months twins have been observed, oblivious of the boundaries between "myself" and "others," sleeping peacefully sucking each other's thumb.

Once a baby has become aware of the boundaries of its own body it begins to move toward emotional separation from its mother during its second year. Separating "myself" from "my twin" may not be easy. The confusion is illustrated in a childhood memory described by Mariam, one of fraternal twins:

> "We must have been about two years old. I can remember very vividly lying on a sofa and opposite me was my twin sister like a symmetrical reflection of myself. We were both holding bottles and feeding . . . I think there was an adult leaning over the back of the sofa. . . . It was my normal view to be lying on my back drinking my milk and watching my sister do the same thing. I think I saw her as myself . . . I was

not sure if she was me or I was her . . . I didn't really quite know who I was!'"

One mother felt she had seen something of a similar reaction in her three-year-olds, who had always been dressed differently. One afternoon the only clean T-shirt for one of the boys was a brightly striped one identical to the one his twin was already wearing:

> "They ran past each other and stopped dead in their tracks. I'll never forget the look of amazement. It was as if they could not comprehend that they could be out there as well as inside themselves. It was over in a moment and they got on with whatever they were doing."

By 20 months most babies can use their own name—an important way of defining oneself. But twins sometimes have difficulties. One study showed that only 40 percent of twins as against 60 percent of singletons could say their own names and some answered to their twin's name. When a pair of two-year-old identical boys were asked their names during one of our interviews, one replied "Anthony Jones" and the other, "Brother." Their responses were the same when they were later asked a second time.

As twins get older there may be areas in which they continue to share some kind of joint identity. Research on twins often mentions situations where one twin is upset or unhappy for both. Lorraine's experience when her girls started nursery school was typical of several others:

> "At first Danielle cried and Linda was as good as gold. This went on for about six months, then they were both fine and the teacher said to me, 'They're both all right now,' and I said, 'No, Linda will do exactly the same as Danielle.' And sure enough, after two weeks she did. She cried about exactly the same things and worried about exactly the same things Danielle had. They did exactly the same things but taking it in turns."

Feelings of confusion about identity can last into adulthood. Pam confessed to occasional feelings of strangeness in the presence of her identical twin, Carol:

"It happens sometimes when we are together in a group. . . . It shakes my confidence. I feel I am an individual and then I catch sight of Carol making the same gestures, using the same tone of voice and I think, why are we so alike? It's a weird feeling. . . . It's like catching sight of yourself in a mirror or a shop window and thinking it isn't you and then realizing that it is."

Esther Goshen-Gottestein suggests that it is more complex for multiple children to identify with their mother (a first step in finding their own identity) when her attention is shared with the other(s). She found that multiple children are sometimes perceived by their mother and relate with her as if together they make up a complete personality. A mother of triplets told us:

"They're all three so different. None of them is my ideal child but all of them have something that the others haven't got and I find that now if you take one away I really miss it. I think, God, these two are boring, because that third element isn't there. I find two alone quite flat. I feel they tend to fit in with one another and make themselves into a person for me. It's weird. And yet I can get a lot of satisfaction out of being alone with one of them."

Some small twins may occasionally wonder if they are a complete person or half of a whole. An older twin (a fraternal boy) confessed:

"When I was five I used to think because me and David were twins we were half everything. My dad was so big I thought I'd be half the usual size."

It is not surprising if it sometimes takes twins and more longer to learn that they are distinct individuals separate from one another.

An adult triplet commented:

For parents it's all very well understanding the concept of individuality. It is often impractical. I think the temptation [i.e., to treat triplets alike] is there for the parents because it makes their life that much easier. . . . To ask a parent to have the understanding and the patience, above all the patience, to allow three children of the same age to express themselves in

the way they want is, quite frankly, probably asking too
much. Parents of triplets do have my sympathy."

For practical reasons, parents of twins, triplets and more cannot get away from sometimes treating them as a unit, but there
are ways parents can help them find their own identity.

• Choose names that sound quite different and cannot be
confused.

• Use their names and address them individually when talking to them even as babies. As they learn to talk, help each to
learn his or her own name. Never address them as "the twins"
and try to avoid using their names together too often. This also
helps other children to learn the twins' names. A small friend
of one pair of two-year-old twins thought that one of them was
called Tom 'n Sally and did not know the name of the other!
Swapping the order when they are named together, i.e., sometimes Sally and Tom as well as Tom and Sally, will help avoid
the names becoming a unit.

• Take advantage of opportunities for feeding them separately during the first year. A meal on their own even just once
or twice a week will help them realize they are separate and
different.

• Help them to look differently from each other so that not
only outsiders but they themselves can easily distinguish one
from the other.

• Make sure that when they are small they have easy access to
a mirror. Small children are very perceptive and see tiny details
that adults often miss. If they are able to see that there are two
(or three or more) of them they will perceive differences between them that will help them strengthen their sense of self.

• Encourage each twin to have his or her own friends and to
spend time with them away from each other.

• Encourage a willing friend or relative to take an interest in
the twins and to take them occasionally for separate outings
and treats—better still, find them an adult each.

• Try to find ways for each child to have some time now and
then on his or her own with one or other parent.

• Encourage individual choices wherever possible. The items
may be quite small: a new pair of socks, spending a few coins of

pocket money, choosing a card for a friend. They may choose the same things. This is not important as long as they have made their own choice.

• Give them their own possessions when they seem ready. They may have to share many things with each other and the rest of the family—this does not matter as long as some things belong to each individual. The important possessions are the ones they seem to care about. It could be toys, clothes, drinking cups, a special spoon.

• As they get older, encourage different interests and hobbies where they develop. It may be a chore to get one to ballet and one to tap; one to cub scouts and the other to a swimming lesson, but most parents accept these divergences of interests in brothers and sisters of different ages, so it is unfair to look for economy with two or more of the same age!

• Be ready to separate them at the appropriate moment at playgroup, nursery school, elementary or junior-high school.

Where am I in the family?
Another factor that helps a child determine his self image is his position in the family. It would be surprising if the need for each twin or triplet to find a role for him or herself was not sometimes a source of tension. The fact that twins of opposite sex have a more distinct role—if firstborn they are at least the eldest son and the eldest daughter—undoubtedly accounts for them being the least rivalrous of fraternal pairs.

Many African tribes leave their twins in no doubt about their position in the family. Among the Yoruba, a firstborn twin is called Taiwo, meaning "he or she who has the first taste of the world" and the second Kehinde, meaning "he or she who lags behind." The firstborn is believed to be the younger paving the way for the elder. A single child following twins also has a special name, Idowu, meaning "the servant of twins" (with triplets, the thirdborn is also called Idowu). Any other subsequent siblings have special names, too, and the children are believed to have special characteristics according to their birth order (e.g. Idowu is considered to be stubborn).

There is a growing body of research that shows that a child's position in the family has a considerable bearing on his or her future development. There is fairly general agreement that, for instance, the oldest child tends to be conforming, dominant and ambitious, the secondborn more easygoing, creative and well adjusted, the middle child aggressive, jealous, suffering from feelings of inadequacy, while the youngest child tends to be immature and good-natured but prone to feelings of inferiority. In a few pairs, both twins may display characteristics typical of their being the oldest, youngest or middle children. But what seems more common is that each will take on a particular family position, usually according to their birth order. When twins come first in the family, for example, the firstborn may display the characteristics of an oldest child and the secondborn of the more relaxed second child.

A factor that may override the influence of birth order on a twin's self-image and self-confidence is his size and weight in a relation to his twin's. Studies have suggested that the heavier twin tends to go on to be dominating and to do better academically. Kenneth, one of an identical pair, though firstborn was 2 lb. lighter than his brother at birth and continued to be smaller. Despite their parents' tendency to treat them as a unit, the boys quickly developed distinctive roles: "He was strong, I was weak. He was bright and I was stupid." Throughout the interview Kenneth frequently referred to himself as the younger brother.

Parents reported that as the twins grew older they were generally very interested to know who was firstborn. Some reacted quite strongly to this information:

> "Neither knew who was born first till they asked when they were around four. Paul, who came second—by a mere six minutes—has developed quite strong feelings about it. I've always played it down, emphasizing that it was only a few minutes' difference and that we will never know who really started first, and I handed on a theory a friend who is a twin suggested: 'First in, last out.' But he seems to have decided that he is younger. When Helen was born when they were five he insisted he was the middle one."

With a short biology lesson you can at least tell identical twins they both started at the same time!

One or two adult twins with older siblings mentioned their awareness as children that their parents had found the unexpected expansion of the family unwelcome:

> "There was a kind of feeling that twins was the last straw, that two were too much to cope with. It made me feel that I was a real trouble for them,"

said a secondborn twin who was fifth and last in the family.

The co-twin's influence

Probably the most significant single influence in a twin's environment is his or her co-twin. In the preschool years a twin is likely to spend far more time with a co-twin than with anyone else, the mother included. Sometimes he or she will want to be and do much the same as the twin, especially during the early years. But more often the response is to strive to be different.

In the Minnesota study the identical twins who were separated at birth and brought together as adults have been found to be more alike than identical twins reared together.

A Norwegian study has suggested that fraternal twins are far less alike in temperament than singleton brothers and sisters and often less alike than any two children picked at random.

This tendency in twins to polarize, or to pull apart from their co-twin is a strategy toward their developing and establishing a clear identity for themselves. It need only be of concern if it is taken to extremes, i.e., if their need to be different (or to be the same for that matter) imposes limitations on their development.

Pulling together . . .

Twins can and do learn a lot from each other. Often just seeing one achieve something will spur the other on to do the same. A number of parents reported their pairs reaching important developmental milestones such as sitting unsupported, crawling or walking "within minutes of each other." These parallel achievements were by no means confined to identical pairs. Sue's non-identical triplets walked within ten minutes of each other. They encouraged each other in their speech too, she felt. "Ned was quite an early talker because he's a very good mimic and that egged the girls on."

While a need to keep abreast of each other may spur twins on once they begin school, parents need to look at markedly similar progress with caution. Twins who want to be exactly the same and to do exactly the same may continue to achieve exactly the same regardless of any differing talents they may have. Sometimes it may mean working extra hard to level up to the co-twin. Sometimes it may mean leveling down, or under-achieving, just to stay in line.

. . . and apart

> "There was a strong pull to be an individual in all spheres—academic ones, sporting ones, social ones—any way in which you could establish an evident or an apparent degree of difference or identity."

Twins may polarize in their temperament, behavior and interests from an early age: introvert v. extrovert; quiet v. noisy; equable v. quick-tempered; well behaved v. badly behaved; scruffy v. neat; indoor v. outdoor; feminine v. masculine—all of these were mentioned by parents. The difference may even extend into areas such as food fads and preferences.

These differences may originally be insignificant but can become more exaggerated as time goes by and the children "pull apart" in search of their own identity:

> "At primary school I became the one who helped people to draw and Leilah helped them to read. And that pattern continued. She's always had the feeling that I was the artistic one and therefore she was the completely scientific one, which isn't true."

Sometimes they may switch roles:

> "Throughout their third year David was a very sunny child and Paul was a misery most of the time. Soon after their fourth birthday David went through a very difficult stage and Paul was then much easier. It was as if he could only allow himself to be pleasant when David wasn't."

While the roles that twins adopt within their pair will probably reflect their natural tendencies and abilities, there is a danger that one or both may put limits on developing their full potential because, like Leilah, she believes the other twin has the monopoly in a particular area of talent, achievement or behavior. Having once adopted a role, it may be very difficult to break out of it.

Parents inevitably contribute toward this tendency to polarize when they stress differences between the twins as a way of helping both the twins themselves and the parents to perceive their individuality.

A number of parents said that when praising one child, they would often praise the other for a different achievement— "Well done, Romulus, that is a lovely sand castle, and what a beautiful hole Remus has dug"—but one mother felt that this, too, could backfire:

> "Once they started school Luke forged ahead at reading while Rachel was really good at drawing, and we would praise each for their achievements and gradually they began to say, 'Luke is good at reading and Rachel is good at drawing' and she didn't really try with her reading. It was really difficult to persuade her that she could read and him that he could draw."

Carol, one of close identical sisters, felt that it was their father who had stressed and even created their different roles:

> "Pam was expected to be very feminine while I was treated as a tomboy. I could get away with things while she was expected to conform. She responded to it and she cared how she looked while I would refuse to have a bath for weeks or cut all my hair off. . . . It started quite young. When I look at photos I'm the one dressed as a mountaineer or a cowboy and she's the one with the veil or a crown."

The acquisition of sex roles was commented on by parents of opposite-sex twins. One lamented, "I was appalled how early they seemed to diverge: by eleven months he was copying little boys aiming pretend guns, and at fourteen months she had little dolls' beds all over the house." Several other mothers, however, remarked on the fact that their little boys up until nursery school or playgroup had wanted to join in their sister's games and preoccupations:

> "He was quite happy to wheel a doll carriage and tuck up dolls. He sometimes insisted on wearing a skirt and having bows in his hair when she had them. He went to playgroup a few times with a ponytail but soon got the message that boys didn't do that."

Opting out

At its most extreme, polarizing may end in one twin completely or partially opting out of a particular activity. It happens when one twin feels that he or she cannot compete with the co-twin and rather than risk failure may quietly abandon any attempt to participate. One or two mothers felt that they had observed this with walking: seeing a more competent twin taking off, the second abandoned the precarious attempts at locomotion for some months. The problem Dawn had with her two fraternal girls at nursery school was not uncommon:

> "I asked the teacher if they always played together and she said, 'Oh no, they separate.' But she said, 'The funny thing is if I take Emily and I say, 'Come on, Emily, we'll do this jigsaw puzzle, or whatever' Emily will say, 'I can't do that, Mrs. Morgan, Helen can,' and she just won't bother to do it."

This pattern of behavior may persist as long as the children are together:

> "For a long time Sam [a triplet] wouldn't use a pencil because Max [the older boy of the trio] was really good at it from an early age. He wouldn't even paint. . . . Quite recently it suddenly clicked. Max had bad flu and was away for over two weeks. Sam went to school enthusiastically and the teacher commented on how well he was doing."

We were very struck at how two of the adult twins we interviewed, an identical man and a fraternal woman, consistently lagged behind, or somehow contrived to lag behind, their twin throughout their schooldays. Kenneth said he had "felt thick" from an early age:

"Derek had a native intelligence, whereas I never even dared
to put anything original down. I think in a way it was because
I was convinced I was thick."

Kenneth consistently trailed behind his twin at school but
in spite of "feeling thick" was accepted at college a year after
Derek.

Mariam had been with Leilah all the time they were at grade
school. They were put in separate classes on entering junior
high school:

"That was my first experience ever of not being with Leilah.
And I think I was so panic-stricken that I wouldn't be with
her again that I worked like mad in the first year at junior
high school to make sure that I'd be top of the form. In fact,
I came top of the form. That's the only time I've ever been
top . . . I just assumed that she'd get in the top stream and I
made damn sure I'd get in, too. And once I was back with her
she always came about third from the top and I always came
about third from the bottom. This was in the second year
onward. We maintained that right the way through, so I must
have been doing it deliberately. It was just too regular."

A refusal to compete with an apparently more competent
twin can usually be dealt with by separating them at school. If
problems of opting out are not dealt with swiftly, it becomes
very difficult to build up the confidence of the one who has
opted out.

Where there is strong competition for attention, a child may
opt out of seeking it. A triplet, quad or quint or a child with
younger twins close in age is most likely to withdraw from seeking affection. Mothers of twins at least have a hand for each:

"Max [a triplet] always used to walk alone because the other
two sat down if their hands weren't held. When they were
just walking he used to plod ahead on his own. I used to talk
to him to encourage him. But I realized recently that he'd
always done this and was becoming withdrawn and cold. He
is very tough and macho now. I think it is partly because of
having to be strong and on his own. Now I don't let the other
two do that. It caused a lot of trouble to change it, but I find
he appreciates it. I feel sad he had to do it for so long. While
he was going ahead on his own he slept badly and cried at

night. He always came into our bed; it was a chance for a cuddle. I'm sure it's because he didn't have a hand to hold. If ever there was competition for my attention he would retreat. If the others were on my knee he wouldn't fight but got off. He's getting over it now but he was loath to be affectionate for a while."

Comparisons

Opting out is the result of an unfavorable comparison, often in the mind of the twin himself, but it is no doubt bolstered by feedback from the outside world. Having a much closer object to compare themselves against than any other child, twins may be unduly sensitive about fairly small differences between them. Some may have a totally distorted perception of these differences:

"When he was nearly five Barry was very intrigued by a photo of a gathering of dwarfs in a color supplement. It took him several days to pluck up the courage to ask if he was a dwarf. His height is, if anything, above average but his brother has always been a bit taller. It had obviously been weighing quite heavily on his mind."

Size was also the focus of a seven-year-old's feeling about his twin sister who was a good half head taller than he was. "Sometimes I feel as though she's a mountain and I'm a pin," he said.

One of the adult twins we talked to felt that it was comparisons with her twin sister that had made her feel that she was an ugly little girl:

"She was the only one in the family with blue eyes and a lot was made of this . . . I remember one day in the convent some fathers from the local monastery came around. This particular father was a great favorite. He had a camera with him on this occasion and he took a snapshot of my sister but not of me. I remember, he said to her, 'You're a pretty little girl. Let me take a picture of you,' and that meant that by default I wasn't a pretty little girl."

Parents will naturally want to respond to the personality and progress and achievements of each twin, triplet or quad as they would to their other children but in so doing it may be difficult to avoid making implicit comparisons: the easy one and the difficult (or "problem") one; the bright one and the not-quite-as-bright (and before you know it "slow") one. Several parents expressed concern over the ease with which others and they themselves labeled their twins:

> "You don't mean to do it, but it's difficult not to think of them in terms of each other and then before you know it you expect them to conform to your label—and they do!"

Stories about how the babies were born that assign a particular role to one baby—"You won the fight to get out first," "She was patient and let you go first"—often said jokingly may be taken to heart, and may even lead to their adopting these roles vis-à-vis each other:

> "The family myth was that she came out first, breech, and pulled me around the right way and I always had this feeling that if it hadn't been for her I wouldn't have come out properly. It reinforced the feelings I had that her opinion was more reliable than mine, that I couldn't compete."

You cannot protect your children from every chance remark that may be perceived by one or the other as a very hurtful comparison. But you can minimize the effect these are likely to have on their self-esteem if they know they are valued for themselves, regardless of an extra inch or curl, gold star or black mark. It is also up to parents to put a stop to any tendency in friends, grandparents and teachers to compare and measure one against the other.

Dominance and dependency
One of the misconceptions about twins that many parents encounter is that one of them must be "in charge" of the relationship. Neither Lytton nor Koch found much evidence of one twin seriously dominating the other, and most parents we talked to were hard put to say which if either of the twins was dominant. Sometimes one twin would dominate a particular area of the relationship and many parents had observed swings in the relationship as the pair developed:

"No, neither are dominant overall but it was quite amazing how they seemed to take turns at being aggressor and victim when they were small. One would seem to be in charge and hit and push the other around for weeks on end. Then I'd have a day or two of peace and then the other would take over—so effectively I'd think that was that, he had it clinched, there'd be no going back. And then a couple of months later there'd be another reversal. That went on till they began to retaliate rather than sit and wail, and then the fun and games really began!"

With children of different ages there is an underlying understanding of some kind of social order wherein one or the other is expected to give way on account of being older or younger. With twins and more there is none, unless one of them is prepared to be submissive—and they usually are not! Mike (adult triplet) expressed exasperation at the impossibility of "establishing any degree of seniority." A mother of triplets said:

"They are each dominant in different ways and they seem to take it in turns. Max is physically vicious; he belts the others. Sam is really nasty. Jenny barges in and grabs. They're always trying to establish a pecking order. Who's got what. Who's winning. Who's deciding and who's got the least of anything. That's what all the fighting is about all the time."

It was also evident that in pairs where one twin was noticeably quieter and more introvert, it was often this twin who had the final say:

"Jason is the more aggressive and cheeky while Kevin is quiet and more sensitive but when it comes to it, he is the leader."

Where one twin tends to dominate or take the lead in a particular area the other may show some degree of dependency. This may be unimportant or it may mean he is failing to develop essential skills:

"We were quite happy about them starting school in the same class. They'd always seemed pretty independent of each other. She was more outgoing and confident, he was quieter and got on with his own thing. They didn't seem particularly competitive so there was no problem. . . . It wasn't until later when they went into different classes that we realized that Duncan had been depending quite strongly on his sister to relate to his teacher. He found settling in with a new teacher on his own pretty tough. It was quite a shock for us because it simply hadn't been obvious while they were together."

Twins will often develop their own strategies when one is in danger of being swamped by the other:

"Sarah is very outgoing while Sharon is rather shy and they have this pattern of Sarah being in full flow in the daytime and then Sharon comes into her own in the evenings . . . I've noticed it particularly when there have been people here . . . Sharon lets Sarah sparkle to begin with and when she's flaked out, Sharon will begin."

Achieving their full potential

Twins, whether they are close or not, have a profound influence on each other. They and their parents are often unaware of the extent of this influence. It can be quite difficult for a child to grow up with another (or more) of exactly the same age, but children are remarkably adaptable. Giving a twin the encouragement and the opportunities he needs to "do his own thing," to be an individual, will allow him to find an identity for himself. Giving a twin the chance to be separate, a space where he can feel free of the need to look over his shoulder the whole time, will allow him to find his own potential in his own time:

"In their last term at nursery school the boys were each given a large scrapbook to draw pictures in, and the teacher then wrote the title underneath. Alexander had been a competent drawer from an unusually early age and got on with his picture book with no trouble at all—'a ship with rigging,' 'a crane lifting up a heavy thing,' 'a car drilling down into the road,' all easily recognizable. . . . Barry still had difficulty even holding a pencil correctly and produced miserable or angry scribbles. His creativity seemed to come out in the weird and wonderful titles he gave to his scribbling, such as 'disappearing magic,' 'somebody nothing who can't see,' 'if you look through the telescope you can see the bullet bigger.' They all seemed to be a denial in one way or another.

"Partly for that and partly for other reasons we put them into separate classes when they went on to infant school. Barry was obviously miserable with a pencil in his hand. He was very negative about 'work,' which I think to him meant showing himself up as a rotten drawer—he is very inclined to measure himself in relation to Alexander. . . . In the second term he began to be more relaxed. And then suddenly he was drawing in a very imaginative and powerful way. He has since gone from strength to strength."

Speech development

Language is a vital tool for relating to the outside world. A mother said of her fraternal boys, "At their nursery they stayed together until they could speak reasonably well and then they went their own way and found their own friends."

Two of the most widely held beliefs about twins concern language: that twins have a private language and twins are slower in their speech development.

Private language?

The first belief is largely based on a few bizarre cases, often widely publicized, where twins, who for one reason or another have had very limited contact with adults, have developed a language beyond the comprehension of anyone else. Certainly in none of the families we saw did any of the twins evolve what we would call an exclusive or secret language.

It used to be believed that so-called autonomous or private speech existed in about 40 percent of twin pairs. The experience of the families we saw reflects the findings of more recent research that had been based on direct observation of twins interacting with their mothers rather than on mothers' reports of their twins' immature speech.

Lytton, in his observations of 46 twins in their homes, reported a few instances of autonomous speech but there was no case of a whole language system developing exclusively between the twins. The "autonomous" or "private" speech usually amounted to no more than a few private exchanges between mother and twin and between twin and twin. (Such exchanges, incidentally, are also sometimes a feature of a mother's interaction with a singleton child.) This, Lyton found, was only a transitory phase and it quite soon evolved into normal adult speech.

Svenka Savic, the author of *How Twins Learn to Speak,* which draws largely on her own recent research, maintains that so-called autonomous speech in twins may be unintelligible to outsiders but is not intended to be so.

A number of the twins we saw had, according to their mothers, developed a means of communicating early by babbling, grunts, giggles and signs and strange words. In some cases these were incomprehensible to the mother but often she could understand, too:

> "I remember an incident when Nathalie called out an unintelligible phrase to Lucy in another room and Lucy dancing with delight in response. I suppose there must have been some kind of private communication but that's the only event I can recall specifically."

> "When they first started speaking there were a few words that both used that did not remotely resemble English. For example a dog was a 'burr' and 'Dee-dah' meant 'All gone.' I knew what they meant and the words were addressed to me rather than to the other, so it could hardly be called a private language."

A twin has a constant companion at the same stage of development and may pick up sounds from the other twin rather than from the mother simply because it is easier for the twins to formulate childlike sounds. "Dee-dah," for example, is much easier to articulate than "All gone." A twin, like any baby, is primarily concerned with communicating with her mother, or her mother-substitute, and will strive to use her mother's language. The twins will resort to a primitive type of language as a principal means of communication only if, during their babyhood and early childhood, they are left for long periods without an adult companion.

Slower to speak?

The second widely held belief that is of concern to some parents is that twins are backward in their speech development.

Research leaves us in no doubt that twins as a whole are slower to acquire speech. But it seems that the tendency to lag behind singletons in language is most marked in the preschool years and that they usually begin to catch up once they are in school.

In what ways have twin children been found to lag behind children of the same age in the preschool period? They are slower to start speaking and also to articulate clearly. Not only do they use shorter sentences but some researchers have noticed a tendency to omit verbs. Their use of language tends to be less sophisticated and less varied.

The fact that twins acquire speech more slowly is only a tendency and needs to be placed in the context of other tendencies, e.g., girls are quicker to speak than boys, the speech of firstborn singletons and only children is often more sophisticated at an earlier age than that of other children. Your twins' language may reflect none, any or all of these tendencies. Certainly among the parents we saw many felt their twins were very much in line with their singleton peers.

A few pairs were well ahead. Sian from a boy/girl pair got lost on a beach when she was 18 months old. Her parents finally found her in the middle of a cluster of people saying "My name is Sian Hughes and I'm lost"—a very sophisticated utterance for any 18-month-old.

Not enough is known to determine exactly which factors affec⁺ speech development in twins. It is highly likely, though, that reduced attention from parents plays a part. Only recently have researchers begun to look at communication between mother and baby in the first year and the bearing this has on subsequent language development.

In his study of twins aged around 2½, Lytton observed that "mothers and fathers of singletons simply spoke more to their children than twin parents did to theirs." In particular, parents of twins reacted *much less* to speech initiated by the children than did the singleton parents. He also noted that twin mothers used shorter and grammatically less complicated sentences. He acknowledges that "such reduced speech is understandable in view of the greater demands on parents' time and attention that a pair of twins makes."

He also reports several mothers mentioning that a "dominant" twin talked more. Dominance, he found, seemed to be related to a child's ability to cope with the environment. Very few of our mothers reported one twin being dominant in language or acting as an interpreter for the other. One of the few was Sian, the child who got lost. Her brother Paedar, though he was ahead of average, was a few months slower than Sian to reach early language milestones. From an early stage, Sian tended to try to protect her brother and boss him: "She'd be his mouthpiece, really." In their third year Paedar began to object to her answering for him and put a stop to her being in charge of speech. Clearly, if a child continued to miss out on opportunities for developing speech, it would be necessary to give him time on his own where he had a chance to get a word or two in.

Some studies suggest that the twins' position in the family and the composition of the pair, i.e., whether they are identical or fraternal, of like or mixed sex, has some bearing on their language development, but the results are so far conflicting. What is important for language development as for everything else is the individual attention each child receives. Identical twins who are addressed and treated as individuals are more likely to speak earlier than if they are regarded as a unit.

Twins coming at the end of a large family will usually get less individual attention than they would if their siblings are close to them in age. Of the three pairs we saw whose speech development was deemed by their mothers to be well behind their peers, two sets had followed fairly closely after two or three older siblings. The other set, firstborn fraternal boys, were growing up with two languages in the home.

Helen found her triplets were slow to learn to talk:

> "I did talk to them as a group but it was a very different experience than with Louisa when I would instinctively talk with her all the time. With the triplets I tended to organize them rather than let speech happen. I had got to the point where I would turn the radio on to drown out their noises. Then I suddenly realized I wasn't talking to them enough, not pushing it enough. So while changing them I used to systematically do a word a day. I did it like a job. Once they got going they caught up pretty quickly. Earlier, they didn't seem

to be bothered about trying. I found that once I had given them that incentive and got them going, they took over and learned."

Diana's quads appeared to be slow to start speaking, and then—at around two—they were suddenly stringing words together.

It's different with twins

Svenka Savic conducted a study comparing three sets of twins and three singletons from the age of one to three. Once a week for two hours all the speech used in the family was noted and once a month the children's speech was recorded on tape. She looked closely at the many interactions between mother and child or children and found that the way twins learn to use language is *different*. To measure their progress against singletons by using the same criteria will often be meaningless, she maintains. She challenges many previously held assumptions, e.g., the fact that twins use shorter sentences has been used to indicate backwardness. She would rather see it as a need or habit.

A singleton, when addressed by an adult, has time to formulate his response. If a twin wants to respond he has to find a way of getting in quickly. He has to develop special strategies for listening to speech and for joining and staying in a conversation. These needs will take precedence over grammar and will also affect the length of his sentence. He has to find "short, brief, efficient" ways of using language.

Singletons are always expected to respond. Twins are not. Savic observed that when an adult addressed twins, the adult was often content to get only one response, so that twins may develop a habit of not answering directly. Like Lytton, Savic found that the most usual form of conversation used by twins was between the parent and one child.

Trying to communicate in a group of three is much more complex and accounted for only 6.5 percent of the total speech in Savic's twins. When all three are involved twins will need to evolve special techniques for contributing to parts of a whole message or idea. A mother had made a note of the following exchange when her twins were just over two years old:

Mother: That was Carly on the phone. She's going to call Andy later.
Tom: Carly phone "Allo Andy."
Robin: Andy ni'[ce] ma'[n].
Tom: Carly like nice man.
Robin: Carly like Andy.

Acquiring speech, according to Savic, is more complicated for twins. Rather than seeing twins as backward she concludes, "It would be more accurate to say that twins pass through the stages of general development, including speech development, *differently*, in comparison with singletons."

What can parents do?
What can parents do to give their twins the best opportunity of developing their language?

• Give them as much individual time and attention as is reasonably possible from birth onward. Talk to each individually, looking at him or her, responding to the noises he or she makes. If one is more vocal than the other, don't forget the quiet one."

• When they get older and you find yourself doing things with both of them and talking to them together more, make a point of addressing some remarks to each individually.

• Twins will often tolerate their mother's absence for longer periods than singletons do. Even so, most will not allow you to stay out of sight for too long. Some may be quiet, cooperative characters who are happy with just their twin for company. However tempted you may feel, don't leave them on their own for prolonged periods on a regular basis.

• Encourage outside social contacts. Especially encourage opportunities for the twins to visit and have friends in on their own.

• Times for each parent to be with a twin on his or her own will give each opportunities to use evolving language without the risk of distraction or intervention by the other. This is particularly important where one twin seems to be dominating the other.

• Some twins may communicate for a time in a "private" language. There is no need to be too concerned about this as long as they are also beginning to develop normal speech.

• It is normal for twins and triplets to reach language milestones anything from one to several months after singletons. If they are very behind and you are concerned about one or both, consult your family doctor or pediatrician, who will recommend a speech therapist if there is cause for further help.

• "Twin parents react much less to speech initiated by their children" (Lytton). Parents who take care of their own needs (see Chapter 7) will be more alert and so more likely to hear their children and respond to them.

Out into the world

However willing parents and family are to see twins as distinct individuals, outsiders often cling to the beliefs and expectations we described at the beginning of this chapter. All the adult twins we talked to expressed annoyance at people's inability or unwillingness to distinguish between them. One suggested: "I think sometimes people want you to be like each other—they get confused because they want to." A mother with fraternal boys who were different in every respect—height, body shape, coloring, clothes—reported how the mother of one of their nursery school friends said with a sigh of relief, "Now Paul has got glasses I can tell them apart at last." Another adult twin had a fairly jaded view of the way she had been treated outside the family. She felt that being a twin was a phenomenon, one that:

> "Somehow meant that people never noticed me as an individual. So it was rather a mixed blessing. You could be asked these questions about whether you were identical or not or which was which and so on, going through that sort of game. No one actually expected much more of you. You weren't expected to have anything else in your life except that. My older sisters might be asked about themselves in different ways. We were never expected to have anything else to offer except the twinship.'"

Society will to a large extent reinforce your attitudes toward your twins. If you see them essentially as individuals and present them as such, that will go a long way toward their being treated as such by people outside the family.

Helping others tell twins apart

A mother of identical twins reported her twins' nursery school teacher saying, "I hope you don't mind us calling them 'twin' when we don't know which one is which?" Her girls were dressed alike, however. Staff dealing with up to 30 active children do need help identifying like twins.

Parents of identical or very similar fraternal twins have a particularly difficult task in ensuring that society sees them as individuals. Suggestions we received included:

• Each twin wearing a badge with his or her name or initial on the front or shoulder.

• T-shirts or sweaters with names or initials.

• One or both twins consistently wearing something of a particular color or style associated with her or his name, e.g., Red Rachel, Cheryl in checks, Duncan in dungarees.

• Each consistently having different hair styles, e.g., Long (-haired) John, Frances with a fringe, or being distinguished by hair color or texture, e.g., fair Philip, curly Clare.

The differences should be clear and obvious at a glance. Having to search for the color of a hairclip, a name engraved on a bracelet or having to look at a child's feet to check shoe color before addressing him or her is not practical.

For fraternal pairs who are different, some of these tactics will be necessary when they first come into contact with outsiders. Names or initials somewhere on their clothing the first few days at playgroup or school will help everyone to get it right from the start. If they do not, the twins may find themselves stuck with Ann-or-is-it-Mary for months.

You have to make it as easy as possible for the outside world. Once you have done that you are on much firmer ground for ensuring that outsiders, and particularly their teachers, make the effort to distinguish between the two. It may prove to be hard work but it will pay in the end. This account from the Mothers of Twins Club 1981 bulletin was one mother's very effective way of handling the situation:

> "The boys attend a small nursery school and they thoroughly enjoy the time spent there. However, we experienced a small problem with Robert not being too keen to attend or cooperate when he was in the classroom. After a fair amount of

gentle probing as to what is wrong at nursery school, Robert replied, 'I don't want to be a twin—I was a twin when I was a little baby. I'm a big boy now.'

"I immediately assured Robert that he was a boy just like the other boys in nursery school, but then I had to shatter his little world by telling him he was born a twin and will always be a twin.

"On my next trip to nursery school I made some inquiries and discovered that *even* the boys' teacher was saying 'twins' rather than Robert and Hugh—I read the riot act and without waiting for comment left. That evening when we got back from nursery school I sat down with Robert and taught him to reply, 'My name is not twin, my name is Robert'—end of problem. Robert felt very confident equipped with this reply to all who used the word twin. All the teachers now use the boys' names when addressing them!"

Starting School

Playgroup and nursery school

Apart from visiting friends, being at playgroup or nursery school is usually the first real step into society for young children. In nearly every family we saw, the twins adapted to their new environment much as any three-year-old singleton would. By and large they went their separate ways and occasionally came together. Most appeared to have different friends. There were three pairs where the twins tended to stay together and where friends or a friend were shared. All three were identical pairs.

Some mothers did not feel the need to get their twins a place any earlier than usual. Others did!

"Yes, my God, I needed it certainly at that age. With twins that are two-ish you really must find something. They need so much stimulation then, and you're feeling pretty shattered and it's difficult in an individual setup to say, 'Will you have both my riotous children and I'll have your one in exchange.'"

"Playgroup helped to give the day a routine . . . I feel that's awfully necessary. I'm not a very organized person and it did fill me with horror to get up and have the whole day stretching ahead with these three little toddlers and nothing really planned."

Playgroups are as much for a mother's benefit as for the children's. But twins and more are rare enough for some preschool teachers and workers to have had little experience of them, and therefore little understanding of the pressures some mothers experience in trying to keep two or three, rather than one small child, occupied. If you meet with a lack of understanding for your own or your twins', triplets' or quads' needs for an early place, get in touch with your local Mothers of Twins Club which may be able to provide assistance in securing appropriate placement for your children when you need it.

A number of mothers used nursery school or playgroup times to separate their twins or triplets and so be able to give each some individual attention.

Occasionally being at nursery school or playgroup on his or her own gives each twin an early opportunity to meet the world as an individual.

Together or apart?
Apart from a few pairs, the twins we saw had not yet started school proper. However, the issue of whether to separate them or not arises for many parents well before they do start.

Some parents decided to separate their twins from the outset. This decision was based on a particular conviction, or on the evidence of the way the twins were currently interacting, or on their playgroup or nursery school experience:

> "I wouldn't want too much direct comparison."

> "One of mine would not even attempt to sing 'Away in a Manger' because the other knew it and it turned him off all Christmas carols. We were not prepared to risk his being turned off something as important as reading."

> "I feel they need to experience situations where it's not ambiguous who's done what. They tend to shift responsibility on to the unit. I feel they need to learn where their responsibility starts and the other's ends."

Others felt they would like them to be together until they found it necessary to separate them:

> "We'd like to keep them together unless there are problems. Should any arise, for example one working through the

other, we would separate them but we would like to avoid it if possible."

"They are not bothered by what the other's doing so they'll be in the same class. Being together is not a problem but we would take action when and if it became one."

"There was only one first grade class, so we had no choice. If they relied too much on each other we feel we would have to send them to separate schools. But I'd be loath to do it. I feel it would be cruel."

The main advantage of twins starting school in the same class is that they are likely to have fewer difficulties in settling than other children, particularly if they go to a school where they do not know anyone else.

Against this advantage parents need to consider the way their twins relate and possibly restrict each other's behavior, whether it be consciously or unconsciously. Any of the patterns discussed in the section on the co-twin (trying to be exactly the same, polarizing, opting out, feeling inferior when compared, dominating or being dominated—pages 241–250) could inhibit one or the other from participating fully in an area of school-work or play if they are kept together.

Other factors that can become apparent quite early include:
• *Disruptive behavior.* "They'd egg each other into trouble because of increased confidence." Even as early as playgroup, mothers reported a tendency for boy pairs to form the nucleus of a gang! If your twins combine forces to be disruptive or if the presence of one is a constant distraction for the other, they will probably settle down to work more readily if separated.

A twin who feels he is second best within the pair may be disruptive as a means of getting attention. He is likely to fare better with his own teacher and in an environment where he cannot constantly compare himself with his twin:

"The teacher seems to prefer Michael, who is good and very willing to work. Christopher is a more disruptive influence in the class. He is now being quite difficult and won't join in, partly because he is perhaps less bright and has great difficulty in 'knuckling down' and partly because he knows his teacher doesn't like him."

• *Parental anxiety over progress.* Children develop and make progress at very different rates. A period of rapid progress is usually followed by a period of assimilation. Even though identical pairs are more likely to progress at a similar pace, do not expect your twins, whether they are identical or not, to follow similar patterns. If Twin A seems to be "stuck" while Twin B is forging ahead, it may well be that Twin A needs more time to assimilate that particular piece of learning. It by no means follows that he or she is "slow." If you tend to be anxious about your children's progress at school, it is more than likely that your twins will pick up your anxiety and that in itself may create learning problems. Placing the twins with different teachers will help you to get a fuller, more balanced picture of each twin's progress.

• *Lack of privacy.* Children enjoy the opportunity being at school offers of having a life of their own. There are aspects of their life there they want to keep to themselves and not share with their family. If one twin has a habit of embarrassing the other by reporting to the parents what has happened to her (whether it be good or bad), the second is being denied the right to privacy. Separation will ensure that each enjoys that basic right.

It is more than likely that by the time your twins reach third grade one of these factors, or a combination, will have become apparent. A local Mothers of Twins Club did a survey among their members and found that a large majority had started together but nearly all had been separated by the time they were eight.

Choosing a school

When deciding on the type of school you want your twins to attend you will want to know how much of their time they are likely to spend together. Nearly all primary schools belong to one of these three broad types.

• *Small single stream.* The twins will inevitably be put in the same class. Children usually work in groups in the early grades so it will often be possible for the twins to work separately even though they are in the same room.

• *Two or three parallel classes in each year.* The twins can be together as above or apart.

• *Cross grade vertical grouping.* Children are in classes with a mixed age range, i.e., there are two or more classes each with ages ranging from five to seven. The twins can be placed together or apart. The children might be grouped according to age for certain activities, e.g., physical education, so that your twins may occasionally be together even if they are in separate classes. If you put them in the same class they will inevitably be doing a lot of work together, as children tend to be grouped according to age within the larger group.

It is a good idea to visit possible schools well before the twins are due to start, to discuss their policy on twins. Find out if they have any set attitudes and beliefs, e.g., "We always keep twins together," "Twins like to be the same." If you choose to start them together and then separate them, find out when would be appropriate stages within that particular school's system.

When you have a choice, a school with a flexible policy that will take into account your individual twins' needs at each stage is likely to be the most suitable, as will a readiness to involve the parents in important decisions, such as whether to separate and when.

Where you have no choice and find the only school has a rigid attitude, there is a lot you can do to enlighten the staff. Their attitudes may be based on one of the many myths around twins or on one or two other pairs whose needs may have been very different from those of your twins. If you still meet with resistance and feel the individual school or district could do more, ask your Mothers of Twins Club for support in backing your requests.

Useful preparations for starting school—a checklist

• Encourage their individuality from the outset (see pages 238–239).

• Make sure they each have the experience of going to playgroup or nursery school on their own a few times. This should minimize the possibility of a major crisis arising every time one of them is not well enough to attend school. The chances of twins coming out in spots on the same day are relatively slim.

• Talk in advance with the principal and, if possible, their teacher(s). Put any misconceptions right. Make sure they know what you want regarding the together/apart issue. Discuss and resolve any difficulties well before the twins start.

• Talk with your twins in advance and explain what is going to happen. This is particularly important if they are starting in separate classes.

• If at all possible take each in turn to meet his or her teacher and see the classroom. If they are going to be separate show each the other's classroom, too.

• Last but not least, think of yourself. If the twins are the last in your family, make plans for when they are off your hands all day.

Early days at school
Whether they are together or apart, it is very important that not only their own teacher but also the head and other teachers, the children, playground assistants and cafeteria workers know which is which. Hints on helping people to identify your twins easily and quickly are listed on page 257.

For twins in the *same class* it will help the teacher if you point out any individual differences that will help identification. Let her know, if you have not already done so, that you would like them to be able to function as individuals within the classroom and that it is not necessary or even advisable for them to be in the same group or paired for activities and outings. If there are any signs of their being compared or "lumped together" either by name or as a working unit, take steps to ensure the practice stops at the outset.

One mother told us how she helped the teacher to see her boy/girl twins as separate individuals:

> "It wasn't that she was insensitive or unaware—I'd talked to her about the problems that I had comparing them. But she seemed unable to think about them separately. Whenever she began talking about one of them she had referred to the other by the end of the sentence. In the end I used to arrange to go up to the classroom to look at the work of just one of them and I'd say I'm coming to discuss Sophie's work today and I'd like to talk about Lawrence's next week. I think it helped me and her and I wished I'd done it right from the beginning."

If your twins are in *separate classes* and the school encourages parents to stay a little till they have got going, try to arrange that each has a familiar adult with him:

> "They started in separate classes and it was hard for all of us. The school is very liberal and happy for parents to come in and settle new children. The real difficulty for me was who to say good-bye to first when they were both feeling anxious. What I eventually did was to leave James first so I could give Nick more time to settle into his classroom. He found it particularly difficult to settle. . . . I think James was bolstered by the prospect of school lunches—his belly has always been pretty important to him. . . . Both had been very happy at their nursery school and I had not anticipated how different this would be. Had I known I'd have done my level best to visit the school in advance with each in turn several times so that each one could begin to feel at home with his teacher."

If your twins are very close make sure the teachers know it is a particularly stressful time for them:

> "When Richard and Nicholas started school their behavior was abominable for the first week at least. Richard actually kicked his teacher. He was rude to her, too. I went in to explain that it was a particularly difficult time for them. I felt it was very important to reassure them as the boys could well have been labeled bad at this point . . . I also asked them to allow Richard and Nicholas to see each other in class from time to time and let them sit together at lunch. This did help a lot."

Into separate classes
Some twins may encounter no problems, or only a few minor ones, when they are first separated at school. When twins are very close, being separated can, to begin with, be a great wrench—maybe even greater than leaving mother is for some children when they first go to school. Such twins may be sad and disorientated for a while, like Richard and Nicholas:

> "Their behavior at home became virtually uncontrollable. Nothing I could do short of murder seemed likely to break the wall they'd erected around themselves. Any attempt at discipline just provoked worse behavior. This seemed to last an eternity—at least three to four weeks.

"It took them a term to settle down to both work and play but all in all it's been a big success. They are now liked and respected by children and staff alike for themselves. Each twin is seen as an individual . . . At first it was awful. I had no idea until they were separated just how dependent they were on each other. I'm glad we stopped it at the age of five years. I wish they had been separated earlier at nursery school."

Those who have begun to learn to "go it alone" in the relative safety of their primary school environment will be that much better prepared for handling the stresses of finding their own feet and making their own way in adolescence and early adulthood.

·9·

Special Problems: Bereavement, Handicap, Illness

It does not lie within the scope of this book to cover all serious illnesses or handicaps and the varying difficulties parents and twins might come across when one or both of the twins are ill or handicapped. Within the last ten years or so national support groups have been set up to help parents with special difficulties. Addresses of helpful groups and associations are given in Appendices 2 and 3 on pages 289–292.

Here we aim to look at the particular difficulties twins and their parents face when one or both are seriously ill or handicapped. From the moment of conception the lives of twins are bound up in each other's. They share a birth. The most constant feature of their environment in the early years is usually their twin. Because of these special links a twin will probably feel the impact of illness, handicap or death much more than another sibling.

In a crisis, parents' attention will naturally and inevitably be largely focused on the ill or dying child, sometimes almost to the point of forgetting the other, who may feel very cut off and neglected.

Stillbirth and neonatal death

The loss of a baby at birth is a tragedy. The loss of two babies is a double tragedy that may be compounded by the loss of the pride and excitement that anticipated the "special" event of their birth and sometimes by a sense of guilt if the parents did not want to have twins in the first place. Parents need to express their anger, guilt and sadness at their loss and need the understanding and support of family, friends and hospital staff.

When a birth and a death occur at the same time, when one twin is stillborn or dies soon after birth and the other survives, the situation is very unclear for parents. They may find it difficult to handle their emotional confusion and so will the people around them. Because talking about death is so difficult, friends, relatives, and sometimes even hospital personnel are likely to take refuge from facing the death by focusing on the live baby and encouraging the parents to do the same. But the parents have lost a baby and need to grieve for this loss like any other parent. At the same time the mother has given birth and there is a live baby demanding her love, care and attention.

The following accounts highlight the difficulties of this situation.

Marion's story
Marion felt "quite faint" when she learned at 34 weeks that she was going to have twins. And then she soon started to be very jubilant and excited. Her husband, Anthony, was very upset at the news and continued to be doubtful for the rest of the pregnancy because of his age and his poor health. They already had a three-year-old daughter, Helen.

Marion: "I went into labor nine days before I was due . . . Jamie was born . . . I was delighted. They held him up to me and I kissed his feet or something and they whisked him away again. Then I drifted off into another dream world with gas and air. Then I heard a lot of dismayed noises round me, lots of groans and "oh no's" and this sort of thing. . . . The registrar put his face close to me and said, "I'm sorry, Mrs. Collins, your baby's dead." I was completely paralyzed. I couldn't believe it.

"Then I had a general anesthetic as I had a retained placenta. I started to cry as soon as I came round from the anesthetic. The first thing I said to my husband was "I'm sorry." He said he didn't mind.

"Jamie was brought in. He was in this incubator in my room and I could just see this baby moving and I wasn't really interested. I thought, 'Oh, there he is, there's the baby and where's the other one'. . . . No, I didn't see the baby who'd died. Now I wish like anything that I'd seen him or that I had a photograph, I really do. I feel very, very strongly about this. I'm still wondering. I don't even know if they were identical twins.

"All the staff were very bright and brisk and I felt very cut off. Later that first day the nurse on the ward wanted to know what to do about the baby. I didn't want to deal with it then. My husband didn't want me to be any more worried and upset, so they decided the hospital would take care of it . . . I remember a staff nurse I'd got to know on the ward visiting me a few days later. She said, 'Oh' at the news and vanished. Later I saw she had red eyes but she didn't talk with me again. . . .

"I didn't cry very much. I felt shut in on myself and lonely . . . I felt guilty, really. I felt bad. I felt as if I had killed the baby . . . as if it was my fault.

"I loved my existing baby. I really did. I cuddled him a lot. I was breast-feeding him. . . .

"There was one evening when I went to have a bath and I suddenly wondered what was happening to my dead baby. I had no idea and yet I didn't dare ask. And I cried in the bath. It happened in November and it was very rainy and horrible and cold outside and that seemed to fit in with the way I was feeling. . . .

"When I had visitors I didn't want to be congratulated on the birth of my son because I didn't feel it was the proper time. When we got home I just felt dreadful. I don't think my husband could understand why I was crying. He just felt we had a lovely healthy boy. We had a nice daughter. We were a happy family. He was, well, not pleased it happened but relieved that we wouldn't have two babies to deal with.

"People on the whole were embarrassed. I wanted to talk. I wanted to talk to everybody I could grab hold of. I talked a lot to a friend who had lost a baby. That was marvelous. But then I felt she must have got fed up. My family doctor was very good. One lunch hour he spent an hour and a quarter with me. . . . "

Marion continued to feel cut off and mourn inwardly for a long time. Her unresolved grief became part of her relationship with her surviving child.

"I felt as if Jamie was half a baby instead of a whole one. One arm felt empty. I'd been planning to breast-feed them both. And I'd been thinking about how I'd do it. I felt very deflated in all senses. As I said, right at the beginning my head was rather swollen with all this twin business. I was treated like a star patient during my prenatal visits. Afterward it was as if the whole thing had been snatched away from me. . . .

"When I looked at Jamie I was trying to form a picture of the other baby in my mind the whole time. I was wondering whether it had Jamie's nose and Jamie's mouth and Jamie's hair and all the rest of it."

Two years after the birth she still had not found an outlet for her grief and had begun to feel "an absolute freak, an abnormal person."

In desperation she got in touch with the Stillbirth and Perinatal Death Assocation. "It was a tremendous relief. It was the first time I'd met people with the same experience. I found they were normal and able to cope. And now I really feel I can go on living instead of being this useless failure."

In the United States, information about parent support groups for those who have suffered a stillbirth or neonatal death can be obtained from The Compassionate Friends, Inc. (see Appendix 2, page 289). A number of the local chapters of this self-help organization for bereaved parents now provide special help to parents who have lost a child at birth or shortly thereafter.

Bill and Margaret's story

Bill and Margaret learned they were expecting twins in the 18th week of pregnancy. Both were very pleased at the news. Right at the end of the pregnancy at a routine prenatal visit it was found that one of the babies had died.

Margaret: "We were immediately admitted for induction. I was dying to just be left on our own."

Bill: "We couldn't cry on the ward. We decided we should go out for a bit and asked them to check to make sure the other baby was all right and discharged ourselves for two or three hours."

Margaret: "It was very good to get out of the hospital. We had a cry. Then we went to have a meal and were so worried the next one was going to die we went back."

Bill: "We felt a lot better going back in again because to some extent we then could concentrate on the live baby and separate the bad news from the good news.

"The whole labor was concentrating on Karen. I wasn't thinking one of them is dead. It was very good that Karen was coming first. The labor was Karen's labor."

Margaret: "She was born and I held her. . . . The second delivery wasn't painful. I pushed and it was over in a short time."

Bill: "It was very painful for me. I was crying quite a lot as the second baby came out and trying not to let Margaret see me cry. They took her away immediately. . . ."

Margaret: "After I'd been stitched Bill came back in and asked if I'd like to see the baby and I remember asking him if he'd seen the baby—it shows what a dopey state I was in—and he said "Yes" so I said I'd like to see her and they brought her back in again and I didn't hold her. Nobody suggested holding her actually, and it didn't occur to me either. Afterward I regretted that. And if it hadn't been suggested to me I wouldn't even have asked to see her. I was so exhausted at the time. But I was very glad later that I had seen the baby. . . . She was an identical twin but because she had been dead some days she was discolored. She was a brown color."

Bill: "But she had exactly the same features, a tiny little upturned mouth."

Margaret: "Immediately after, it was very good . . . I had a room of my own and Karen was there all the time. We weren't separated at all. . . . For a short time I just forgot about the other baby . . . I found I was very busy with Karen feeding her. I remember feeling generally cheerful when there were visitors and to be honest it wasn't really until two or three days had passed that I began really to start thinking about the other baby. I was in a kind of limbo at first.

"Then there were two things that I really directed my feelings into, one was an obsession with getting to find out why. . . . Then I think that I would tend to do the being upset on my own. In the maternity hospital you can go outside and occasionally when Karen was asleep I would leave her in the room and go out into the garden and have a cigarette."

Bill: "Actually we both went out and cried there quite a few times."

Margaret: "It was almost as if it was unfair to do it in front of Karen. I think I felt it was a bit ungrateful and disloyal to be unhappy.

"The hospital staff were very good on the whole. Unlike a lot of friends and relatives they didn't make any assumptions that it didn't matter. . . . Most of the staff accepted it was a bereavement and encouraged me to have a good cry. . . .

"The head nurse came two or three times and she handled all the official side of it . . . and then she came and discussed with us what we wanted to do about a funeral. It was a few days after the birth. She suggested the hospital would arrange the funeral and asked if we wanted to be notified and to go and we said yes. . . .

"When visitors came I wanted to talk about it . . . I wanted to make it clear to everybody that it wasn't a vetoed subject."

Bill: "It was mainly people without children who would try to look on the bright side and there was no way we wanted to look on the bright side because I think that would have been terribly disloyal. . . . We wanted to let them know quite clearly that we weren't having anything like 'Well, two would have been an awful lot of trouble,' which is the kind of thing some people did say."

Margaret: "They're trying to do you out of your right to grieve.

"We were discharged after about a week. We'd just got home with Karen and the very next morning we got the notification that the burial was taking place that very day at half past ten. . . ."

Bill: "It was a mad rush to get Karen all wrapped up."

Margaret: "We still had a big bouquet. We picked out the best flowers and made our own bouquet. It was only ourselves. We hadn't really fixed on a name for the baby at that stage but we had decided that we were going to name her. In the waiting room we decided the name. . . . We were left at the burial place for five or ten minutes, and we walked around the cemetery and sat at the end of the garden.

"The funeral was just over a week from the birth and I think it marked an end to the immediate period of grieving about it because once the baby was buried there was great relief, really. You weren't wondering anymore when it was going to be or what was going to happen and we knew where she was. . . .

"After that we just got on with living, I was very preoccupied with feeding. Every time I looked at Karen I didn't think how upset I was or anything, I really only did get upset or cry when I heard about women losing their babies.

"I didn't have any problem relating to Karen except from wanting to separate the two. All along, right from the start we wanted to separate the unhappy from the happy . . . not being unhappy when Karen was there. So she was completely separate from the grief of the other baby."

Bill: "We've been talking about the dead baby but really all that time from when we went into the hospital up till now, always Karen's been in the front of our minds and lives all the time. I think it was a terrific help to know before we went into labor.

"I don't think for me that there's been any time that the dead baby was more important to us than Karen. The time in the hospital and when we came home were also very happy times."

Ill or dying babies

Because of the increased risks of prematurity, parents of multiple children are more likely than most to experience a very worrying time after the birth of their babies. One or all may be seriously at risk in an intensive-care unit. You may think they are going to die and feel helpless about doing anything. The one thing you can do is to be with them as much as possible. Touching them or holding them, where it is possible, will help you feel very close to them in their struggle for life. And, if they pull through, it will be a very important early step in building your relationship with them. If one or both die, you will have been close to them during their short life and will have very real memories of your babies and know you have done all you can for them.

An excellent resource book for parents of one or more infants requiring intensive care is *The Premature Baby Book,* by Helen Harrison with Ann Kositsky, R.N. (New York: St. Martin's Press, 1983). Chapter 6, "The Death of a Baby," deals directly and sensitively with the problems faced by grieving parents.

Where only one twin is at risk, you may want to devote more of your time to that baby, to being with him during his, possibly, short life. If you are anxious about a lack of feeling for your well baby, remember there will be plenty of time for you to get to know and love him later once you are through the crisis.

Some mothers deal with their deep distress at the possible loss of one baby by blotting it out and focusing all their concern on to the baby who is well. However hard it is, we do suggest you visit the ill baby if at all possible. Whatever the outcome, you will later be glad to have had contact with him or her at this critical time. When a mother is ill, her partner has a very important role in keeping her in touch with a baby or babies who are in special care.

In the intensive-care unit ask any questions you need to about the equipment and machines, and the treatment your babies are receiving. Doctors and nurses will also be upset and anxious about the babies' condition and may need to be reminded that you want to know what is going on.

When a baby dies
Parents need to give expression to their grief. A few suggestions follow of things you can do to help deal with it. They apply as much to parents who have a surviving baby as to those who have lost both babies.

It may be a particularly difficult and lonely time for a father. With your partner in a hospital bed and needing comfort you may feel that you have to be strong and must put your own feelings aside so you can give her support. Talking and crying together will probably help you both.

• Ask the hospital for any available reading material that might be helpful. A number of books on the subject are listed in Appendix 4, on page 294.

• Like Marion, many mothers subsequently regret deeply

that they had no contact with the baby after birth. If you feel you want to, ask to see and hold the dead baby.

• When you are asked what you want the hospital to do with the baby, delay your decision for a few days. There is no need to rush. Parents often want to attend the burial but may feel they are not ready to make a decision while they are still in shock.

• Give your baby, or babies, a name.

• Ask to have a private room if you feel it will help, or draw your cubicle curtains or ask if there is a room where you can go to talk and cry with your partner.

• Talk as much as you feel you need to. You may need to let it be known to visitors, nurses and doctors that you want to talk about the baby who died.

• Ask to see the hospital social worker or priest if you feel you want to talk through some of your feelings with them.

• Ask whether the babies were identical or non-identical.

• Ask for any explanation you need about the cause of death and continue your inquiries until you are satisfied you have been told all there is to know.

• When you get home continue to talk about the baby who has died as often as you feel you need to. Do not be surprised if you find it hard to love or relate to a twin. Some mothers find it difficult to build up an attachment with a surviving twin while they are still mourning the baby who died. It may help to find some form ot counseling to help you come to terms with the loss, so you can then focus on your relationship with the live baby.

• Other mothers may find they are unduly anxious about the surviving baby. If this continues to be a feature of your relationship, again it may help to speak to your doctor or to find some form of counseling.

• If you want to talk with other mothers who have shared the same experience, contact the Mothers of Twins Clubs Association and/or The Compassionate Friends. There is no need to fell anxious about approaching the latter because you have a live baby.

• Some couples find it difficult to share their grief with each other. You may find talking about your loss together with your family doctor or someone else will then enable you to help each other share your feelings about your loss at home.

Death of a twin—baby or child

Once the twins are at home and the parents are seen to have separate and individual relationships with them, once friends and relatives have begun to see them as two distinct beings, it is far less likely that the parents will be denied their right to grieve if one twin dies. However, they may still meet with some of the dilemmas parents have to contend with at a stillbirth or neonatal death.

Crib death (Sudden Infant Death Syndrome)

Crib deaths are still something of a mystery to the medical profession. Because so little is known, when one twin dies in this way, the other may be admitted to the hospital for a short while during the period immediately following the death for close observation. In this very upsetting situation many mothers will want to be admitted with the twin, particularly if they are breast-feeding. Others may feel more comfortable handing the surviving baby over into safe care while they stay at home to be comforted and to mourn their loss without having to meet any further demands.

In some cases a mother may subsequently lose confidence in her ability to care for her surviving baby and feel so afraid of the same thing happening to him that it ruins her enjoyment of her relationship with him. This is quite understandable. If you find you continue to be unduly anxious about handling or leaving the baby, it is important to talk about any fears or guilt you may feel—perhaps with your doctor or with other mothers who have shared the same experience. Crib deaths are inexplicable and happen to the best-cared-for babies.

Parents who have lost a child to crib death can get information and assistance from the National Sudden Infant Death Syndrome Foundation, Two Metro Plaza, Suite 205, 8240 Professional Place, Landover, MD 20785.

When a twin is dying
In the very distressing circumstances of one of your twins being close to dying you may be unsure of what to do about his well twin. You may want to protect him from the deep hurt you are experiencing. What do you tell him? Won't he be desperately upset to see his brother so ill? Will he be better off staying with grandparents until it is all over?

Being kept in the dark about events that are clearly deeply upsetting to his parents, and so in a way being excluded by them, is likely to be more frightening and disturbing to a child than to know what is happening. Gently tell him why you are so sad and preoccupied. Let him know the truth about his twin in quantities he or she can handle. You will be the best judge of how much to tell him at any one time. If at all possible, allow him to spend time with his dying twin. They may both welcome the experience.

The surviving twin
Twins, especially those who have a very close understanding of each other, will be deeply affected by the death of the other and will need much support to help them deal with their grief.

Children show grief in different ways. They live much more from moment to moment and soon after crying may be able to play quite cheerfully. This does not mean they are unaffected by their loss. Some bereaved children may become very withdrawn and retreat into a shell, a behavior that may pass unnoticed for some time by parents who are preoccupied with their own distress. Yet other children express their grief by behaving "badly," by being unduly rowdy and destructive. Parents may particularly resent this last reaction and come to feel hostile to this twin who has survived while the "good" twin has died.

Recent studies have shown that bereaved children, and particularly twins who have lost a twin, are more likely to need psychiatric treatment in later life. Studies have also shown that the risk is considerably reduced if a child is encouraged to express his or her grief at the appropriate time. Grieving is a healthy, natural process.

How do you help a child to grieve the loss of his or her twin?

• A child needs to know the truth about an event that is clearly overwhelming the family. Tell the truth in quantities he or she can handle.

• Encourage the child to cry and share his or her feelings with you. Don't avoid situations that remind the child of the twin. Rather, use them to allow the child to express sadness or anger.

• Whether a child attends a funeral or not will depend on the age, understanding, his or her own and the parents' wishes. Parents will be caught up in their own grief, so it is useful to have another adult to take care of the child. Prepare the child by explaining in advance what is going to happen. Death and funerals are handled simply and sensitively in *The Body Book* by Claire Rayner (see Appendix 4, page 294).

• Children under the age of about four or five do not understand the finality of death. A small twin may want to keep half a bar of chocolate to share with the dead twin, or wrap up a present for him at Christmas time or keep on asking when he is coming back. Gently tell the child that the brother, or sister, can no longer eat, drink, sleep, move, see, hear or feel and little by little the understanding will come that the other twin's life has ended.

• Very young children may be helped to express their feelings, fears and fantasies and also be helped to understand what has happened through drawing, painting, photographs, or through playing with dolls or other small figures, or with dough or plasticene.

• Young children may have strange fantasies about death. Encourage them to tell you what they know and what they think so any misconceptions can be cleared up. A twin has shared most of the important events of the early years with his or her sister or brother. When one twin has died, the surviving twin may be afraid he or she is going to share this event and soon die, too. The twin may often have wished the other out of the way when competing for the mother's attention and now may be wondering whether by some magical power this wish has come true. The survivor may be angry with the other twin for deserting him or her or for causing their parents such distress. The remaining twin may even feel responsible for the distress and feel the need to compensate the parents for the twin's desertion.

• If you find you are unable to talk with the child about the twin's death, it is important that you find someone else who can, a close friend or relative perhaps, or someone through the school, church or your doctor.

• If in spite of talking the surviving twin continues to show signs of being disturbed by the death, again consult your doctor for possible referral for counseling. The sooner the child's fears and anxieties are dealt with the better.

Parents' feelings

Any surviving twin will be a very close and sometimes very painful reminder of the child who has died. None more so than a surviving identical twin, who may share, or sometimes unconsciously adopt, many of his twin's mannerisms and expressions. Some mothers may find much comfort in the surviving twin. Some may be afraid he or she too will die and become unduly protective. Some may, for a while, not want to have anything to do with the child that shared her womb and a birth with the one who is now dead, and yet still feel able to relate to their other children. Some may feel angry toward the survivor and resent any apparently unfeeling behavior in him. Some may experience an extra burden of guilt at the many times they wished they had only had one child to deal with.

Fathers, too, are likely to experience similar reactions but may find it more difficult to express their grief.

Bereaved parents may try to hide some of the very intense feelings of anger, resentment and guilt that accompany the sadness and loneliness of loss. The best way of dealing with them is to share them with someone you can trust, with each other, with a close friend or relative, or with an outside helper. You will never forget the death, but through allowing yourself to mourn, the pain will, in time, grow less intense and less frequent. Continue to talk about your loss and any fears, resentments or guilt for as long as you need to.

A mother who held on to her grief over a long period said, "When I looked at Tony I would always see Mark and I used to feel dreadful that Mark was lying in a grave when Tony was playing around." It was only after a lot of talking and grieving later on that anxiety and sadness did not regularly intrude on her relationship with Tony.

If you have difficulty talking with your partner or if you find your family life has been seriously disrupted by your loss, your doctor may be able to help or put you in touch with a counselor or family therapist.

Handicap

Able-bodied twins are hard work. The load is inevitably increased when one or both are handicapped.

One disabled and one able-bodied twin

At about six weeks Kate was led to believe that one of her twins might be spastic, although at about a year her development was found to be normal. In spite of the already heavy demands, she was able to find time to give that twin the special attention she needed:

> "Rosie's exercises took priority over everything. I put everything out of the way for that. Even if the diapers were totally out of hand and I hadn't got a clean one in the house and I knew I was going to have a riot on my hands, her exercises had to be done . . . I felt guilty about neglecting Leo, but then I used to say to myself, 'Well, Leo . . .' I mean, at that stage I thought she was never going to walk or anything, so, putting it into perspective, I said, 'Well, Leo, you've got your health so I'm afraid you've got to put up with this.' I used to say to myself, 'I'll explain when he's older.'"

A toddler twin with a serious handicap again poses problems of priorities for the mother. One of Susie's boys, Yuan, was found to be deaf when he was about a year old:

> "I'm supposed to do much more with him than I can. They're both very possessive. When I take him on my lap Lin sees and wants to come on my lap as well . . . Yuan's powers of concentration are not as good as Lin's and I think the fact that Lin's always buzzing about doesn't help him. . . . Sometimes he gets angry and screams and throws the book away. Other times he's fairly passive about it . . . I feel very guilty about

not doing more work with Yuan, but I get so tired, especially in the late afternoon."

At that time Susie was a single parent and was unable to find individual time for each in the evenings or on weekends.

Later on a handicapped twin will need much sensitive support in coming to terms with accepting the disability with the ever-present reminder of what he or she might have been and and done that is seen in the co-twin.

A normal twin growing up with a severely handicapped twin brother or sister, will, as he or she becomes aware of the differences, need to talk a lot about them. The normal twin will need to know why he or she is so different and may harbor secret anxieties that he or she will become like the twin. The normal twin will need to be reassured of separateness and that he or she is in no way responsible.

Martin, now in his forties, talked of his identical brother, who was a severely disabled spastic. His parents, he felt, had not resolved their own feelings of guilt and shame and never discussed his brother's handicap with him:

> "I somehow felt, I think, that I was responsible for him, for the fact that he was as he was, though this was never said to me directly. I suppose I always experienced myself as strong and felt guilty about that in various ways . . . I respond quite emotionally to people who are disabled so I suppose I must have suppressed quite a lot quite early around the whole thing. . . . He was threatening in that he was clear evidence of what I might have been or what I avoided being. . . . He was frighteningly like me. He was a caricature of me. He had the same face, same body configuration, same hands and feet but it was all disfigured, so it was a very excruciating comparison and very difficult to face him. And also the sense of responsibility about him made it worse."

Now that there is much more support for parents of handicapped children, the situation Martin had to contend with is less likely to occur. If you find you are still unable to talk easily about the handicap and so help a twin or close sibling to discuss their fantasies or fears, you can seek help through your family doctor or parent support group for those whose children are similarly handicapped.

Both twins handicapped

Evelyn's twins were very slow to reach the normal milestones of physical development; when they were about seven months some disability was suspected, and then confirmed for her soon after they were one. Both have cerebral palsy with a mild-to-moderate degree of spasticity. She has found support through various channels that enabled her to be active beyond the daily coping with two handicapped children who fight and demand her attention like any other young twins. She and a friend run their local Mothers of Twins Club. From the club she has gained practical support. For instance, when things have been bad at bedtime she has on occasion phoned a friend from the club who has gone straight over to help. When we spoke to her she had recently joined a local center for handicapped children for support in coping with her twins' handicap. She gets some at-home assistance from social services as well as a small allowance. But it has not been easy to set this up. It has meant making numerous inquiries and then asking for the support. "I think you have to fight a lot," she said. Evelyn, understandably, feels very bitter that both her babies are handicapped.

Rosemary had suspected that one of her girls might have hearing difficulties. Then both were found to be deaf when they were 13 months old. She was devastated at the news:

> "It was unbelievable. . . . I had all the usual reactions—It's not going to happen to me. . . . The fact that both were deaf? Oh, that made it much worse. I felt that if it was only one the other one would help, and they were just neither of them ever going to get enough attention and I was just completely pulled apart really. I felt like crying all the time. But when I was actually with them, they were so happy and so gay and so alive I just couldn't burst into tears, in fact."

Keeping a hearing aid on one toddler is difficult enough. On two it was a nightmare:

> "I can remember being a jittering wreck, shaking from the effort of trying to keep it all on and all together and endlessly searching for little bits and pieces in the car and on the sidewalks . . . if ever they were not doing something they used to take them to bits. They used to stick them in each other's mouths and have wrong bits in each other's ears."

The usual twin difficulties in learning side by side, such as opting out, are often exacerbated by the handicap, with possible serious consequences. Rosemary has to do extra language work with her twins at home. Alice, a willful young lady, found it particularly difficult to sit still and concentrate on it:

> "Rebecca loved it from the word go and picked it up and started to speak. . . . Obviously when you start getting feedback you are much more likely to respond. And when children are deaf you emphasize whenever you speak so Alice is bound to notice. Alice doesn't consciously think, Rebecca is succeeding, I'll fail, but that is what she in fact does."

The twins and Rosemary went to a special teacher of the deaf once a week. During the sessions each adult helped one of the girls. At the time of the interview Alice had started having extra time with the teacher at the end of the lesson to try to catch up on what she had missed through opting out.

Rosemary foresaw particular difficulties in ensuring that her girls continued to interact with the family and, later on, in the mainstream of life:

> "If they go to a school where they learn to sign to each other and cut us off, there'll be the twins v. the family . . . if they go to a school where they aren't taught to sign, they would pick it up from the other children and might evolve their own sign language, which nobody would understand."

Rosemary hopes to send them to an ordinary school.

When either or both of your twins are handicapped you, even more than other twin mothers, will need a break from the double stress from time to time. Somehow or other, try to have as much help as you can on a regular basis so you can occasionally give one twin your undivided attention and so that you know you can sometimes escape from the pressures. First try to arrange some kind of home help or practical support through your local Social Services Department or your family doctor. If you don't get very far, seek support from the Mothers of Twins Clubs and/or the association relevant to your children's handicap, to press your claims. As Evelyn said, "I think you have to advise parents to fight for their rights."

Illness

The ill child has a twin
A twin with chronic ill health may feel he has let the side down:

> "I think that a lot of my pattern of feeling that people are
> disappointed with me comes from having been the weaker
> twin. My health wasn't very good as a child. I think I felt very
> compared to my physically stronger, more robust twin. I
> think I felt that the fact that I had special needs as a child was
> a worry to people and it was more of a worry because he
> didn't have those needs."

A well twin on the other hand may be resentful, with some
justification, at the loss of her mother's attention:

> "On the big journey we took from Calcutta to England when
> we were both just five we came by sea and Leilah developed
> acute appendicitis and for the first few days of the voyage was
> doubled up. She got more and more ill. I think I must have
> been quite disturbed on that journey because so much was
> going on with her. It was such a big drama. I was unhappy. I
> remember sitting on deck completely paralyzed with rage be-
> cause I had been asked to compete in a race and I think it
> might have been due to the fact that I couldn't compete with
> her because she was ill. There was no way I could be as ill as
> her."

A well child may suffer restrictions imposed on him because
of his brother's poor health or handicap:

> "I think it was because of my brother's physical health that I
> was overprotected when I was young. I wasn't given the nor-
> mal opportunities of exploring and getting myself dirty . . .
> so that I was both overprotected on the one hand and proba-
> bly physically underloved on the other."

Hospital

Until about the fourth year, when they have some understanding of numbers and time and can comprehend what is
happening, a long separation from their mother can be a be-
wildering and upsetting experience for small children.

More and more hospitals are providing facilities for a mother to stay in with her sick child. But what do you do if only one of your twins needs hospitalization when they are both too young to be away from you for a long time? The twin in the hospital certainly needs you with him but so does the twin who is left behind. Twins who are close may find it hard to tolerate prolonged absences from one another, too.

When circumstances do not allow the well twin to stay in the hospital all or part of the time, parents usually find it best to keep the child at home (or in another familiar environment) with a trusted and loved person to care for him. It may be possible for a father to take a few days off and occasionally relieve the mother in the hospital so she can spend some time at home with the well twin. It will probably help both twins to have as much contact with each other as circumstances allow. If visiting is not possible, the well child needs to know where the twin is and what is happening. You can tell him through play and drawings and photographs.

Beth and her three-and-a-half-year-old boys were involved in a traffic accident, in which one of the boys, Adam, suffered serious injury necessitating a 6½ week stay in the hospital. Beth shared her time between the two by spending the morning with Thomas and taking him to friends after lunch on her way to the hospital:

> "Adam didn't seem to notice Thomas' absence as he was in a different situation entirely, but he was delighted when Thomas came to visit him. But Thomas missed Adam a lot and always talked about him when he was playing at home. Both boys kept on going over and over the facts of the accident several times a day for many weeks during and after Adam's stay in the hospital. It wasn't pleasant, but I had to let them go through it again and again and straighten out ideas they had twisted."

It took Adam quite a time to get back on his feet again after he came home:

> "The boys are now turning it all into a game among their many others. One lies down with 'broken legs,' one is a doctor, or a nurse, or an ambulance man, or Mommy. Then they

swap. Thomas can't imagine what Adam really went through. This seems to be his way of sharing being in the hospital. Now it's finally fading, though I doubt if it will ever be forgotten."

Children have a lot to teach adults about coping and coming to terms with painful experiences and, in the process, healing themselves.

APPENDIX 1

Mothers of Twins Clubs

The need
Most of the mothers we interviewed expressed a strong need for contact with other mothers of twins—to share their frustrations, their difficulties, their learning, their successes. Mutual support can alleviate much of the loneliness and stress of dealing with numbers of small children. Being able to share and cry about, or laugh at, the ridiculousness and awfulness of some of the situations you may find yourself in can make the difference between succumbing to the pressures or riding through them. Twins and the way they relate are fascinating. What better place to share this fascination than with other parents of twins?

Mothers/Parents of Twins Clubs (MOTC)
There are local clubs for parents of twins located throughout the country. To find one in your area, check your local telephone directory or ask your doctor. You can also contact the National Organization of Mothers of Twins Clubs, Inc., 5402 Amberwood Lane, Rockville, MD 20853 for the address of the club nearest your home. If there is no club in your area, how about starting one? Most clubs were started by mothers who felt the need. The national Organization of MOTC can give you advice on forming a club if you have none near you.

The National Organization of Mothers of Twins Clubs is an umbrella organization linking local clubs and individual members throughout the United States. The Mothers of Twins Club Association in England performs similar functions for Great Britain. The purpose of these national associations includes the following:

1. To give encouragement and support to parents of twins, triplets or more
2. To publish a National Register of Twins Clubs
3. To promote and establish future clubs
4. To produce and disseminate helpful information and literature to members
5. To increase public and commercial awareness of special needs of twins and their families
6. To promote greater appreciation within the medical profession of the problems of multiple births
7. To raise funds to promote the above aims.

Activities include conferences and meetings, publication of a newsletter, and the distribution of publications that are helpful to parents of twins. Other useful functions include:

• Advice or support for parents experiencing a particular difficulty, either with handling their twins or with convincing an organization such as a hospital, school or social services department of their special needs.

• Registers are kept of parents who have dealt with special experiences and are willing to support others. These include supertwins, adoption, one-parent families, crib deaths, handicapped twins and bereaved families.

The Center for Study of Multiple Gestation
The purpose of the Center for Study of Multiple Gestation is "to stimulate and foster medical and social research in the area of multiple birth and to provide help to mothers with the special problems they and their offspring will encounter." The center, founded in 1977, is located at 333 East Superior Street, Chicago, IL 60611. Telephone: (312) 649-7532. The Center focuses its efforts on the following:

• Increasing the dissemination of information regarding the medical risks of multiple birth and the special problems encountered by mothers and their offspring.

• Sponsoring scientific conferences of the care of twins and other multiples.

• Encouraging funding for the support of medical and social research.

The center is affiliated with the Department of Obstetrics and Gynecology, Northwestern Medical School, and the Prentice Women's Hospital and Maternity Center in Chicago. The center issues a number of helpful publications (see Appendix 4) and distributes publications of other publishers as well.

APPENDIX 2

Helpful Organizations

In addition to the Mothers of Twins Clubs and the Center for Study of Multiple Gestation, both of which are concerned specifically with twins or other multiples, there are numerous organizations that deal with special aspects of parenting that may or may not apply to your situation. A list of these resources follows.

American Academy of Pediatrics
141 Northwest Point Boulevard
Elk Grove Village, IL 60007
(312) 228-5005
This is a source of literature on children, their care, and their health care.

Association for the Care of Children's Health
3615 Wisconsin Avenue NW
Washington, DC 20016
(202) 244-1801

Center for Study of Multiple Birth
333 East Superior Street
Chicago, IL 60611
(312) 266-9093
Write or call for the list of current publications.

The Compassionate Friends, Inc.
National Headquarters
P.O. Box 3696
Oak Brook, IL 60522
(312) 990-0010
This group provides support for bereaved parents.

Double Talk
Box 412
Amelia, Ohio 45102
This is a newsletter for parents of twins.

La Leche League International
9616 Minneapolis Avenue
Franklin Park, IL 60131
(312) 455-7730
Call or write for the address and number of your local La Leche League. Through its local volunteers, La Leche League provides support and encouragement for nursing mothers.

National Health Information Clearinghouse
P.O. Box 1133
Washington, DC 20013
(800) 336-4797 in all states except Virginia
in Virginia (703) 522-2590
This organization provides information to help consumers locate required health care services.

National Organization of Mothers of Twins Clubs
12404 Princess Jeanne NE
Albuquerque, NM 87112
(505) 275-0955
Contact this address for the location of your local Mothers/Parents of Twins Club.

National Sudden Infant Death Syndrome Foundation
Two Metro Plaza   Suite 205
8240 Professional Place
Landover, MD 20785
This organization provides support for parents who have lost a child to crib death.

Nursing Mothers Counsel, Inc.
P.O. Box 500063
Palo Alto, CA 94303

Parents Anonymous
6733 South Sepulveda Boulevard, Suite 270
Los Angeles, CA 90045
(800) 421-0353 in all states except California
(800) 352-0386 in California
This organization provides help for parents under stress. If you are having trouble coping and you are hurting your children or are afraid you might hurt them, give PA a call.

Parents of Premature and High Risk Infants International, Inc.
c/o The National Self-Help Clearinghouse
24 West 43 Street, Room 620
New York, NY 10036
(212) 642-2944
This organization is a source of information, referrals and support for those concerned with infants who require special care. Parents of premature multiples will find useful material through this clearinghouse.

Twinline
P.O. Box 10066
Berkeley, CA 94709
(415) 644-0861
This organization provides advice by phone, leaflets with useful information and a reading list of other useful publications on twins. Write or call for further information.

APPENDIX 3

Suppliers of Specialist Equipment

Because of the wide variation of availability of equipment from one locality to another, and the continuing introduction of new products, the best source of information about where to purchase needed items is your local Mothers of Twins Club. If you live in a large urban area or near a shopping mall with a large supplier of children's equipment, you may be in luck and able to purchase what you require conveniently. If not, the mothers of other multiples near you would be the best source of help in directing you to the right places. Some twins clubs provide an exchange for outgrown and no longer needed used items.

If your twins are premature and require smaller than standard baby clothes, *The Premature Baby Book,* by Helen Harrison (see Appendix 4) lists more than a dozen sources of commercially manufactured and custom-made clothes for tiny children.

Smaller than standard disposable diapers (Pampers) are available directly from Procter & Gamble. Their toll-free number is (800) 543-4932 except in Ohio, where it is (800) 582-2623.

The carriage that converts to a twin stroller (mentioned in Chapter 4) is available from the designer in England. Chances are, however, you'll be able to find something that suits you in your own local stores. Try before you resort to transoceanic ordering.

APPENDIX 4

Recommended Further Reading

Conception
The Biology of Twinning in Man, by M. Bulmer (Clarendon Press, 1970)
The Etiology of Twins, by Benson, Keith and Keith; *Conjoined Twins,* by Ellis, Keith and Keith. This double report is available from the Center for Multiple Gestation, Chicago, for $9.95 plus $1.00 postage and handling.
Human Multiple Reproduction, by I. MacGillivray, P. P. S. Nylander, G. Corney (W. B. Saunders, 1975)

Pregnancy and Birth
The Complete Book of Pregnancy and Childbirth, by Sheila Kitzinger. New York: Alfred A. Knopf, 1981. This beautifully written and comprehensive book is an excellent resource. Although not specifically about multiple pregnancy, the book's author is herself the mother of twins. Most of the information does pertain to any pregnancy, and there are a few helpful pages written directly about a twin pregnancy.
Essential Exercises for the Childbearing Year, by Elizabeth Noble. Boston: Houghton Mifflin Co., 1976. This book contains detailed directions for keeping fit during pregnancy and for restoring oneself as rapidly as possible after delivery.
Having Twins: A Parents' Guide to Pregnancy, Birth and Early Childhood, by Elizabeth Noble. Boston: Houghton Mifflin Co., 1980. This book would be most useful if obtained as early as possible during a multiple pregnancy.
Making Love During Pregnancy, by E. Bing and L. Coleman. New York: Bantam, 1977.
What Every Pregnant Woman Should Know: The Truth about Drugs and Diet in Pregnancy, by Gail S. Brewer with T. Brewer, consultant. Baltimore: Penguin, 1979.
While Waiting: A Prenatal Guidebook, by George Verrilli, M.D., and

Anne Mueser, Ed.D. New York: St. Martin's Press, 1982. This is a handy and easy-to-read reference guide for use during any pregnancy.

Feeding

The Complete Book of Breastfeeding, by Marvin Eiger and Sally Wendkos. New York: Bantam, 1972. This is one of the most useful and widely used books on this topic.

The Experience of Breastfeeding, by Sheila Kitzinger. New York: Penguin, 1980. This very supportive book deals with the pleasures and burdens of breast-feeding. It is one of the few titles that place emphasis on the emotional aspects of nursing and the influence the process has on family life.

Child Care and Development

Babysense, by Frances Wells Burck. New York: St. Martin's Press, 1979. This volume contains much information and supportive reassurance for parents of one or more infants.

Better Homes and Gardens New Baby Book. DesMoines, Iowa: Meredith Corp., 1979.

The Body Book, by Claire Rayner. Woodbury, N.Y.: Barron's Educational Series, Inc., 1980.

The Magic Years, by Selma Fraiberg. New York: Charles Scribner's Sons, 1959.

The Premature Baby Book, by Helen Harrison with Ann Kositsky, R.N. New York: St. Martin's Press, 1983.

Talk and Toddle: A Guide to the First Three Years, by Anne Mueser, Ed.D., and Lynne Liptay, M.D. New York: St. Martin's Press, 1983.

Welcome Baby: A Guide to the First Six Weeks, by Anne Mueser, Ed.D., and George Verrilli, M.D. New York: St. Martin's Press, 1982.

Your Baby and Child: From Birth to Age Five, by Penelope Leach. New York: Alfred A. Knopf, 1981. This beautifully written book is comprehensive, full of sound advice and an excellent resource.

Failed Pregnancy

After a Loss in Pregnancy: Help for Families Affected by a Miscarriage, a Stillbirth, or the Loss of a Newborn, by Nancy Berezin. New York: Simon and Schuster, 1982.

The Bereaved Parent, by Harriet S. Schiff. New York: Penguin Books, 1977.

Motherhood and Mourning: Perinatal Death, by Larry G. Peppers and Ronald J. Knapp. New York: Praeger, 1980.

Surviving Pregnancy Loss, by Rochelle Friedman and Bonnie Gradstein. Boston: Little, Brown and Company, 1982.

When Pregnancy Fails: Families Coping with Miscarriage, Stillbirth, and Infant Death, by Susan Borg and Judith Lasker. Boston: Beacon Press, 1981.

Pamphlets
The Center for Study of Multiple Gestation, Suite 463-5, 333 East
Superior Street, Chicago, IL 60611, distributes their own publications on twins and those of numerous other publishers as well.
Write for their latest list of available books and pamphlets. The center publishes a series of pamphlets that are available singly or as a
complete set. Titles currently available include:

Toddler Growth and Development
Teen Age Twins
Family Adjustments
Premature Twins
Twins in School
Helpful Hints
Twins Private Language (Ideoglossia)
Triplet Management
Disability of One Twin

INDEX